EXMOOR &
North Devon
COAST PATH

SW COAST PATH PART 1 – MINEHEAD TO BUDE

68 large-scale maps & guides to 30 towns and villages

PLANNING – PLACES TO STAY – PLACES TO EAT

HENRY STEDMAN & JOEL NEWTON

TRAILBLAZER PUBLICATIONS

Contents

INTRODUCTION

Exmoor and North Devon Coast Path

PART 1: PLANNING YOUR WALK

Practical information for the walker

Budgeting 28

Itineraries

What to take

Getting to and from the path

PART 2: MINIMUM IMPACT WALKING & OUTDOOR SAFETY

Minimum impact walking

Outdoor safety

PART 3: THE ENVIRONMENT & NATURE

Flora and fauna

PART 4: ROUTE GUIDE AND MAPS

APPENDICES

INDEX 206

ABOUT THIS BOOK

This guidebook contains all the information you need. The hard work has been done for you so you can plan your trip from home without the usual pile of books, maps and guides.

When you're all packed and ready to go, there's comprehensive public transport information to get you to and from the trail and 68 detailed maps and town plans to help you find your way along it.

The guide includes:

● All standards of accommodation with reviews of campsites, hostels, B&Bs, guesthouses and hotels
● Walking companies if you want an organised tour and baggage-carrying services if you just want your luggage carried
● Itineraries for all levels of walkers
● Answers to all your questions: when to go, degree of difficulty, what to pack, and how much the whole walking holiday will cost
● Walking times in both directions and GPS waypoints
● Cafés, pubs, tearooms, takeaways, restaurants and shops for buying supplies
● Rail, bus and taxi information for all villages and towns along the path
● Street plans of the main towns both on and off the path
● Historical, cultural and geographical background information

MINIMUM IMPACT FOR MAXIMUM INSIGHT

Man has suffered in his separation from the soil and from other living creatures ... and as yet he must still, for security, look long at some portion of the earth as it was before he tampered with it. **Gavin Maxwell**, *Ring of Bright Water*, 1960

Why is walking in wild and solitary places so satisfying? Partly it is the sheer physical pleasure: sometimes pitting one's strength against the elements and the lie of the land. The beauty and wonder of the natural world and the fresh air restore our sense of proportion and the stresses and strains of everyday life slip away. Whatever the character of the countryside, walking in it benefits us mentally and physically, inducing a sense of well-being, an enrichment of life and an enhanced awareness of what lies around us.

All this the countryside gives us and the least we can do is to safeguard it by supporting rural economies, local businesses, and low-impact methods of farming and land-management, and by using environmentally sensitive forms of transport – walking being pre-eminent.

In this book there is a detailed and illustrated chapter on the wildlife and conservation of the region and a chapter on minimum-impact walking, with ideas on how to tread lightly in this fragile environment; by following its principles we can help to preserve our natural heritage for future generations.

INTRODUCTION

This book covers the first 124¹/₂ miles (200.3km) of the South-West Coast Path (hereafter known as SWCP), Britain's longest national trail. The trail in this book starts at Minehead in Somerset and, after navigating the whole of North Devon's coastline, ends just across the border at Bude in Cornwall.

This book covers the first 124¹/₂ miles of the 630-mile South-West Coast Path

Together with the two other books in this 'mini-series', the entire length of this 630-mile-long coast path is covered.

This first section of the path is also by some distance the shortest section of the three. But size isn't everything, as they say, and there's plenty here to tempt the discerning walker. Look at a map of the British Isles and this part of the coastal path – meandering as it does

Rhododendron blooms in springtime; on the way to Lynmouth.

along some of Britain's most exquisite shoreline, backed by a vast swathe of green, a verdant outlook unbroken save for tiny villages and hamlets scattered here and there – is a logical place to go for an amble. That vast swathe of green is Exmoor National Park, the most delightful of wildernesses and one through which the route saunters along the coastal cliffs for 34 miles and includes Great Hangman, at 318m (1043ft) the highest point on the entire trail. Nor does the fun stop there for no sooner does the path leave the park than it immediately joins the North Devon coast, luxuriating in its designation as an Area of Outstanding Natural Beauty (AONB). It is here you'll find enormous beaches stretching for miles; Braunton Burrows, part of a UNESCO Biosphere Reserve and the largest sand dune system in the country; plenty of pretty little historical towns and gorgeous villages where one can rest and recuperate, including the breathtaking harbour of Clovelly; and we haven't even mentioned the walk around Hartland Peninsula, the toughest, most isolated and the most spectacular walking – in most experts' opinions – on the entire SWCP. Clearly, God was in a rumbustious mood when He designed this gorgeous little corner of England.

> Clearly, God was in a rumbustious mood when He designed this gorgeous little corner of England

The North Devon AONB continues all the way to the border with Cornwall, though this book actually finishes just across the border at Bude – a more logical end to a walk, with fine accommodation, good restaurants in which to celebrate and half-decent (by the standards of the South-West at least!) transport links back to the everyday world.

Another sunny day above Welcombe Mouth (see p192). It's a steep descent to reach it, though.

Sounds perfect doesn't it? A dozen days or so of walking along romantic, windswept cliffs, through Elysian fields and sylvan valleys, a small yet vital part

This is actually the toughest leg of the entire South-West Coast Path

of a mammoth odyssey around England's most idiosyncratic corner. But such rewards are not gained easily; for one thing, the weather in this blessed corner of England takes a perverse pleasure in its unpredictability – though boy, it does have more than its fair share of good weather too, especially compared to the rest of the UK. But there's also some hard walking to be done; by many people's estimates, this is actually the toughest leg of the entire SWCP, with plenty of fiercely undulating sections guaranteed to torment calf muscles and sap morale. Indeed, it can't be denied that there are a couple of days that will truly test your mettle.

But then again, few if any will disagree that the obstacles and difficulties this path presents to those who dare to pit themselves against it, are far outweighed by its compensations...

History

The Somerset and North Devon section of the South-West Coast Path is the youngest part, having only been created and added to the rest of the path in 1978 – five years after the Cornish section was declared open. The entire path, however, including this section, existed way before its designation as a national

---

❏ The South-West Coast Path

Typing 'Minehead to South Haven Point, Dorset' into Googlemaps, reveals that travelling between the two can be completed in a matter of 3 hours 37 minutes by car, along a distance of 96.6 miles. Even walking, along the most direct route, takes only around 29 hours, so Googlemaps says, with the path an even shorter one at just 89.3 miles.

It is these two points that are connected by the South-West Coast Path (SWCP). This most famous – and infamous – of national trails is, however, a good deal longer than 89.3 miles. Though estimates as to its exact length vary – and to a large part are determined by which of the alternative paths one takes at various stages along the trail – the most widely accepted estimate of the path is that it is about 630 miles long (1014km). That figure, however, often changes due to necessary changes in the path caused by erosion and other factors.

So why, when you could walk from Minehead to South Haven Point in just 29 hours, do most people choose to take 6-8 weeks? The answer is simple: the SWCP is one of the most beautiful trails in the UK. Around 70% of those 630 miles are spent either in national parks, or regions that have been designated as Areas of Outstanding Natural Beauty. The variety of places crossed by the SWCP is extraordinary too: from sunkissed beaches to sandy burrows, holiday parks to fishing harbours, esplanade to estuary, on top of windswept cliffs and under woodland canopy, the scenery that one travels through along the length of SWCP has to be the most diverse of any of the national trails. (*cont'd overleaf*)

❏ The South-West Coast Path (*cont'd from p9*)

Of course, mantaining such a monumental route is no easy task. A survey in 2000 stated that the trail could boast 2473 signposts and waymarks, 302 bridges, 921 stiles, and 26,719 steps. These figures are, of course, out of date now, though they do still give an idea of both how long the trail is, and how much is involved in building and maintaining it to such a high standard. The task of looking after the trail falls to a dedicated team from the official body, Natural England. Another important organisation, and one that looks after the rights of walkers is the South West Coast Path Association, a charity that fights for improvements to the path and offers advice, information and support to walkers. They also campaign against many of the proposed changes to the path, and help to ensure that England's right-of-way laws which ensure that the footpath is open to the public – even though it does, on occasion, pass through private property – are fully observed.

History of the path

In 1948 a government report recommended the creation of a footpath around the entire South-West peninsula to improve public access to the coast which, at that time, was pretty dire. It took until 1973 for the Cornwall Coast Path to be declared officially open and another five years for the rest of the South-West Coast Path to be completed. The section covered in this book, North Devon and Exmoor, is the first part that most coastal walkers complete, though it was actually the last section to be opened to the public, in 1978.

The origins of the path, however, are much older than its official designation. Originally, the paths were established – or at least adopted, there presumably being coastal paths from time immemorial that connected the coastal villages – by the local coastguard in the nineteenth century, who needed a path that hugged the shoreline closely to aid them in their attempts to spot and prevent smugglers from bringing contraband into the country. The coastguards were unpopular in the area as they prevented the locals from exploiting a lucrative if illegal activity, to the extent that it was considered too dangerous for them to stay in the villages; as a result, the authorities were obliged to build special cottages for the coastguards that stood (and, often, still stand) in splendid isolation near the path – but well away from the villages.

The lifeboat patrols also used the path to look out for craft in distress (and on one famous occasion used the path to drag their boat to a safe launch to rescue a ship in distress – see p98). When the coastguards' work ended in 1856, the Admiralty took over the task of protecting England's shoreline and thus the paths continued to be used.

The route – Minehead (Somerset) to Poole Harbour (Dorset)

The SWCP officially begins at Minehead in Somerset (its exact starting point marked by a sculpture that celebrates the trail), heads west right round the bottom south-west corner of Britain then shuffles back along the south coast to South Haven Point, overlooking Poole Harbour in Dorset. On its lengthy journey around Britain's south-western corner the SWCP crosses national parks such as Exmoor as well as regions that have been designated as Areas of Outstanding Natural Beauty (including North, South and East Devon AONB and the Cornwall and Dorset AONBs) or Sites of Special Scientific Interest (Braunton Burrows being just one example – an area that also enjoys a privileged status as a UNESCO Biosphere Reserve), and even a couple of UNESCO World Heritage sites, too, including the Jurassic Coast of East Devon and Dorset and the old mining landscape of Cornwall and West Devon. Other features passed on the way include the highest cliffs on mainland

trail, having been used by the coastguard for centuries to protect against smugglers and aid maritime safety. The nature of the coastguard's job meant that the path had to follow the cliff-tops closely to provide their officers with far-reaching views over land and sea – and to allow them to visit every beach and cove along the way. By chance, these are the exact same qualities that discerning walkers look for in a coastal path!

How difficult is the path?

The South-West Coast Path (SWCP) is just a (very, very) long walk, so there's no need for crampons, ropes, ice axes, oxygen bottles or any other climbing paraphernalia. All you need to complete the walk is some suitable clothing, a bit of money, a rucksack full of determination and a half-decent pair of calf muscles.

That said, the part of the SWCP that is covered by this book is reputed to be the most challenging section, with plenty of steep ups-and-downs. It is also a fairly wild walk in places – to cross Exmoor National Park is to traverse one of the remotest corners of the country. There are also plenty of places on the

Britain (at Great Hangman – also the highest point on the coast path at 318m/1043ft, with a cliff-face of 244m), the largest sand-dune system in England (at Braunton Burrows), England's most westerly point (at Land's End) and Britain's most southerly (at the Lizard), the 18-mile barrier beach of Chesil Bank, one of the world's largest natural harbours at Poole, and even the National Trust's only official nudist beach at Studland! The path then ends at South Haven Point, its exact finish marked by a second SWCP sculpture. The path also takes in four counties – Somerset, Devon, Cornwall and Dorset, and connects with over fifteen other long-distance trails; the southern section from Plymouth to Poole also forms part of the 3125-mile long European E9 Coastal Path that runs on a convoluted route from Portugal to Estonia.

Walking the South-West Coast Path

In terms of difficulty, there are those people who, having never undertaken such a trail before, are under the illusion that coastal walking is a cinch; that all it involves is a simple stroll along mile after mile of golden, level beach, the walker needing to pause only to kick the sand out from his or her flipflop or buy another ice cream.

The truth, of course, is somewhat different, for coastal paths tend to stick to the cliffs above the beaches rather than the beaches themselves (which is actually something of a relief, given how hard it is to walk across sand or shingle). These cliffs make for some spectacular walking but – given the undulating nature of Britain's coastline, and the fact the course of the SWCP inevitably crosses innumerable river valleys, each of which forces the walker to descend rapidly before climbing back up again almost immediately afterwards – some exhausting walking too. Indeed, it has been estimated that anybody who completes the entire SWCP will have climbed more than four times the height of Everest (35,031m to be precise, or 114,931ft) by the time they finish!

Given these figures, it is perhaps hardly surprising that most people take around eight weeks to complete the whole route, and few do so in one go; indeed, it is not unusual for people to take years or even decades to complete the whole path, taking a week or two here and there to tackle various sections until the whole trail is complete.

regular trail where it would be possible to fall from a great height, even if you strayed from the path by only a few metres. Still, with the path well signposted (see p17) all the way along and the sea keeping you company for the entire stretch, it's difficult to get lost (though it's always a good idea to take a compass or GPS unit, just in case).

As with any walk, you can minimise the risks by preparing properly. Your greatest danger on the walk is likely to be from the weather, which can be so unpredictable in this corner of the world, so it is vital that you dress for inclement conditions and always carry a set of dry clothes with you.

How long do you need?

People take an average of around ten days to complete the walk; count on a fortnight away in total to give you time to travel there and back. Of course, if you're fit there's no reason why you can't go a little faster, if that's what you want to do, and finish the walk in eight days or even less, though you will end up having a different sort of walk to most of the other people on the trail. For, whilst theirs is a fairly relaxing holiday, yours will be more of a sport. What's more, you won't have much time to laze in the sun on the beaches, scoff scones in tearooms, visit an attraction or two, or sup local beers under the shade of a pub parasol – which does rather beg the

It takes an average of around ten days to complete the walk

The view from the harbour arm in the lovely village of Clovelly (see p177).

question as to why you've come here in the first place! There's nothing wrong with this approach, of course – *chacun à son goût*, as the French probably say. However, what you **mustn't do is try to push yourself too fast, or too far**. That road leads only to exhaustion, injury or, at the absolute least, an unpleasant time.

When deciding how long to allow for the walk, those intending to camp and carry their own luggage shouldn't underestimate just how much a heavy pack can slow them down. On pp29-30 there are some suggested itineraries covering different walking speeds.

If you have only a few days, don't try to walk it all; concentrate instead on one area such as the coast path

See pp29-30 for some suggested itineraries covering different walking speeds

through Exmoor, the beaches around Woolacombe and Croyde, or the more low-key estuary path along a disused railway from Braunton to Westward Ho!. Or you can really challenge yourself by taking on the trail between lovely Clovelly and Bude.

When to go

SEASONS

'My shoes are clean from walking in the rain.' **Jack Kerouac**

Britain is a notoriously wet country and South-West England does nothing to crush that reputation. Few walkers manage to complete the walk without suffering at least one downpour; two or three per walk are more likely, even in summer. That said, it's equally unlikely that you'll spend a week in the area and not see any sun at all, and even the most cynical of walkers will have to

Few walkers manage to complete the walk without at least one downpour

admit that, during the **walking season** at least, there are more sunny days than showery ones. The season, by the way, starts at Easter and builds to a crescendo in August, before steadily tailing off in October. Few people attempt the entire path after the end of October though there are still plenty of people on day walks. Many places close in November for the winter.

There is one further point to consider when planning your trip. Firstly, remember that most people set off on the trail at a weekend. This means that you'll find the trail quieter **during the week** and as a consequence you may find it easier to book accommodation.

Spring

Find a dry fortnight in springtime (around the end of March to mid-June) and you're in for a treat. The wild flowers are coming into bloom, lambs are skipping in the meadows and the grass is green and lush. Of course, finding a dry week in spring is not easy but occasionally there's a mini-heatwave at this time. Another advantage with walking at this time is that there will be fewer walkers

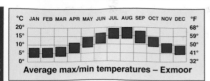

Average max/min temperatures – Exmoor

and finding accommodation is relatively easy, though do check that the hostels/B&Bs are open. Easter is the exception; the first major holiday in the year when people flock to the coast.

Summer

Summer, on the other hand, can be a bit *too* busy, at least in the towns and tourist centres, and over a weekend in August can be both suffocating and insufferable. Still, the chances of a prolonged period of sunshine are of course higher at this time of year than any other, the days are much longer, and all the facilities and public transport are operating. Our advice is this: if you're flexible and want to avoid seeing too many people on the trail, avoid the school holidays, which basically means ruling out the tail end of July, all of August and the first few days of September. Alternatively, if you crave the company of other walkers summer will provide you with the opportunity of meeting plenty, though do remember that you **must book your accommodation in advance**, especially if staying in B&Bs or similar accommodation. Despite the higher than average chance of sunshine, take clothes for any eventuality – it will probably still rain at some point.

Autumn

September is a wonderful time to walk; many tourists have returned home and the path is clear. I think that the weather is usually reliably sunny too, at least at the beginning of September, though I'll admit I don't have any figures to back this claim. The first signs of winter will be felt in October but there's nothing really to deter the walker. In fact there's still much to entice you, such as the colours of the heathland, which come into their own in autumn; a magnificent blaze of brilliant purples and pinks, splashed with the occasional yellow flowers of gorse (it is more usual in spring but can thrive in autumn). By the end of October, however, the weather will begin to get a little wilder and the nights will start to draw in. The walking season is almost at an end and most campsites and some B&Bs and hostels may close.

Winter

November can bring crisp clear days which are ideal for walking, although you'll definitely feel the chill when you stop on the cliff tops for a break. Winter temperatures rarely fall below freezing but the incidence of gales and storms definitely increases. You need to be fairly hardy to walk in December and January and you may have to alter your plans because of the weather. By February the daffodils and primroses are already appearing but even into March it can still be decidedly chilly if the sun is not out.

While winter is definitely the low season with many places closed, this can be more of an advantage than a disadvantage. Very few people walk at this time of year, giving you long stretches of the trail to yourself. When you do stumble across other walkers they are as happy as you to stop and chat. Finding B&B

accommodation is easier as you will rarely have to book more than a night ahead (though it is still worth checking in advance as some B&Bs close out of season), but if you are planning to camp, or are on a small budget, you will find places to stay much more limited.

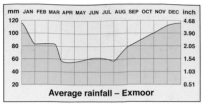

Average rainfall – Exmoor

WEATHER

Before departing on your walk, tell yourself this: at some point on my walk it is going to **rain**. That's not to say it will, but at least if it does you won't be too disappointed and will hopefully have come prepared for this, clothes-wise. Besides, walking in the rain can be fun, at least for a while: the gentle drumming of rain on hood can be quite relaxing, the path is usually quiet, and if it really does chuck it down at least it provides an excuse to linger in tearooms and have that extra scone. And as long as you dress accordingly and take note of the safety advice given on pp57-60, walking in moderate rain is no more dangerous than walking at any other time – though do be careful, particularly on exposed sections, if the path becomes slippy or the wind picks up.

DAYLIGHT HOURS

If walking in winter, autumn or even early spring, you must take account of how far you can walk in the available light. It won't be possible to cover as many miles as you would in summer. Conversely, in the summer months there is enough available light until at least

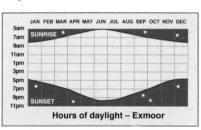

Hours of daylight – Exmoor

9pm – so don't use that as an excuse for finishing your day's walk early! Remember, too, that you will get a further 30-45 minutes of usable light before sunrise and after sunset depending on the weather.

❏ FESTIVALS AND ANNUAL EVENTS

Before leaving home it may be wise to be aware of any cultural events that could turn your peaceful seaside stroll into something resembling the Rio Carnival! You may wish to consider either avoiding or participating in the following events whilst planning your walk.

April/May
● **Ilfracombe Beer Festival** (🖳 www.visitilfracombe.co.uk) Held over May Day weekend and with live music, entertainment, real ales and cider and free admission – the reasons to check this out are manifold!

(cont'd overleaf)

❏ FESTIVALS AND ANNUAL EVENTS *(cont'd from p15)*

June
● **Lynton and Lynmouth Music Festival** (🖥 www.llama.org.uk) Free music festival organised by the Lynton & Lynmouth Arts & Music Association (LLAMA) It was cancelled in 2011 but may be relaunched in June 2012.
● **Ilfracombe** Early in the month, in **Victorian Wee**k (🖥 www.visitilfracombe .co.uk), locals and visitors dress up in Victorian costumes to celebrate the town's past. A variety of events are held culminating in a concert and firework festival on the last night. At the end of the month the **Arts Festival** (🖥 www.ilfracombe-arts-festi val.co.uk) is a four-day event featuring performances and exhibitions staged in various locations about the town.
● **Gold Coast Oceanfest** (🖥 www.goldcoastoceanfest.co.uk) Ostensibly a music festival in Croyde Bay though with as much emphasis on sport, especially surfing. The programme boasted Seasick Steve in 2011.
● **North Devon Festival** (🖥 www.northdevonfestival.org) A month-long shebang that brings many celebrated acts to Barnstaple as well as highlighting homegrown performers. Includes **Barnstaple Fringe Theatrefest** (🖥 www.theatrefest.co.uk).
● **Appledore Visual Arts Festival** (🖥 www.appledorearts.org) Charity-funded family friendly event that celebrates the work of local communities and artists. They are hoping to be back in 2012 following a sabbatical in 2011.
● **Braunton's Festival of music, dance and literature** Held around 26 June to celebrate St Brannock's Day. See p145.

July
● **Combe Martin Music Festival** (🖥 combemartinmusicfestival.vpweb.co.uk) A 'musical extravaganza' held every year over every weekend in July.

August
● **Combe Martin Carnival** (🖥 cmcarnival.freehostia.com) Annual week-long event held in mid-August with kayaking and wheelbarrow races as well as a much-anticipated parade. However, at the time of research it wasn't certain if it would happen in 2012.
● **Bude Jazz Festival** (🖥 www.budejazzfestival.co.uk) Another week-long festival featuring top UK and international musicians; next due in 2013.

September
● **Porlock Arts Festival** (🖥 www.porlockfestival.org) Literary festival including guest speakers, poetry workshops and many other bookish activities.
● **Appledore Book Festival** (🖥 appledorebookfestival.co.uk) Held over a week in late September, this festival attracts many highly regarded authors to the stage.
● **The Doone Run** (🖥 www.northdevonroadrunners.com) See box p106.
● **Barnstaple Fair** (🖥 www.barnstapletowncouncil.co.uk/barnstaple-fair.asp) Held for four days beginning on the Wednesday before 20th September with carnivals and processions before culminating in a firework 'extravaganza'.

This list is by no means comprehensive. For further information on other festivals in the area visit: 🖥 www.visitdevon.co.uk or 🖥 www.exmoor.com.

If continuing along the SWCP you'll find the fun continues over the border in Cornwall (🖥 www.cornwall.gov.uk) too with **Boscastle Food Arts and Crafts Festival** (🖥 www.boscastlefestival.co.uk) – held in October and the first festival venue you come to heading west. They also have a walking festival in April. Further details on festivals around the Cornish Coast can be found in Trailblazer's guide to *Cornwall Coast Path*, part of the series of books for the SWCP.

PLANNING YOUR WALK

Practical information for the walker

ROUTE FINDING

For most of its length the coast path is well signposted. At confusing junctions the route is usually indicated by a finger-post sign with 'coast path' written on it. At other points, where there could be some confusion, there are wooden waymark posts with an acorn symbol and a yellow arrow to indicate which direction you should head. The waymarking is the responsibility of the local authorities along the trail who have a duty to maintain the path. Generally they do a good job but occasionally you will come across sections of the trail where waymarking is ambiguous, or even non-existent, but with the detailed trail maps and directions in this book and the fact that you always have the sea to one side it would be hard to get really lost.

Using GPS with this book

Given the above, modern Wainwrights may scoff while more open-minded walkers will accept that GPS technology can be an inexpensive, well-established if non-essential navigational aid. In no time at all a GPS receiver with a clear view of the sky will establish your position and altitude in a variety of formats, including the British OS grid system, to within a few metres.

The maps in the route guide include numbered waypoints; these correlate to the list on pp204-5, which gives the latitude/longitude position in a decimal minute format as well as a description. Where the path is vague, or there are several options, you will find more waypoints. You can download the complete list of these waypoints for free as a GPS-readable file (that doesn't include the text descriptions) from the Trailblazer website: 🖳 www.trailblazer-guides.com (click on GPS waypoints).

It's also possible to buy state-of-the-art digital mapping to import into your GPS unit, assuming that you have sufficient memory capacity, but it's not the most reliable way of navigating and the small screen on your pocket-sized unit will invariably fail to put places into context or give you the 'big picture'.

Bear in mind that the vast majority of people who tackle this Path do so perfectly well without a GPS unit. Instead of rushing out to invest in one, consider putting the money towards good-quality waterproofs or footwear instead.

ACCOMMODATION

The route guide (Part 4) lists a fairly comprehensive selection of places to stay along the length of the trail. You have two main options: camping or using B&Bs and hotels. There is, perhaps, a third option too, that of staying in hostels, though there aren't many on this stretch of the coast path and sometimes they are too far from the path to be a realistic alternative. Few people stick to just one of these options the whole way, preferring, for example, to camp most of the time but spend every third night in a guesthouse, or perhaps use hostels where possible but splash out on a B&B every once in a while.

Note that when booking accommodation that is far from the path, remember to ask if a pick-up and drop-off service is available (usually only B&Bs provide this service); at the end of a tiring day it's nice to know a lift is available to take you to your accommodation rather than having to traipse another two or three miles off the path to get to your bed for the night. (This is particularly true at the end of this section of the SWCP, around Hartland Point, where there are only a few B&Bs and they are usually a fair walk from the path – and the walking is arduous enough as it is around this peninsula.)

The facilities' table on pp32-3 provides a quick snapshot of what type of accommodation is available in each of the towns and villages along the way, while the tables on p29 and p30 provide some suggested itineraries.

Camping

There are campsites all the way along the South-West Coast Path. That said, few people choose to camp every night. You're almost bound to get at least one night where the rain falls relentlessly, soaking equipment and sapping morale, and it is then that most campers opt to spend the next night drying out in a hostel or B&B. There are, however, many advantages with camping. It's more economical, for a start, with many campsites charging somewhere around £5 (though we have found places that charge £26!).

Campsites vary; some are just a quiet corner of a farmer's field, while others are full-blown caravan sites with a few spaces put aside for tents; since their main customers are families on their annual holidays, backpackers are often low on their list of priorities. Showers are usually available, normally for a small fee. Note that none of the YHA hostels on the path accepts campers. Note, too, that **wild camping** (ie not in a regular campsite) is not allowed.

Camping is not an easy option; the route is wearying enough without carrying your accommodation around with you. Should you decide to camp, therefore, we advise you to look into employing the baggage-carrying company mentioned on pp26-7, though this does, of course, mean that it will cost more and that you will lose a certain amount of freedom as you have to tell the company, at least a day before, of your next destination – and stick to it – so that you and your bag can be reunited every evening.

Rates for camping vary from site to site but for backpackers many charge for two people in a small tent although some charge per pitch and per person.

Hostels

The Exmoor and North Devon Coast Path is not well served by YHA hostels, with only three in total at Minehead, Westward Ho!, and Elmscott, near Hartland Quay, and even then the Minehead one is too far from the path to be of much use and the other two are part of the Enterprise Scheme so are privately owned. There are, however, good independent hostels at Minehead, Ilfracombe (which has two), Croyde and Bude.

If you haven't visited a youth hostel recently because the words 'youth' and 'hostel' still conjure up images of cold, crowded dorms, uncomfortable beds and lousy food all overseen by little-Hitler staff who take a sadistic pleasure in treating you like schoolchildren, we advise you to take a second look. These days, each hostel comes equipped with a whole range of facilities from drying

❏ **Should you book your accommodation in advance?**

When walking any section of South-West Coast Path it's essential that you have your night's accommodation booked by the time you set off in the morning, whether you're planning to stay in a hostel or, a B&B. Nothing is more deflating than to arrive at your destination at day's end only to find that you've then got to walk a further five miles or so, or even take a detour, because everywhere in town is booked.

That said, there's a certain amount of hysteria regarding the booking of accommodation, with many websites, B&Bs and other organisations suggesting you book at least six months in advance. Whilst it's true that the earlier you book the more chance you have of getting precisely the accommodation you require, booking so far in advance does leave you vulnerable to changing circumstances. Booking a full six months before setting foot on the trail is all very well if everything goes to plan but if you break your leg just before you're due to set off or, God forbid, there's another outbreak of foot and mouth, all you're going to end up with is a lot of lost deposits. By not booking so far in advance, you give yourself the chance to shift your holiday plans to a later date should the unforeseen arise.

In my experience, the lack of **B&B-style accommodation** is not as bad as some suggest, at least not outside the high season (ie the summer period coinciding with the long school holidays in the UK). Outside this period, and particularly in April/May or September, as long as you're flexible and willing to take what's offered, with maybe even a night or two in a hostel if that's all there is, you should get away with booking just a few nights in advance, or indeed just the night before. The exceptions to this rule are at weekends and in the high season, when everywhere is busy; at these times you should book as soon as you can, especially if you want to stay in a particular place.

Campers, however, have more flexibility and can often just turn up and find a space there and then, though ringing in advance can't hurt. The exception is at Bude, where you should phone well in advance especially at weekends and in summer.

If staying in **hostels**, the same applies though do be careful when travelling out of high season as sometimes hostels close for a couple of days each week and shut altogether from around November to Easter. Once again, it's well worth phoning at least one night before and well before that if it's a weekend, to make sure the hostel isn't fully booked.

rooms to televisions and fully equipped kitchens for guests to use. Many also have a shop selling emergency groceries, snacks and souvenirs and some offer internet access and/or wi-fi. They are also good places to meet fellow walkers, swap stories and compare blisters.

Weighed against these advantages is the fact that beds are still arranged in dormitories with up to seven beds in a room, thereby increasing your chances of sharing the night with a heavy snorer. The curfew (usually 11pm) is annoying too. A couple of the hostels also suffer from a shortfall in adequate washing facilities, with only one or two showers to be shared between 15 or 20 people. Nor is it really feasible to stay in hostels every night, for there are large swathes where hostels don't exist.

If you are travelling in April/May or September, at the beginning or end of the walking season, you may find many closed for two or three days per week, or entirely taken over by school groups, leaving walkers shut out. Contact the YHA or the relevant hostel to find out the exact opening dates. Finally, the cost of staying in a hostel (around £16-18pp for members, plus an additional £3pp per night for non members), once breakfast has been added on, is in most instances not that much cheaper than staying in a B&B.

Booking a hostel Despite the name, anyone of any age can join the YHA. This can be done at any hostel or by contacting the **Youth Hostels Association of England and Wales** (YHA; ☎ 0800-0191 700 or ☎ 01629-592700, 🖥 www .yha.org.uk). The cost of a year's membership is currently £15.95 (£9.95 for anyone under 26). Having secured your membership, YHA hostels are easy to book, either online or by phone. The hostels also offer a booking service and will reserve a bed at the next stop on the path for you.

Bed and breakfast accommodation

Bed and Breakfasts (**B&Bs**) are a great British institution and many of those along the South-West Coast Path are absolutely charming. Nearly all of the B&Bs on this route have either en suite rooms or rooms with private facilities; only a few have rooms with shared facilities.

The rooms usually contain either a double bed (known as a double room), or two single beds (known as a twin room). Family rooms are for three or more people; they usually contain a double bed and a single bed or a bunk bed but occasionally there are three or four single beds.

Note that in winter some B&Bs close; for those that stay open, make sure that beforehand they will have their heating in your room turned on!

An evening meal (usually £15-20) is often provided at the more remote or bigger places, at least if you book in advance. (Note that if you have any dietary requirements – eg if you're vegetarian, or need a gluten-free meal, you must tell the B&B owner beforehand.) Alternatively, if you want to eat out, there's nearly always a pub or restaurant nearby or, if it's far, the B&B owner may give you a lift to and from the nearest place with food.

The difference between a B&B and a **guesthouse** is minimal, though some of the better guesthouses are more like hotels, offering evening meals and a lounge for guests. **Pubs** and **inns** also offer bed and breakfast accommodation and prices are generally no more than in a regular B&B.

Hotels usually *do* cost more than B&Bs, however, and some might be a little incensed by a bunch of smelly walkers turning up and treading mud into their carpet. Most on the South-West Coast Path, however, are used to seeing walkers and welcome them warmly.

Rates Proprietors quote their **tariffs** either on a **per person** (pp) basis or **per room**, assuming two people are sharing; rates are also sometimes given for single occupancy of a room where there are no single rooms.

Accommodation in this guide starts at around £21pp for the most basic B&Bs rising to around £50pp for the most luxurious places. Most charge around £25-35pp. Prices in hotels start at around £35pp; however, sometimes rates are for the room only and breakfast is additional. Solo walkers should take note: single rooms are not so easy to find and you will often end up occupying a double/twin room and are likely to have to pay a single occupancy supplement (£5-15).

Some places have their own website and offer online/email **booking** but for the majority you will need to phone. Most places ask for a deposit (about 50%) which is generally non-refundable if you cancel at short notice. Some places may charge 100% if the booking is for one night only; they may also charge a single-night supplement or require a stay of at least two nights. Always let the owner know as soon as possible if you have to cancel your booking so they can offer the bed to someone else.

Larger places take credit or debit cards. Most smaller B&Bs accept only cheques by post or payments by bank transfer for the deposit; the balance can be settled with cash or a cheque.

FOOD AND DRINK

Breakfast and lunch

Stay in a B&B and you'll be filled to the gills with a cooked **English breakfast**. This usually consists of a bowl of cereal followed by a plateful of eggs, bacon, sausages, mushrooms, tomatoes and possibly baked beans or black pudding, with toast and butter, and all washed down with coffee, tea and/or juice. Enormously satisfying the first time you try it, by the fourth or fifth morning you may start to prefer a lighter continental breakfast. If you have had enough of these cooked breakfasts and/or plan an early start, ask if you can have a packed lunch instead of breakfast. Your landlady or hostel can usually provide a **packed lunch** at an additional cost (unless it's in lieu of breakfast), though of course there's nothing to stop you preparing your own lunch (but do bring a penknife if you plan to do this), or going to a pub (see p22) or café.

Remember, to plan ahead: certain stretches of the walk are virtually devoid of eating places (the stretch from Porlock Weir to Lynmouth, and from Lynton/Combe Martin to Ilfracombe, or the final stretch from Hartland Quay to Bude) so read ahead about the next day's walk in Part 4 to make sure you never go hungry.

Cream teas

Whatever you do for lunch, don't forget to leave some room for a cream tea (see box below) or two, a morale, energy and cholesterol booster all rolled into one delicious package: a pot of tea accompanied by scones served with cream and jam, and sometimes a cake or two. The jury is out on whether you should put the jam on first or the cream but either way do not miss the chance of at least one cream tea.

Evening meals

Pubs are as much a feature of the walk as seagulls and sheep, and in some cases the pub is as much a tourist attraction as any Roman fort or ruined priory. The Ship Inn at Porlock, The Rising Sun at Lynmouth, The Hunters Inn, nestled in the Heddon Valley, The Pack o' Cards at Combe Martin, harbour-side Red Lion Hotel at Clovelly, 14th-century Bush Inn at Morwenstow ... the list goes on.

Most pubs have become highly attuned to the desires of walkers and offer lunch and evening meals (often with a couple of local dishes and usually a few vegetarian options), some locally brewed beers, a garden to relax in on hot days and a roaring fire to huddle around on cold ones. The standard of the food varies widely, though is usually served in big portions, which is often just about all walkers care about at the end of a long day. In many of the villages the pub is the only place to eat out. Note that pubs may close in the afternoon, especially in the winter months, so check in advance if you are hoping to visit a particular one, and also if you are planning lunch there as food serving hours can change.

❏ **Traditional food in Somerset and Devon**

As a major centre of farming and fishing, it's not surprising that the South-West is a major supplier of food to the rest of Britain and can boast some pretty fine local specialities. In **Somerset** – literally, 'Land of the Summer People' – fruit is unsurprisingly bountiful with apples, the main ingredient for their legendary cider, particularly renowned. However, the cheeses of Somerset are perhaps its most famous export, with the name Cheddar used throughout the world, though only The Cheddar Gorge Cheese Company actually produces the cheese within the parish of Cheddar.

Say '**Devon**' to most Brits and in addition to images of sparkling coastlines and rolling hills, the county's name will also conjure up the delights of clotted cream – best enjoyed as part of a traditional cream tea with a scone or two and some whortleberry jam. This is an Exmoor speciality, whortleberry being the local name for wild bilberry (though they go by several other names including blueberry, heidelberry, huckleberry, hurtleberry and wimberry) and locally they're called 'worts' or 'urts'. Dairy products as a whole are plentiful in this corner of the country including delicious yoghurts and ice-cream. In the sea, South Devon crab is reputed to be the tastiest in the world and smoked eels are a speciality in these parts too. Other fish caught in the Bristol Channel include thornback ray, bass, conger, dogfish, flounder, whiting, dab pout, cod and codling. There's also shellfish: lobsters, crabs, scallops, langoustines, clams and mussels, which are often fished for from the smaller coastal villages.

Even if you're on a tight budget the ubiquitous fish and chips can be satisfying if cooked with fresh fish. At the other end of the scale there are plenty of restaurants around the coast offering mouth-watering dishes concocted from locally caught fish.

That other great British culinary institution, the **fish 'n' chip shop**, can be found in virtually every town on the trail.

As well as the chippies, there are other takeaways (Chinese, Indian etc) in the larger towns en route.

❑ BEERS AND CIDERS

Beers

The process of brewing beer is believed to have been in Britain since the Neolithic period and is an art local brewers have been perfecting ever since. Real ale is beer that has been brewed using traditional methods. Real ales are not filtered or pasteurised, a process which removes and kills all the yeast cells, but instead undergo a secondary fermentation at the pub which enhances the natural flavours and brings out the individual characteristics of the beer. It's served at cellar temperature with no artificial fizz added unlike keg beer which is pasteurised and has the fizz added by injecting nitrogen dioxide.

Based in the Somerset town of Wiveliscombe on the border of the national park, **Exmoor Ale**s (🖳 www.exmoorales.co.uk) produces five permanent ales including Exmoor Stag and Exmoor Beast (6.6%), named after Exmoor's most famous modern mystery (see box p66). Nearby, **Cotleigh Brewery** (🖳 www.cotleighbrewery.com) was originally based in Devon but moved to Wiveliscombe after just one year of trading. They brew around half a dozen real ales, each named after a member of the local avifauna such as Barn Owl or Buzzard.

Next door, Devon is well served with breweries with, according to a CAMRA study, 28 micro-breweries operating within its borders including **Barum Brewery** (🖳 www.barumbrewery.co.uk), a tiny brewery based at the Reform Inn in Pilton near Barnstaple. They are responsible for the dangerously strong 6.6% ABV Barnstablasta!

Country Life Brewery (🖳 www.countrylifebrewery.com) is in the Big Sheep attraction at Bideford, where you can watch the brewing process and pick up a couple of bottles of tipples such as Pot Wallop, Old Appledore Ale or the brain-befuddling 10% ABV Devonshire 10 'Der'. Further west along the trail, **Forge Brewery** (🖳 www.forgebrewery.co.uk) in Hartland is continuing a proud tradition of brewing that was started by the Augustinian monks at the abbey.

Ciders

A pint of **cider** on this section of the walk is pretty much as obligatory as blisters. Somerset in particular is known for its cider farms, with Sheppy's (🖳 www.sheppyscider.com) at Bradford-on-Tone, Torre Cider Farm (🖳 www.torrecider.com) at Washford Watchet, Parson's Choice Cider at West Lyng, Perry's Cider Mills (🖳 www.perryscider.co.uk) of Ilminster, Hecks (🖳 www.hecksfarmhousecider.co.uk) at Street, and the Somerset Cider Brandy Co (🖳 www.ciderbrandy.co.uk) at Martock – though none is particularly near the path. Across the border, Ostlers (🖳 www.ostlerscidermill.co.uk) is a family-run cider mill based in Goodleigh near Barnstaple, Devon, that churns out scrumpy ciders, vinegars and chutneys.

Scrumpy, or rough cider, is a particular form of cider, easy to differentiate from the weaker, more mass-market keg ciders, being cloudy, fizz-free and with bits floating in it too! The only thing to remember before drinking scrumpy is that it should be done in moderation – it's powerful stuff. After you've drunk it, you'll be lucky to remember anything at all.

Buying camping supplies

There is a shop of some description in most of the places along the route, though most are small (and often combined with the post office) and whether you'll be able to find precisely what you went in for is highly unlikely. If self-catering, therefore, your menu for the evening will depend upon what you found in the store that day. Part 4 details what shops are on the path.

Drinking water

On a hot day in some of the remoter parts after a steep climb or two you'll quickly dehydrate, which is at best highly unpleasant and at worst mightily dangerous. Always carry water with you and in hot weather drink 3-4 litres a day. Don't be tempted by the water in the streams; if the cow or sheep faeces in the

---

❑ **Information for foreign visitors**

● **Currency** The British pound (£) comes in notes of £100, £50, £20, £10 and £5, and coins of £2 and £1. The pound is divided into 100 pence (usually referred to as 'p', pronounced 'pee') which comes in silver coins of 50p, 20p, 10p and 5p, and copper coins of 2p and 1p.

● **Money** Up-to-date **rates of exchange** can be found on 🖥 www.xe.com/ucc, at some post offices, or at any bank or travel agent. **Travellers' cheques** can be cashed only at banks, foreign exchanges and some of the large hotels; it is probably better to use a debit card or bring cash.

● **Business hours** Most shops and main post offices are open at least from Monday to Friday 9am-5pm and Saturday 9am-12.30pm but many shops open earlier and close later, some open on Sunday as well. Occasionally, especially in rural areas, you'll come across a local shop that closes at midday during the week, usually a Wednesday or Thursday, a throwback to the days when all towns and villages had an 'early closing day'. Many supermarkets remain open 12 hours a day; the Spar chain usually displays '8 till late' on the door. Banks typically open at 9.30am Monday to Friday and close at 3.30pm or 4pm, but of course ATM machines are open all the time (if they are outside). Pub hours are less predictable; although many open daily 11am-11pm, often in rural areas, and particularly in winter months, opening hours are 11am-3pm and 6-11pm Mon-Sat, 11am/noon-3pm and 7-11pm on Sunday.

● **National holidays** Most businesses in the South-West are shut on 1 January, Good Friday (March/April), Easter Monday (March/April), first and last Monday in May, last Monday in August, 25 December and 26 December.

● **School holidays** State-school holidays in England are generally as follows: a one-week break late October, two weeks over Christmas and the New Year, a week mid-February, two weeks around Easter, one week at the end of May/early June (to coincide with the bank holiday at the end of May) and five to six weeks from late July to early September. Private-school holidays fall at the same time, but tend to be slightly longer.

● **Documents** If you are a member of a National Trust organisation in your country bring your membership card as you should be entitled to free entry to National Trust properties and sites in the UK. See also p38.

● **EHICs and travel insurance** Although Britain's National Health Service (NHS) is free at the point of use, that is only the case for residents. All visitors to Britain should be properly insured, including comprehensive health coverage. The European Health Insurance Card (EHIC) entitles EU nationals (on production of the EHIC card so ensure you bring it with you) to necessary medical treatment under the NHS while on

water don't make you ill, the chemicals from the pesticides and fertilisers used on the farms almost certainly will. Using iodine or another purifying treatment will help to combat the former, though there's little you can do about the latter. It's a lot safer to fill up from taps instead.

MONEY

There are several banks on the trail, most equipped with an ATM (cash machine). You'll also find cash machines in many shops and stores though these tend to charge around £1.75 to withdraw money. The only place where you need to be careful is from Westward Ho! to Bude where there are no cashpoints on the path (the nearest place to get money being Hartland, several miles inland).

a temporary visit here. For details, contact your national social security institution. However, this is not a substitute for proper medical cover on your travel insurance for unforeseen bills and for getting you home should that be necessary. Also consider cover for loss and theft of personal belongings, especially if you are camping or staying in hostels, as there will be times when you'll have to leave your luggage unattended.

● **Weights and measures** The European Commission is no longer attempting to ban the pint or the mile: so, in Britain, milk can be sold in pints (1 pint = 568ml), as can beer in pubs, though most other liquid including petrol (gasoline) and diesel is sold in litres. Distances on road and path signs will continue to be given in miles (1 mile = 1.6km) rather than kilometres, and yards (1yd = 0.9m) rather than metres. The population remains divided between those who still use inches (1 inch = 2.5cm), feet (1ft = 0.3m) and yards and those who are happy with millimetres, centimetres and metres; you'll often be told that 'it's only a hundred yards or so' to somewhere, rather than a hundred metres or so.

Most food is sold in metric weights (g and kg) but the imperial weights of pounds (lb: 1lb = 453g) and ounces (oz: 1oz = 28g) are frequently displayed too. The weather – a frequent topic of conversation – is also an issue: while most forecasts predict temperatures in Celsius (C), many people continue to think in terms of Fahrenheit (F; see the temperature chart on p15 for conversions).

● **Smoking** The ban on smoking in public places relates not only to pubs and restaurants, but also to B&Bs, hostels and hotels. These latter have the right to designate one or more bedrooms where the occupants can smoke, but the ban is in force in all enclosed areas open to the public – even if they are in a private home such as a B&B. Should you be foolhardy enough to light up in a no-smoking area, which includes pretty well any indoor public place, you could be fined £50, but it's the owners of the premises who carry the can if they fail to stop you, with a potential fine of £2500.

● **Time** During the winter, the whole of Britain is on Greenwich Meantime (GMT). The clocks move one hour forward on the last Sunday in March, remaining on British Summer Time (BST) until the last Sunday in October.

● **Telephone** From outside Britain the international country access code for Britain is ☎ 44 followed by the area code minus the first 0, and then the number you require. Within Britain, to call a landline number with the same code as the landline phone you are calling from, the code can be omitted: dial the number only. If you're using a mobile phone that is registered overseas, consider buying a local SIM card to keep costs down. See also box p38.

● **Emergency services** For police, ambulance, fire or coastguard dial ☎ 999 or ☎ 112.

PLANNING YOUR WALK

Make sure you take enough out at Westward Ho! (where you'll be charged) or Bideford (where there are free ATMs). Another way of getting money in your hand is to use the **cashback system**: find a store that will accept a debit card and ask them to advance cash against the card.

However, with few local stores, pubs or B&Bs accepting credit or debit cards, and few places where you can get money out along the way, it is essential to carry plenty of cash with you, though do keep it safe and out of sight (preferably in a moneybelt). A chequebook could prove very useful as back-up, so that you don't have to keep on dipping into your cash reserves, especially as most B&Bs don't accept debit/credit cards.

Using the Post Office for banking

Several banks have agreements with the Post Office allowing customers to make cash withdrawals free of charge using a debit card at branches throughout the country. Given that many towns and villages have post offices this is a very useful facility. However, check with the Post Office Helpline (☎ 08457-223344, 🖥 www.postoffice.co.uk) that the post offices en route are still open and that your bank has an agreement with the post office. If using the website click on Counter services, then Counter money services, then Pay in and withdraw money under Use your bank account for a full list of banks offering withdrawal facilities through post office branches and for a list of the branches with an ATM.

OTHER SERVICES

There is **internet access** in the libraries along the trail as well as at several shops and other private enterprises. Many pubs, restaurants and B&Bs also have wi-fi, useful for those who've brought their own laptop/mobile. Most villages have a **grocery store**; nearby you'll usually find a **phone box**. There are **outdoor equipment shops** in Porlock, Lynmouth, Combe Martin, Barnstaple and Bude.

WALKING COMPANIES

It is, of course, possible to turn up with your boots and backpack at Minehead and just start walking, with little planned save for your accommodation (see box on p19). The following companies, however, are in the business of making your holiday as stress-free and enjoyable as possible.

Baggage carriers

For those who don't fancy being burdened while on the path, it is possible to arrange to have your luggage transferred to the end of each day's destination. The main baggage company on the SWCP is the aptly named **Luggage Transfers** (☎ 01326-550721, 🖥 www.luggagetransfers.co.uk), who cover the whole of the path, charging from £13 for a two-bag transfer; the rate depends on the distance. They deliver to B&Bs and campsites (as long as you have rung the campsite by the night before to give your name).

Alternatively, some of the **taxi** firms listed in this guide can provide a similar service within a local area if you want a break from carrying your bags for a day or so. Also, don't rule out the possibility of your B&B/guesthouse owner taking your bags ahead for you; plenty of them are glad to do so. Depending on the distance they may make no charge at all, or charge £10-15; this may be less than a taxi so is worth enquiring about.

Self-guided holidays

Useful for those who simply don't have the time to organise their trip, several companies now offer what are known as self-guided holidays, where your accommodation, transport at the start/end of the walk and baggage transportation along the trail are arranged for you.

Unless specified, all the companies below offer walks on the whole South-West Coast Path (SWCP) and they can tailor-make holidays and arrange accommodation only if required. Detailed information and maps are also provided as a matter of course, thereby allowing you to just turn up and start marching!

● **Budget Walking** (☎ 01326-565114, 💻 www.budgetwalking.co.uk; Cornwall) Claims to be the cheapest self-guided walking holidays along the SWCP. Most of their holidays are seven-night, six-days, though they do a ten-day Minehead to Bude holiday and can also organise dog-friendly walking holidays.

● **Celtic Trails** (☎ 01291-689774, 💻 www.celtic-trails.com; Chepstow) Long-established company that offers walks all over the UK. They divide the SWCP into nine sections; their Minehead to Westward Ho! section is spread over seven days of walking. You have a choice of two levels of accommodation.

● **Contours** (☎ 01629-821900, 💻 www.contours.co.uk; Derbyshire) They divide the SWCP into ten sections and offer walks from three days to four weeks and more. Their itineraries from Minehead to Westward Ho! last six, seven and eleven days.

● **Encounter Walking Holidays** (☎ 01208-871066, 💻 www.encounterwalking holidays.com; Fowey, Cornwall) Operating tailor made short breaks and walking holidays around whole SWCP. Will help everyone from individual walkers to large groups and specialise in assisting overseas walkers along the route.

● **Explore Britain** (☎ 01740-650900, 💻 www.explorebritain.com; Co Durham) Walks on the SWCP include six days from Minehead to Barnstaple, five days from Minehead to Woolacombe, and four days from Minehead to Combe Martin.

● **Footpath Holidays** (☎ 01985-840049, 💻 www.footpath-holidays.com; Wilts) Arrange a six-day Exmoor Coast walk from Minehead to Instow, and a five-day section along the North Devon Coast from Instow to Bude.

● **Let's Go Walking!** (☎ 01837-880075, 💻 www.southwestcoastpathwalking holidays.com; Devon) Covers the SWCP in ten sections including an eight-day stretch from Minehead to Barnstaple and another eight-day section from Barnstaple to Crackington Haven, with an optional trip to Lundy Island.

● **Macs Adventure** (☎ 0141-530 8886, 💻 www.macsadventure.com; Glasgow) Have walks covering the whole SWCP including Minehead to Westward Ho! (6-7 days) and Westward Ho! to Padstow (6-8 days).

● **Westcountry Walking Holidays** (☎ 0845-094 3848, 💻 www.westcountry-walking-holidays.com; Middlesex) They specialise in walking holidays in south-west England and offer a nine-day Minehead to Hartland Quay walk as well as short (two-night) and tailor-made breaks anywhere along the SWCP.

Group/guided walking tours

These are ideal for those who want the extra safety, security and companionship that comes with walking in a group. Accommodation, meals, transport to and from the trail, baggage transfer – all of these are usually included in the price.

● **HF Holidays** (☎ 0845-470 7558, 🖳 www.hfholidays.co.uk; Herts) Offers guided walks to various parts of the SWCP including the seven-night Somerset & North Devon Coast Path (Minehead to Croyde).

Budgeting

England is not a cheap place to go travelling and the accommodation providers on the South-West Coast Path are more than used to seeing tourists and charge accordingly. You may think before you set out that you are going to try to keep your budget to a minimum by camping every night and cooking your own food but it's a rare walker who sticks to this rule. Besides, the B&Bs and pubs on the route are amongst the path's major attractions and it would be a pity not to sample the hospitality in at least some of them.

If the only expenses of this walk were accommodation and food, budgeting for the trip would be a piece of cake. Unfortunately, in addition there are all the little extras that push up the cost of your trip: getting to and from the path, beer, cream teas, stamps and postcards, internet access, buses here and there, baggage carriers, phone calls, laundry, souvenirs, entrance fees ... it's surprising how much all of these things add up.

CAMPING

You can survive on less than £15 per person (pp) if you use the cheapest campsites, don't visit a pub, avoid all the museums and tourist attractions in the towns, cook all your own food from staple ingredients and generally have a pretty miserable time of it. Even then, unforeseen expenses will probably nudge your daily budget above this figure. Include the occasional pint, and perhaps a pub meal every now and then, and the figure will be nearer £20-25pp a day.

HOSTELS

There are only three YHA hostels, with charges ranging from £9.99pp (when there's a special offer on at the hostel in Westward Ho!) to £18.40pp (Minehead). There are, however, several independent hostels at Minehead, Ilfracombe (two of them), Croyde and Bude. Rates are £10pp (Ilfracombe) to £30pp (though the latter is unusual and refers to the hostel at Croyde). These rates don't usually include breakfast but you may be able to order one for around £5; which means that, overall, it can cost around £30-35pp per day, or £40-50pp to live in a little more comfort and enjoy the odd beer or two.

B&Bs, GUESTHOUSES AND HOTELS

B&B rates start at £21pp per night but can be at least twice this, particularly if you are walking alone and are thus liable to pay single supplements. Add the cost of lunch and dinner and you should reckon on about £40-45 minimum. Staying in a guesthouse or hotel will push the minimum up to £55-60. See also pp20-1.

Itineraries

To help you plan your walk there is a **planning map** (opposite the inside back cover) and a **table of village/town facilities** (pp32-33), which gives a run-down on the essential information you will need regarding accommodation possibilities and services.

SUGGESTED ITINERARIES

The itineraries in the box below and on p30 are based on different accommodation types (camping or B&B/hotel), each divided into three options depending on your walking speed. They are only suggestions so feel free to adapt them. Don't forget to **add on your travelling time** before and after the walk. If using public transport to get to the start and end of the walk see the **public transport map and service details and map** on pp44-51. Once you have an idea of your

PLANNING YOUR WALK

STAYING IN B&B-STYLE ACCOMMODATION

	Relaxed		Medium		Fast	
Night	**Place**	**Approx Distance** miles/km	**Place**	**Approx Distance** miles/km	**Place**	**Approx Distance** miles/km
0	Minehead	0	Minehead	0	Minehead	0
1	Porlock Weir	9/14.5	Porlock Weir	9/14.5	Lynmouth	21.25/34.2
2	Lynmouth	12.25/19.7	Lynmouth	12.25/19.7	Ilfracombe	19.5/31.3
3	Combe Martin	13.75/22.1	Combe Martin	13.75/22.1	Croyde	14.75/23.7
4	Ilfracombe	5.75/9.3	Woolacombe	14.25/22.9	Barnstaple	13.5/21.7
5	Woolacombe	8.5/13.7	Braunton	14.75/23.7	W'ward Ho!	18.5/29.8
6	Saunton	8.5/13.7	Instow	12.5/20.1	Clovelly	11/17.7
7	Barnstaple	11.25/18.1	Westward Ho!	11/17.7	H'land Quay	10.5/16.9
8	Instow	7.5/12.1	Clovelly	11/17.7	Bude	15.5/25
9	Appledore	6.25/10.1	Hartland Quay	10.5/16.9		
10	Westward Ho!	4.75/7.6	Morwenstow	8/12.9		
11	Clovelly	11/17.7	Bude	7.5/12.1		
12	Hartland Quay	10.5/16.9				
13	Morwenstow	8/12.9				
14	Bude	7.5/12.1				
Total		**124.5/200.3**		**124.5/200.3**		**124.5/200.3**

CAMPING					
Relaxed		Medium		Fast	
Place	Approx Distance	Place	Approx Distance	Place	Approx Distance
Night	miles/km		miles/km		miles/km
0 Minehead	0	Minehead	0	Minehead	0
1 Porlock*	7.25/11.7	Porlock*	7.25/11.7	Lynton*	22/35.4
2 Lynton*	15.25/24.5	Lynton*	15.25/24.5	Watermouth	16/25.75
3 Watermouth	16/25.75	Combe Martin	14/22.5	Woolacombe	12.25/19.7
4 Woolacombe	12.25/19.7	Woolacombe	14.25/22.9	Chivenor	16/25.7
5 Croyde	6.25/10.1	Saunton(Lobb)*	10.5/16.5	Appledore*	18/29
6 Chivenor	9.75/15.7	Chivenor	9.5/15.3	Clovelly*	17.25/27.8
7 Appledore*	18/29	Appledore*	18/29	H'land Quay*	12/19.3
8 Westward Ho!	5.25/8.45	Clovelly*	17.25/27.8	Bude	16/25.7
9 Clovelly*	12/19.3	Hartland Quay*	12/19.3		
10 Hartland Quay*	12/19.3	Bude	16/25.7		
12 Bude	16/25.7				
Total	**130/209.2**		**134/215.6**		**129.5/208.4**

* **Note**: In this chart we have included in the mile counts an approximate figure for places where the campsite is out of town. For example, the campsite at **Lynton** is half a mile outside of the town, so that those who are staying there have to walk half a mile further to reach it – and another half-mile the next day to return to the path. The other places where this is relevant are: **Porlock** (quarter of a mile to Lobb Campsite from path); **Saunton** (two miles to Lobb Campsite from path); **Appledore** (half a mile to Knapp House from path); **Clovelly** (one mile to get to Dyke Green Farm at Higher Clovelly from path); **Hartland Quay** (half a mile to Stoke Barton from path).

approach turn to Part 4 for detailed information on accommodation, places to eat and other services in each village and town on the route. Also in Part 4 you will find summaries of the route to accompany the detailed trail maps.

WHICH DIRECTION?

It's more common for walkers attempting the entire trail to start from Minehead and head west. This is also the logical way to walk and thus the way we have chosen to describe the route in this direction in Part 4. If this is your first taste of the South-West Coast Path – but think you may like to do it all one day – obviously this is the way to head, with the Cornwall section next up. Furthermore, many will argue that Bude is a more picturesque place to celebrate the end of your walk than Minehead!

That said, this may of course be the final leg of your walk on the South-West Coast Path and thus Bude to Minehead would probably be the way to go. What's more, the prevailing wind usually comes from the west, so by walking in this direction you'll find you have the weather behind you, pushing you on rather than driving in your face. If you prefer to swim against the tide of popular opinion and walk west to east you should find it easy to use this book too.

THE BEST DAY AND WEEKEND WALKS

Trying to pick one particular section that is representative of the entire trail is impossible because each is very different. The wilds of Exmoor, the beaches of Woolacombe and Croyde, the estuaries of Bideford and Barnstaple, and the windswept cliff-top beauty of Hartland – each region enjoys its own character and to think that, by visiting one, you have a flavour of the entire region, is erroneous. That said, if you don't have the time to walk the entire route the following will allow you to savour at least some of the joys of the Exmoor and North Devon Coast Path. The main obstacle to preparing a short itinerary of a few days or less along the cost path is the lack of regular transport connections to towns and villages on the way. For example, on possibly the most spectacular part of the entire SWCP, Clovelly to Bude, public transport is scarce and it is thus very difficult to divide this section into day walks. However, if you have three days spare this section is both achievable and most definitely worth it!

All of the routes below are designed to link up with public transport (see pp49-51) at both their start and finish.

Minehead to Porlock   7½ miles/12km (see pp79-89)
A splendid introduction to Exmoor with varied terrain, tremendous views out to sea as well as the option of an alternative rugged route. Parts of this walk are quite tough – although the hardest part may well be turning back and going home after just one day.

Lynton to Combe Martin   13½ miles/22.1km (see pp105-16)
You may wish to get up early for this one, a long and strenuous day's walk that will truly whet the appetite for both Exmoor and the coastal path. Highlights include the extraordinary Valley of Rocks as well as the SWCP's highest point – Great Hangman.

Woolacombe to Croyde   6¼ miles/10km (see pp130-9)
A moderate to easy day's walk that could be completed in one morning. There is the option of either walking through Woolacombe Warren or making your way along the beach before both paths unite for a stroll around Baggy Point: the views from here over Croyde Bay and Saunton Sands are terrific.

Croyde to Braunton   8¾ miles/14km (see pp139-47)
Ambling hand-in-hand with the Tarka Trail around Saunton Down and through the Braunton Burrows, this is an easy to moderate day's walk.

Bideford to Westward Ho!   8¼ miles/13.2km (see pp162-73)
An easy day's walk that includes both the lovely village of Appledore – an ideal location for lunch – and Northam Burrows Country Park.

Weekend walks – 2-3 days
● **Exmoor: Porlock Weir to Combe Martin** 26 miles/41.8km (see pp89-116)
A strenuous couple of days with an overnight stop in Lynmouth/Lynton; this section offers some of the best walking in England – fact!   (*cont'd on p34*)

VILLAGE AND

Place name (Places in brackets are a short walk off the path)	Distance from previous place § approx miles/km	Bank/ Cash Machine (ATM) *	Post Office	Tourist Information Centre (TIC) Visitor Centre (VC)
Minehead	0	✓	✓	
Bossington	**6/9.7**			
(Porlock)	(1.25/2)	✓	✓	VC
Porlock Weir	**3/4.8**			
Countisbury	**10.75/17.3**			
Lynmouth	**1.5/2.4**	✓		VC
Lynton	**0.25/0.4**	✓	✓	TIC
Combe Martin	**13.5/21.7**	✓	✓	TIC
Watermouth	**2/3.2**			
Ilfracombe	**3.75/6**	✓	✓	TIC
(Lee)	(2.5/4)			
Woolacombe	**8.5/13.7**	✓	✓	TIC
Croyde	**6.25/10.1**	✓	✓	
Saunton	**2.25/3.6**			
Braunton	**6.25/10.1**	✓	✓	
Chivenor	**1.25/2**			
Barnstaple	**3.75/6**	✓	✓	TIC
Fremington Quay	**2.5/4**			
Instow	**5/8**	✓	✓	
Bideford	**2.75/4.4**	✓	✓	TIC
Appledore	**3.5/5.6**		✓	IN LIBRARY
Westward Ho!	**4.75/7.6**	✓	✓	
Clovelly	**11/17.7**			VC
Hartland Quay	**10.5/16.9**			
(Stoke)	(0.5/0.8)			
(Hartland)	(2.5/4)	✓	✓	
(Elmscott)	(2/3.2)			
(Morwenstow)	(8/12.9)			
Bude	**15.5/24.9**	✓	✓	TIC

TOTAL DISTANCE   **124.5 miles/200.3km**

§ The distances between a place **and the previous place** *on* **the path** are given in brackets; distances in **bold** are between places directly on the trail.

* CASH MACHINE ✓ Cash machine (ATM) available;
                    ✓ ATM available but charges for use

PLANNING YOUR WALK

TOWN FACILITIES

Eating Place ✔=one ✔✔=two ✔✔✔=three + (✔)=seasonal	Food Store	Campsite	Hostels YHA/ H (IndHostel)	B&B-style accommodation ✔=one ✔✔=two ✔✔✔=three+	Place name (Places in brackets are a short walk off the path)
✔✔✔	✔	✔	YHA/H	✔✔✔	**Minehead**
(✔)				✔	**Bossington**
✔✔✔	✔	✔		✔✔✔	(Porlock)
✔✔✔	✔			✔✔✔	**Porlock Weir**
✔				✔	**Countisbury**
✔✔✔	✔	✔		✔✔✔	**Lynmouth**
✔✔✔	✔			✔✔✔	**Lynton**
✔✔✔		✔		✔✔✔	**Combe Martin**
✔		✔		✔	**Watermouth**
✔✔✔	✔		H	✔✔✔	**Ilfracombe**
✔				✔	(Lee)
✔✔✔	✔	✔		✔✔✔	**Woolacombe**
✔✔✔	✔	✔	H	✔✔✔	**Croyde**
✔✔		✔		✔✔✔	**Saunton**
✔✔✔	✔			✔✔✔	**Braunton**
✔		✔			**Chivenor**
✔✔✔	✔			✔✔✔	**Barnstaple**
✔					**Fremington Quay**
✔✔✔	✔			✔✔✔	**Instow**
✔✔✔	✔			✔✔✔	**Bideford**
✔✔✔	✔	✔		✔✔✔	**Appledore**
✔✔✔	✔	✔	YHA	✔✔✔	**Westward Ho!**
✔✔✔		✔		✔✔✔	**Clovelly**
✔				✔	**Hartland Quay**
		✔		✔	(Stoke)
✔✔	✔			✔✔✔	(Hartland)
			H	✔	(Elmscott)
✔✔				✔✔	(Morwenstow)
✔✔✔	✔	✔	H	✔✔✔	**Bude**

Weekend walks – 2-3 days (cont'd from p31)
● **Beaches and Burrows: Ilfracombe to Braunton** 23$^1/_2$ miles/38km (see pp120-47) This is a relatively easy couple of days; highlights include the beaches of Woolacombe and Saunton as well as Braunton Burrows.

● **The best of the best: Westward Ho! to Bude** 37 miles/59.5km (see pp172-203) A long, strenuous and truly spectacular three-day walk, but the scenery is some of the best on the entire SWCP. Highlights include the village of Clovelly and the remarkably dramatic views of the sunset over the Atlantic at Hartland Quay.

SIDE TRIPS

The South-West Coast Path cuts through some of the richest walking territory in the UK and there are plenty of opportunities for short (or long) diversions off the trail. Such trips are beyond the scope of this book but a glance at the box below and an Ordnance Survey map will give you some idea of the other walks available.

PLANNING YOUR WALK

> ❏ **Other trails**
> Whilst the SWCP follows the coastline of Exmoor, other walking trails meander through its interior and some, at points, cross over or join the coastal path.
> ● **The Coleridge Way** (🖳 www.coleridgeway.co.uk) Starting in Nether Stowey, where Coleridge lived from 1797, The Coleridge Way crosses 36 miles of the Quantock Hills, Brendon Hills and Exmoor, ending in Porlock (where the Man who notoriously interrupted the writing of the poet's *Kubla Khan* originated). In 1956 the Quantock Hills was the first area of England to be designated an Area of Outstanding Natural Beauty (AONB). The trail is well-serviced by pubs and tea-rooms.
> ● **The Tarka Trail** (🖳 www.devon.gov.uk/tarkatrail) Following in the paw-steps of Henry Williamson's famous *Tarka the Otter*, this 180-mile path runs in the shape of a figure-of-eight and centres on Barnstaple. It joins the SWCP at Lynton and colludes with it as far south as Bideford. The stretch between Braunton and Meeth is part of Sustrans' National Cycle Network (🖳 www.nationalcyclenetwork.org.uk), and there's a section where you even take a train! Whilst the chances of seeing an otter are slim there is an abundance of other wildlife to be seen.
> ● **The Two Moors Way/Erme-Plym Trail** (🖳 www.devon.gov.uk/twomoorsway .pdf) The Erme-Plym Trail begins in Wembury on the South-Devon coast and travels as far North as Ivybridge where The Two Moors Way begins. Climbing onto Dartmoor can be strenuous but the effort is worth it. The trail then heads north, traversing the length of Dartmoor to Drewsteignton before passing through Morchard Bishop and Witheridge, eventually entering Exmoor from the south before culminating in Lynmouth. Splendid scenery, and real solitude are just two of the joys of this trip.
> ● **The Samaritans Way** (🖳 www.samaritansway-southwest.org.uk) Beginning at Clifton Suspension Bridge in Bristol this 100-mile jaunt heads south through the Mendip Hills to Glastonbury before turning west and passing through the Quantock Hills and Exmoor to end in Lynton. For those after a really long walk, The Samaritans Way can be joined to The Cotswold Way via The River Avon trail which runs from Bath to Bristol.

What to take

'When you have worn out your shoes, the strength of the shoe leather has passed into the fiber of your body. I measure your health by the number of shoes and hats and clothes you have worn out.'
Ralph Waldo Emerson

Deciding how much to take can be difficult. Experienced walkers know that you should take only the bare essentials but at the same time you must ensure you have all the equipment necessary to make the trip safe and comfortable.

KEEP YOUR LUGGAGE LIGHT

Experienced backpackers know that there is some sort of complicated formula governing the success of a walk, in which the enjoyment of the walk is inversely proportional to the amount carried.

Carrying a heavy rucksack slows you down, tires you out and gives you aches and pains in parts of the body that you never knew existed. It is imperative, therefore, that you take a good deal of time packing and that you are ruthless when you do; if it's not essential, don't take it.

HOW TO CARRY IT

If you are using one of the baggage-carrier services, you must contact them beforehand to find out what their regulations are regarding the weight and size of the luggage you wish them to carry.

Even if you are using one of these services, you will still need to carry a small **daypack** with you, filled with those items that you will need during the day: water bottle or pouch, this book, map, sun-screen, sun hat, wet-weather gear, some food, camera, money and so on.

If you have decided to forego the services of the baggage carriers you will have to consider your **rucksack** even more carefully. Ultimately its size will depend on where you are planning to stay and how you are planning to eat. If you are camping and cooking for yourself you will probably need a 65- to 75-litre rucksack, which should be large enough to carry a small tent, sleeping bag, cooking equipment, crockery, cutlery and food. Those not carrying their home with them should find a 40- to 60-litre rucksack sufficient.

When choosing a rucksack, make sure it has a stiffened back and can be adjusted to fit your own back comfortably. Don't just try the rucksack out in the shop: take it home, fill it with things and then try it out around the house and take it out for a short walk. Only then can you be certain that it fits. Make sure the hip belt and chest strap (if there is one) are fastened tightly as this helps distribute the weight more comfortably with most of it being carried on the hips. Carry a small daypack inside the rucksack, as this will be useful to carry things in when leaving the main pack at the hostel or B&B.

One reader wrote in with the eminently sensible advice of taking a **water-proof rucksack cover**. Most rucksacks these days have them 'built in' to the sack, but you can also buy them separately for less than a tenner. Lining your bag with a **bin liner** is another sensible, cut-price idea. Finally, it's also a good idea to keep everything wrapped in plastic bags inside the rucksack; I usually place all these bags inside a bin-bag which then goes inside the rucksack. That way, even if it does pour with rain, everything should remain dry.

FOOTWEAR

Boots
Only a decent pair of strong, durable walking boots is good enough to survive the rigours of the South-West Coast Path. Don't be tempted by a spell of hot weather into bringing something flimsier. Make sure, too, that your boots provide good ankle support, for the ground can occasionally be rough and stony and twisted ankles are commonplace. Make sure your boots are waterproof as well: these days most people opt for a synthetic waterproof lining (Gore-Tex or similar), though a good-quality leather boot with dubbin should prove just as reliable in keeping your feet dry.

In addition, many people bring an extra pair of shoes or trainers to wear off the trail. This is not essential but if you are using one of the luggage-carrying services and you've got room in your luggage, why not?

Socks
If you haven't got a pair of the modern hi-tech walking socks the old system of wearing a thin liner sock under a thicker wool sock is just as good. Bring a few pairs of each.

CLOTHES

In a country notorious for its unpredictable climate it is imperative that you pack enough clothes to cover every extreme of weather, from burning hot to bloomin' freezing.

Modern hi-tech outdoor clothes come with a range of fancy names and brands but they all still follow the basic two- or three-layer principle, with an inner base layer to transport sweat away from your skin, a mid-layer for warmth and an outer layer to protect you from the wind and rain.

A thin lightweight **thermal top** of a synthetic material is ideal as the base layer as it draws moisture (ie sweat) away from your body. Cool in hot weather and warm when worn under other clothes in the cold, pack at least one thermal top. Over the top in cold weather a mid-weight **polyester fleece** should suffice. Fleeces are light, more water-resistant than the alternatives (such as a woolly jumper), remain warm even when wet and pack down small in rucksacks; they are thus ideal walking gear.

Over the top of all this a **waterproof jacket** is essential. 'Breathable' jackets cost a small fortune (though prices are falling all the time) but they do prevent the build-up of condensation.

Leg wear

Many walkers find walking trousers an unnecessary investment. Any light, quick-drying trouser should suffice. Jeans are heavy and dry slowly and are thus not recommended. A pair of waterproof trousers *is* more than useful, however, while on really hot sunny days you'll be glad you brought your shorts. Thermal **long johns** take up little room in the rucksack and could be vital if the weather starts to close in.

Gaiters are not essential but, again, those who bring them are always glad they did, for they provide extra protection when walking through muddy ground and when the vegetation around the trail is dripping wet after bad weather.

Underwear

Three or four changes of underwear is fine. Any more is excessive, any less unhygienic. Because backpacks can cause bra straps to dig painfully into the skin, women may find a **sports bra** more comfortable.

Other clothes

You may like to consider a woolly **hat** and **gloves** – you'd be surprised how cold it can get up on the cliffs even in summer. A **sun hat** (see p60) is vital given the strength of the sun sometimes.

TOILETRIES

Once again, take the minimum. **Soap**, **towel**, a **toothbrush** and **toothpaste** are pretty much essential (although those staying in B&Bs will find that most provide soap and towels anyway). Some **toilet paper** could also prove vital on the trail, particularly if using public toilets (which occasionally run out).

Other items: **razor**; **deodorant**; **tampons/sanitary towels** and a high factor **sun-screen** should cover just about everything.

FIRST-AID KIT

A small first-aid kit could prove useful for those emergencies that occur along the trail. This kit should include **aspirin** or **paracetamol**; **plasters** for minor cuts; Compeed, **Second Skin** or some other treatment for blisters; a **bandage** or elasticated joint support for supporting a sprained ankle or a weak knee; **antiseptic wipes**; **antiseptic cream**; **safety pins**; **tweezers** and **scissors**.

GENERAL ITEMS

Essential

Everybody should have a **map**, **torch**, **water bottle or pouch**, **spare batteries**, **penknife**, **whistle** (see p58 for details of the international distress signal), some **emergency food** and a **watch** (preferably with an alarm to help you make an early start each day). Those with weak knees will find a **walking pole** or **sticks** essential. Those who've also walked in Scotland will recognise the importance of taking **insect repellent** to ward off midges, though they're not so bad here. **Sun screen**, however, is vital; see p60.

❏ **Mobile phone reception and internet connections on the trail**
While many people view their walk in this remote corner of England as an escape from the modern world, for some people a decent connection with the outside world is vital. In our research we found Orange (together with its partner T-Mobile under the name Everything Everywhere) provided the best coverage for mobile and internet connections (with Vodaphone pretty good too); those who need to stay in touch, and who are taking a laptop, may like to consider investing in an Orange dongle (a small device that plugs into a USB port and connects your computer to the internet) – though many B&Bs and pubs also offer wi-fi.

A **mobile phone** (see box above) is invaluable too – and reception is usually pretty good – for arranging a lift from the path to the B&B, booking a table at a restaurant etc; just don't forget the charger! If you know how to use it properly you'll also find a **compass** handy.

Useful items and luxuries

Suggestions here include a **book** for days off or on train and bus journeys, a **camera**, a pair of **sunglasses**, **binoculars** and a **radio or iPod**.

CAMPING GEAR

Campers will find a sleeping bag essential. A two- to three-season bag should suffice for summer. In addition, they will also need a decent bivvy bag or tent, a sleeping mat, fuel and stove, cutlery/pans, a cup and a scrubber for washing up.

MONEY

Cash machines (ATMs) are fairly common along the Exmoor and North Devon Coast Path as are banks. However, not everybody accepts **debit** or **credit cards** as payment – though some B&Bs and many restaurants now do.

As a result, you should carry a fair amount of **cash** with you, just to be on the safe side. A **cheque book** from a British bank is useful in those places where debit/credit cards are not accepted.

Crime on the trail is thankfully rare but it's always a good idea to carry your money safely in a **moneybelt**.

DOCUMENTS

National Trust and English Heritage membership cards, as well as student (ISIC) and YHA hostel cards could save you money on the trail. Some sort of ID, such as a driving licence, might also prove useful.

MAPS

It would be perfectly possible to walk long stretches of the coastal path unaided by map or compass. Just keep the sea to your right (or left, depending on which way you're heading) and you can't go too far off track. The **hand-drawn maps in this book**, which cover the trail at a scale of 1:20,000, should provide sufficient aid in areas where navigation is slightly more problematic.

Nevertheless, having other maps will paint a more fulfilling picture of your surroundings and will allow you to plan much more effectively for any accommodation or other facilities that lie off the trail. **Ordnance Survey** (OS; 🖳 www.ordnancesurvey.co.uk) produce their maps to two scales: the 1:25,000 Explorer series in orange and the 1:50,000 Landranger in pink (which is less useful for walking purposes). Alongside the paper versions OS also produce an 'Active' edition of both which is 'weatherproof' (covered in a lightweight protective plastic coating). Those needed for the stretch of the SWCP covered by this book are as follows: Explorer: Outdoor Leisure (OL) 9 Exmoor; 139 Bideford, Ilfracombe and Barnstaple; 126 Clovelly and Hartland, and 111 Bude, Boscastle and Tintagel. The fourth map is really essential only if you plan to continue past Bude, as the section of path missing between Map 126 and Bude is only about a mile or two of fairly uneventful walking. If you don't feel that such precise cartography is needed the Landranger may be sufficient; of the 14 to cover the SWCP you will need the following three to cover the initial 115 miles: 181 Minehead and Brendon Hills; 180 Barnstaple and Ilfracombe; and 190 Bude and Clovelly. While it may be extravagant to buy all these maps, Ramblers (see box p41) allows members to borrow them at just 50p per map, or £1 for waterproof maps. Alternatively, members of Backpackers are entitled to discounts.

OS also offer **digital maps** of the region. You can get them from Memory Map at a scale of 1:25,000. They cover the whole SWCP in two volumes. Minehead to Falmouth and Falmouth to Poole. Each volume costs £99.95.

Harvey Maps (🖳 www.harveymaps.co.uk) produce a series of maps that cover all the designated National Trails to a scale of 1:40,000. For full coverage of the SWCP you will need six, but if you are intending to walk the section covered by this book just Map One (Minehead to Bude) will suffice. This of course will save on weight and cost compared to buying the four OS maps, though the OS has more detail and will show you what is further inland.

RECOMMENDED READING

Below is a by no-means exhaustive but hopefully helpful introduction to some of the literature available in regards to the SWCP and, in particular, the Exmoor and North Devon coast.

Guidebooks
If you're willing to also carry separate maps, undoubtedly the most detailed guide to the accommodation, tide tables and other useful information on the entire SWCP is the South West Coast Path Association's companion to the path, called simply **The South-West Coast Path** and currently priced at £9.95. Alongside this annual guide they also produce and sell pamphlets for each section which can be found in tourist information centres en route or ordered via post or online for £1; see 🖳 www.southwestcoastpath.org.uk for details.

Flora and fauna

For identifying obscure plants and peculiar looking beasties as you walk, Collins and New Holland publish a pocket-sized range to Britain's natural riches. The Collins Gem series are tough little books; current titles include guides to *Trees*, *Birds*, *Mushrooms*, *Wild Flowers*, *Wild Animals*, *Insects* and *Butterflies*. In addition, for any budding crustacean connoisseur there is a *Seashore* book, and there is also handbook to the *Stars*, which could be of particular interest for those who are considering sleeping under them. Also in the Collins series, there's an adapted version of Richard Mabey's classic bestseller *Food for Free* – great for anyone intent on getting back to nature, saving the pennies, or just with an interest in what's edible outside of a supermarket. You could also consult *Wild Food: Foraging for Food in the Wild*, written by Jane Eastoe and published by the National Trust.

New Holland's Concise range covers much the same topics as the Gem series and comes in a waterproof plastic jacket and include useful quick reference foldout charts. Both series contain a wealth of information.

If you have a smart phone it's worth investigating the rapidly increasing range of flora and fauna identification apps that are becoming available.

Autobiography and fiction

With the Falklands War imminent Mark Wallington set off to walk the SWCP in an attempt to impress a girl that he had met at a party. Accompanied by the more-loathed-than-loved Boogie the dog, man and beast survive all that the path can throw at them on a diet of tinned soup and Kennomeat. *Travels with Boogie: 500 Mile Walkies* is Wallington's humorous account of his time spent on the trail. If you have walked and camped or have ever walked a long distance with a dog many of the author's anecdotes will ring true – a light-hearted and thoroughly enjoyable read. Another dog goes walking in *Two feet, four paws*, Spud Talbot-Ponsonby's tale of her time circumnavigating Britain (Chapter 15: Bristol to Boscastle is the relevant chapter to this section of the SWCP).

The Tarka Trail is a local path named after Henry Williamson's much-loved *Tarka the Otter*, just one of many books in which Williamson's extraordinary ability to evoke the Devonshire countryside gilds every page. Perhaps the most famous book, however, is the most dense 19th-century classic, *Lorna Doone: A Romance of Exmoor*, by Richard Doddridge Blackmore. Margaret Drabble's witty 1998 novel *The Witch of Exmoor* is also set near the Lyn Valley.

Possibly the only piece of fiction to inspire the name of an English village, *Westward Ho!* (see p171) is a Spanish Armada adventure-romp written by Charles Kingsley.

History

Hope Bourne had four books published during her 91-year lifetime that vividly describe life in the wilds of Devon, beginning with 1963's *Living on Exmoor* and ending with 1993's *My Moorland Life*.

One thousand years of farming, quarrying and the Home Guard are crammed into Felicity Goodall's *Lost Devon*, which is good for those with an interest in the lost heritage of the county; while for those interested in the development of

❏ SOURCES OF FURTHER INFORMATION

Online information

● **www.southwestcoastpath.com** The official and most useful website to Britain's longest national trail. Good for background information on the trail and has the latest news on the path, details about river crossings and army ranges, as well as lots of information on accommodation, suggested itineraries and distance and timing calculators.

● **www.southwestcoastpath.org.uk** The site for the SWCPA, a registered charity that exists to support users of the path. Many of the features on the official site are replicated here – distance calculators, river crossing details etc – though there is much more detail here too. The Association is also very active politically, pressurising government bodies to ensure that the path is highly maintained along its length. Membership is available at £12.50/14/21 for single/joint/group memberships for UK residents (£19 for both single and joint membership for non-UK residents) and includes a free copy of their guidebook and twice-yearly newsletters.

● **www.southwestcoastalpath.co.uk** Unusual website that concentrates on day walks along short stretches of the Coast Path. Also includes information on accommodation, pubs and restaurants.

● **www.exmoor-nationalpark.gov.uk** The official site of the Exmoor National Park – home to both the country's longest wooded coastline and its highest tree!

● **www.everythingexmoor.org.uk** A community website that publishes news stories about the park that are sent in by members of the public. It's currently a little shambolic but if the links aren't broken you should be able to unearth a lot of information.

● **www.northdevon-aonb.org.uk** Official website of the North Devon Areas of Outstanding Natural Beauty. Good for background information on the geology, flora and fauna of the region.

Tourist information centres (TICs)

As one of the busiest tourist areas of the country, it is no surprise to find that the South-West is well served by tourist information offices. Centres close to this section of the coastal path are: **Lynton** (see p102); **Combe Martin** (see p114); **Ilfracombe** (see p120); **Woolacombe** (see p130); **Barnstaple** (see p151); **Bideford** (see p163); **Appledore** (see p167); and **Bude** (see p199). At the time of research the offices in Minehead and Braunton had closed.

Organisations for walkers

● **The Backpackers' Club** (🖳 www.backpackersclub.co.uk) A club aimed at people who are involved or interested in lightweight camping through walking, cycling, skiing and canoeing. They produce a quarterly magazine, provide members with a comprehensive advisory and information service on all aspects of backpacking, organise weekend trips, offer discounts for maps and at outdoor stores, and also publish a farm-pitch directory. Membership is £12 a year.

● **The Long Distance Walkers' Association** (🖳 www.ldwa.org.uk) Membership (£13 a year) includes a copy of their journal *Strider* three times per year giving details of challenge events and local group walks as well as articles on the subject. Members also receive a discount on maps and also on the UK Trailwalker's Handbook which details 730 trails across the UK.

● **Ramblers** (formerly Ramblers' Association; 🖳 www.ramblers.org.uk) Looks after the interests of walkers throughout Britain. They publish a large amount of useful information including their quarterly *Walk* magazine (£3.60 to non-members). The website also has a discussion forum. Membership costs £31/41/19.50 individual/joint/concessionary; £10 discount for individual/joint membership if paid by direct debit.

the moor's landscape and archaeology, *The Field Archaeology of Exmoor* by Hazel Riley and Robert Wilson-North is published by English Heritage.

A broader, more conventional historical summary can be found in Mary Siraut's *Exmoor: The Making of an English Upland*. Local historian Dennis Corner has written several books on the local area including *Porlock in those Days*. Derrick Warren's *Curious Devon* examines the quirkier side of the county, while for something a little darker there's John Van Der Kiste's *Grim Almanac of Devon* that recounts 366 of the county's more macabre episodes.

❏ TAKING DOGS ALONG THE COAST PATH

The South-West Coast Path is a dog-friendly path and many are the rewards that await those prepared to make the extra effort required to bring their best friend along with them. However, don't underestimate the amount of work involved in bringing your pooch to the path. Indeed, just about every decision you make will be influenced by the fact that you've got a dog: how you plan to travel to the start of the trail, where you're going to stay, how far you're going to walk each day, where you're going to eat in the evening etc, etc. The decision-making begins before you've set foot on the trail. For starters, you have to ask – and be honest with – yourself: can your dog really cope with walking ten-plus miles a day, day after day, week after week? And just as importantly, will he or she actually enjoy it? If you think the answer is yes to both, then the best starting point is the Village & town facilities table on pp32-3 (and the advice below), and plan where to stop, where to eat, where to buy food for your mutt.

Looking after your dog

To begin with, you need to make sure that your own dog is fully **inoculated** against the usual doggy illnesses, and also up to date with regard to **worm pills** (eg Drontal) and **flea preventatives** such as Frontline – they are, after all, following in the pawprints of many a dog before them, some of whom may well have left fleas or other parasites on the trail that now lie in wait for their next meal to arrive. **Pet insurance** is also a very good idea for a trip such as this; if you've already got insurance, do check that it will cover the kind of walk you are planning.

Perhaps the most important implement you can take with you is the **plastic tick remover**, available from vets for a couple of quid. Ticks are a real problem on the SWCP. These removers, while fiddly, help you to get rid of the tick safely (ie without leaving its head behind buried under the dog's skin).

Being in unfamiliar territory also makes it more likely that you and your dog could become separated. For this reason, make sure your dog has a **tag with your contact details on it** (a mobile phone number would be best if you are carrying one with you); you could also consider having it **microchipped** for further security.

Dogs on beaches

There is no general rule regarding whether dogs are allowed on beaches or not. Some of the beaches on the SWCP are open to dogs all year; some allow them on the beach only outside the summer season (1 May to 30 September); while a few beaches don't allow dogs at all. (Guide dogs, by the way, are usually excluded from any bans.) If in doubt, look for the noticeboards that will tell you the exact rules. On the beaches, the rules vary: at Woolacombe (see p130), they have an area where dogs are forbidden, another where they need to be on a lead, and a third area where they can run free. At Croyde you will have to walk across a part where dogs are banned – keep the dog on a tight lead here.

Dogs on beaches *(continued)* There are leaflets produced by 🖥 www.visitdevon .co.uk and 🖥 www.n-somerset.gov.uk that detail which beaches allow dogs and which don't.

Where dogs are banned from a beach there will usually be an alternative path that you can take that avoids the sands. If there isn't, and you have no choice but to cross the beach even though dogs are officially banned, you are permitted to do so as long as you cross as speedily as possible, follow the line of the path (which is usually well above the high-water mark) and keep your dog tightly under control.

Whatever the rules of access are for the beach, remember that your dog shouldn't disturb other beach-users – and you must always **clean up after your dog**.

Finally, remember to bring drinking water with you as dogs can over-heat with the lack of shade.

When to keep your dog on a lead
● **On cliff tops** It's a sad fact that, every year, a few dogs lose their lives falling over the edge of the cliffs. It usually occurs when they are chasing rabbits (which know where the cliff-edge is and are able, unlike your poor pooch, to stop in time).
● **When crossing farmland**, particularly in the lambing season (around May) when your dog can scare the sheep, causing them to lose their young. Farmers are allowed by law to shoot at and kill any dogs that they consider are worrying their sheep. During lambing, most farmers would prefer it if you didn't bring your dog at all. The exception is if your dog is being attacked by cows. A couple of years ago there were three deaths in the UK caused by walkers being trampled as they tried to rescue their dogs from the attentions of cattle. The advice in this instance is to **let go of the lead**, head speedily to a position of safety (usually the other side of the field gate or stile) and call your dog to you.
● **On National Trust land**, where it is **compulsory** to keep your dog on a lead.
● **Around ground-nesting birds** It's important to keep your dog under control when crossing an area where certain species of birds nest on the ground. Most dogs love foraging around in the woods but make sure it's allowed; some woods are used as 'nurseries' for game birds and dogs are only allowed through them on a lead.

What to pack
You've probably already got a good idea of what to bring to keep your dog alive and happy, but the following is a checklist:
● **Food/water bowl** Foldable cloth bowls are popular with walkers, being light and compact in the rucksack. You can get also get a water-bottle-and-bowl combination, where the bottle folds into a 'trough' from which the dog can drink.
● **Lead and collar** An extendable one is probably preferable for this sort of trip. Make sure both lead and collar are in good condition – you don't want either to snap on the trail, or you may end up carrying your dog through sheep fields until a replacement can be found. It is worth taking a spare.
● **Medication** You'll know if you need to bring any lotions or potions.
● **Tick remover** See opposite.
● **Bedding** A simple blanket may suffice, or you can opt for something more elaborate if you aren't carrying your own luggage.
● **Poo bags** Essential (see p44).
● **Hygiene wipes** For cleaning your dog after it's rolled in stuff.
● **A favourite toy** Helps prevent your dog from pining for the entire walk.
● **Corkscrew stake** Available from camping or pet shops, this will help you to keep your dog secure in one place while you set up camp/doze.   *(continued overleaf)*

PLANNING YOUR WALK

TAKING DOGS *(continued from p43)*

What to pack
● **Food/water** Remember to bring treats as well as regular food to keep up the mutt's morale. That said, if your dog is anything like mine the chances are they'll spend most of the walk dining on rabbit droppings and sheep poo anyway.
● **Raingear** It can rain a lot!
● **Old towels** For drying your dog after the deluge.

When it comes to packing, I always leave an exterior pocket of my rucksack empty so I can put used poo bags in there (for deposit at the first bin we come to). I always like to keep all the dog's kit together and separate from the other luggage (usually inside a plastic bag inside my rucksack). I have also seen several dogs sporting their own 'doggy rucksack', so they can carry their own food, water, poo etc – which certainly reduces the burden on their owner!

Cleaning up after your dog
It is extremely important that dog owners behave in a responsible way when walking the path. Dog excrement should be cleaned up. In towns, villages and fields where animals graze or which will be cut for silage, hay etc, you need to pick up and bag the excrement. In other places you can possibly get away with merely flicking it with a nearby stick into the undergrowth, thus ensuring there is none left on the path to decorate the boots of others.

Staying with your dog
In this guide we have used a symbol 🐕 to denote where a hotel, pub or B&B welcomes dogs; however, this always needs to be arranged in advance and some places may charge extra. Hostels (both YHA and independent) do not permit them unless they are an assistance (guide) dog; smaller campsites tend to accept them, but some of the larger holiday parks do not. Before you turn up always double check whether the place you would like to stay accepts dogs and whether there is space for them; many places have only one or two rooms suitable for people with dogs.

When it comes to **eating**, most landlords allow dogs in at least a section of their pubs, though few restaurants do. Make sure you always ask first and ensure your dog doesn't run around the pub but is secured to your table or a radiator.

Getting to and from the Coast Path

Given that it is one of the most popular holiday destinations in the UK, the South-West is surprisingly poorly served by public transport connections. Indeed, getting to the start of your walk can be quite laborious – and returning home at the end can be equally painful.

Those who wish to take a train (see opposite) will soon discover that neither Minehead nor Bude has a mainline rail connection. The best way to get to Minehead by train is to go to Taunton, Barnstaple, or Tiverton Parkway. Barnstaple, Exeter and Okehampton are best for Bude. See below for more details. National Express coach services only go to Minehead in the summer months and also serve the Butlins there rather than the centre of town and the fare is quite expensive. A service to Bude only operates weekly late May to early September. See p47-8 for options for coach travel.

Given the above, the temptation to drive (see p48) to the start of your walk is understandable. This may be the most convenient way to get there but it will also probably be the most expensive and you may not feel comfortable abandoning it on the side of the road for a couple of weeks. Nor have we mentioned the ecological considerations of driving.

NATIONAL TRANSPORT

By train

Neither Minehead or Bude is served by a regular rail service (though see box below). **Taunton**, however, *is* well connected by rail (Bristol is less than an hour away, Exeter half an hour and even London Paddington is within a two-hour journey) and there are regular bus services (First Group's No 28) from there on to Minehead (90 mins). This journey is, whilst slow, enjoyable: if you have already travelled by train from London, or indeed any other metropolis, you will feel life pleasantly decelerating around you as you approach the northern end of Exmoor. Another option is to go to **Tiverton Parkway** and take

---

❏ **Rail services**

Note: not all stops are listed.
● London to Penzance via Reading, Taunton, Exeter, Plymouth & Bodmin Parkway, Mon-Sat approx 10/day, Sun approx 8/day, some services go via Bristol, some call at Tiverton Parkway;
● Cardiff to Taunton via Bristol (some services continue to Tiverton Parkway, Exeter & Plymouth), Mon-Fri 1/hr, Sat & Sun no direct services;
● Glasgow/Edinburgh to Plymouth via Newcastle, York, Leeds, Birmingham, Bristol, Taunton, Tiverton Parkway & Exeter, Mon-Sat 7-day, Sun 5/day for the full route
● Exeter to Barnstaple (The Tarka Line), Mon-Sat approx 12/day, Sun 7/day.

The West Somerset Railway Arriving in Minehead by rail is undoubtedly the most attractive way of arriving in town (apart from walking from Porlock, of course!), the steam train chuffing its way through the rolling Somerset countryside before terminating its journey right in the centre of town, just a few steps from the seafront and only a couple of hundred metres from the start of the SWCP itself.

Unfortunately, the only train service that operates a service to/from Minehead is the West Somerset Railway (🖳 www.west-somerset-railway.co.uk). It may be one of the most picturesque services imaginable – but it's also one of the most pointless, in that it doesn't go anywhere particularly useful. Running between Minehead and Bishops Lydeard, on the way to Taunton, the railway offers a choice of transportation by either steam or diesel, the entire journey taking around 1¹/₄ hours to cover the 20 miles.

If you're determined that this is how you want to arrive, Bishops Lydeard is a half-hour bus ride from Taunton on First Somerset's 28 service. The train operation's regularity differs daily so it would be wise to check the website (or phone ahead) for up-to-date timetabling information.

PLANNING YOUR WALK

Stagecoach's No 1 (Exeter to Tiverton via Tiverton Parkway, Mon-Sat 1/hr, 20 mins) and then Beacon's No 398 (see box p49; approx two hours) to Minehead.

As for the other end of the walk, the nearest train stations to Bude are at Exeter, Okehampton and Barnstaple, and each boasts some sort of bus service to Bude (see box p49-50).

Barnstaple is actually the only location on the path that *is* served by a regular rail service, though it's a 3½-hour train-ride from London, two hours from Taunton and a good 80 minutes from Exeter. The quickest way from Barnstaple to Minehead (at least three hours) is to take a bus to Tiverton (Stagecoach's No 155) and then Beacon Bus's No 398 to Minehead.

From Barnstaple there is a daily service (No 85) to Bude. Alternatively Stagecoach's No 319 to Hartland connects with Jackett Coaches No 219 to Bude but neither of these operates on a Sunday; see box pp49-50 for details.

❏ GETTING TO BRITAIN

● **By air** Exeter (🖥 www.exeter-airport.co.uk), Bristol (🖥 www.bristolairport.co .uk), Southampton (🖥 www.southamptonairport.com) and Bournemouth (🖥 www .bournemouthairport.com) have international flights though mostly from Europe only. However, Exeter, Southampton and Bournemouth are not well connected to Minehead (there is, surprisingly, no direct bus from Exeter to Minehead) and the start of the trail, so for this reason London's Heathrow (🖥 www.heathrowairport.com) and Bristol remain the nearest airport of significance.

National Express (see box opposite) operates coach services from Heathrow (and also from Bristol – take a bus from the airport to the main coach station) to Taunton and Barnstaple. There are also rail services between Bristol Temple Meads and Heathrow to Taunton. From Taunton you can catch First Group's No 28 (see box p49) to Minehead at the start of the trail.

● **Eurostar** (🖥 www.eurostar.com) operates a high-speed passenger service via the Channel Tunnel between Paris, Brussels and Lille and London. The Eurostar terminal in London is at St Pancras International station with connections to the London Underground and to all other main railway stations in London. Trains to Somerset and Devon leave from Paddington station.

For more information about rail services to Britain contact Railteam (🖥 www .railteam.eu).

● **From Europe by coach** Eurolines (🖥 www.eurolines.com) have a wide network of long-distance bus services connecting over 500 destinations in 25 European countries to London (Victoria Coach Station). Visit the Eurolines website for details of services from your country. Check carefully: often, once expenses such as food for the journey are taken into consideration, it doesn't work out much cheaper than flying, particularly when compared to the prices of some of the budget airlines.

● **From Europe by car** Ferries operate between Calais and Dover; Rotterdam/ Zeebrugge and Hull; Bilbao and Portsmouth; Santander/Roscoff and Plymouth; as well as Cherbourg, St Malo and Caen to Poole and Portsmouth. There are also several other ferries plying routes between mainland Europe and ports on Britain's eastern coast. Look at 🖥 www.ferrysavers.com or 🖥 www.directferries.co.uk for a full list of companies and services.

Eurotunnel (🖥 www.eurotunnel.com) operates a shuttle train service for vehicles via the Channel Tunnel between Calais and Folkestone.

PLANNING YOUR WALK

National Rail (☎ 08457-484950, 💻 www.nationalrail.co.uk) is the best source of rail information. The lines throughout the South-West are run by **First Great Western** (☎ 08457-000125, 💻 www.firstgreatwestern.co.uk). **Arriva Cross Country Trains** (💻 www.crosscountrytrains.co.uk) also run services linking the Midlands, North and Scotland with the South-West.

Finally, one tip for when buying tickets: it's always worth checking the fares on the relevant train company's website or 💻 www.thetrainline.com – you'll normally find significant reductions, especially if booking 8-12 weeks in advance. However, be aware of additional charges such as a booking fee, or for using a debit/credit card.

If you plan to take a bus when you arrive consider getting a plusbus (💻 www .plusbus.info) ticket and if you want to book a taxi Traintaxi's website (💻 www .traintaxi.co.uk) gives details of the companies operating at railway stations.

By coach

Although coach travel can take significantly longer than getting a train and is susceptible to traffic jams – especially in the summer months when the South-West is choked with tourists – it is generally cheaper than train travel and can, on some of today's newer coaches, also be far more salubrious than coach travel of old.

National Express (see box below; 💻 www.nationalexpress.com) runs several services to Taunton (from here take Webberbus's No 18 or First's No 28 to Minehead); services also go to Barnstaple, Bideford and Ilfracombe.

However, it is not easy to reach Bude by coach. There is a seasonal service (Saturday only) from London and several services to Westward Ho! but it is not easy to get to Bude from there. Your best bet is to travel to Exeter and from there take First Group's No X9 or Western Greyhound's No 599 service (see box p50).

Megabus (💻 uk.megabus.com), part of Stagecoach, is a cheap and expanding bus company but to take advantage of this service you would need

(see box p50)

❏ **National Express coach services**
Note: not all stops are listed.

328   Birmingham to Penzance via Worcester, Bristol, Tiverton, **Barnstaple**, **Ilfracombe**, **Bideford**, Plymouth, Truro, Redruth & Camborne, 1/day

337   Bristol to Paignton via Taunton, **Barnstaple**, **Ilfracombe**, **Bideford**, **Westward Ho!**, Exeter & Torquay, 1/day

339   Birmingham to **Westward Ho!** via Cheltenham, Bristol, Taunton, Tiverton, **Barnstaple**, **Ilfracombe** & **Bideford**, 1/day

406   London Victoria to Taunton via Heathrow Airport, 1/day

501   London Victoria to Taunton via Heathrow Airport, 3/day

502   London Victoria to **Ilfracombe** via Heathrow Airport, Taunton, Wellington, Tiverton, **Barnstaple**, **Chivenor** & **Braunton**, 1-2/day

502   London Victoria to **Westward Ho!** via Heathrow Airport, Taunton, Wellington, Tiverton, **Barnstaple**, **Chivenor**, **Braunton**, Fremington, Yelland, **Instow** & **Bideford**, 2/day (plus late May to early Sep Sat 1/day to **Bude**)

532   Birmingham to Plymouth via Bristol, Taunton, Tiverton, **Barnstaple**, **Ilfracombe** & **Bideford**, 1/day

to continue on down the coastal path to Newquay – and from here it's about three hours back to Bude by at least two more buses!

By car

Driving to the start of the path raises as many questions as it does answers: Where do you leave your car while you're walking? Will it be safe? And how are you going to get back to it at the end of your trip? Furthermore, given the ever-rising price of fuel and the fact that you'll probably have to pay to leave your car somewhere, taking your car will almost certainly be the least financially viable option.

For those who do decide to drive, the best way to access both ends of the path is to use the M5. Approaching from the North, exit at junction 23 and then follow the A38 to Bridgwater and the A39 to Minehead. From the South, depart the motorway at junction 25 and proceed along the A358 to Williton before again using the A39 to complete your journey. Alternatively, if coming from Exeter or the South-West you could exit the M5 at junction 27 and take the more scenic A396 through Exmoor. If starting your walk in Bude and arriving from London or the North, use junction 27 of the M5 and follow the A361 to Barnstaple and the A39 through Bideford and to Bude. Whereas if travelling from the south coast via Exeter, take the A30 across the top of Dartmoor before getting on the A39 northwards.

A great way to look at the varying options in regards to route planning is to use the AA's website and route planner (🖥 www.theaa.com/route-planner/index.jsp).

Minehead has no long-stay parking and the last time we were there the tourist office recommended parking on a residential side street; leaving your vehicle in a designated car park for over a week would be more of a risk, apparently. Some campsites and other accommodation providers may assist you with a parking spot whilst you're walking but enquiries regarding this should always be made in advance of leaving home.

One idea that is popular with drivers is to park in Barnstaple (the train station has long-term parking where you can pay (about £3 per day) for nine days and update it by phone if necessary. The advantage with parking in Barnstaple is that your vehicle is left at a point approximately half-way along the trail – allowing you to leave items in the car and pick them up when you walk past – or jump in and drive home if you've found the walking too taxing! It also means you won't have quite such an arduous journey to get back to the car from Bude at the end of the trip.

By air

In addition to the airports mentioned in the box on p46, there is the option of flying (mostly domestic flights) into Newquay (🖥 www.newquaycornwallairport.com). However, Newquay lies 70 miles along the coast from Bude. What's more, it isn't particularly well placed even for Bude (and not really a realistic option for Minehead) – a bus between Newquay and Bude takes at least three hours.

LOCAL TRANSPORT

Bus services

All places along the trail (or at least those with inhabitants) boast at least some sort of bus service except for Hartland Quay, the penultimate stop on the path. Nearly all of the buses servicing points on the trail run at least once daily and usually more, which makes the chances of getting stuck somewhere gratifyingly slim – you may just have to wait a while.

The main problem with public transport in the area is the time it takes to get anywhere. Things are further complicated by the fact that local buses have been organised by county, meaning that while Minehead and Bude may have good connections within their respective counties (Somerset and Cornwall), they have pretty lousy connections with their neighbour Devon, which means that if you want to cross a county border you've often got to change buses somewhere along the way. Planning ahead is a must as services change and may have been cut.

Timetables for the services should be available for free at bus stations and tourist information centres (the North Devon booklet covers all services) and can also be found online on either their own websites or 🖥 www.travelinesw.com.

❏ **BUS SERVICES**

Beacon Bus (☎ 01805-804240; 🖥 www.beaconbus.co.uk)
33 Ilfracombe to Berrynarbor via Hele & Watermouth, Mon-Fri 2/day
35 Ilfracombe to Lee, Mon-Sat 4/day
398 Tiverton to Minehead via Dulverton & Dunster, Mon-Sat 5/day

Filers Travel (☎ 01271-863819, 🖥 www.filers.co.uk)
300 Lynmouth to Ilfracombe via Lynton, Berrynarbor & Combe Martin, late May to mid Sep daily 3/day; rest of year Sat & Sun only 2/day
301 Combe Martin to Barnstaple via Berrynarbor & Ilfracombe, Mon-Sat 4/day; plus Ilfracombe to Barnstaple, Mon-Sat 4/day
302 Ilfracombe to Woolacombe, Jul to mid Sep Sun/bank hol Mons 8/day
303 Barnstaple to Woolacombe via Braunton and Mortehoe, Mon-Sat 4-5/day
309/310 Lynton to Barnstaple via Martinhoe Cross, Mon-Sat 8/day (2/day start in Lynmouth)

First (🖥 www.firstgroup.com)
1   Barnstaple to Westward Ho! via Fremington, Instow & Bideford, Mon-Sat 2/hr, Sun 1/hr
2   Barnstaple to Appledore via Fremington, Instow & Bideford, Mon-Sat 2/hr, Sun 1/hr
3   Ilfracombe to Barnstaple via Braunton & Knowle, Mon-Fri 4/hr, Sat & Sun via Braunton & Chivenor, Sat 4/hr, Sun approx 1/hr
28 Taunton to Minehead, Mon-Sat 2/hr, Sun approx 1/hr
30 Combe Martin to Ilfracombe via Watermouth & Hele, Mon-Sat 1/hr
31 Ilfracombe to Woolacombe via Lee Cross, Mon-Sat 6/day
76 Plymouth to Bude via Launceston, Mon-Sat 5-6/day
303 Woolacombe to Barnstaple via Braunton, Mon-Sat 5/day, Sun 3/day
X9 Bude to Exeter via Holsworthy & Okehampton, Mon-Sat 5/day

(continued overleaf)

PLANNING YOUR WALK

BUS SERVICES *(continued from p49)*

Jackett Coaches (☎ 01752-787797, ⌨ jacketscoaches.com)
219 Hartland to Bude, Mon-Sat 4/day
X85 Plymouth to Barnstaple via Holsworthy, Bideford, Instow & Fremington, Sat 1/day (see also Stagecoach 85/85C)

Quantock Motor Services (☎ 01823-430202, ⌨ www.quantockmotorservices.co.uk)
39   Minehead to Porlock Weir via Bossington & Porlock, Mon-Sat 8-9/day
300 Minehead to Lynmouth via Porlock, Porlock Weir & Countisbury, open-top bus Apr-Oct Mon-Sat 4/day, Sun and bank hols 3/day

Stagecoach (⌨ www.stagecoachbus.com)
21   Barnstaple to Westward Ho! via Fremington, Instow Quay, East-the-Water & Bideford, Mon-Sat 2/hr, Sun 1/hr
21A Ilfracombe to Appledore via Braunton, Chivenor, Barnstaple, Fremington, Instow, East-the-Water & Bideford, Mon-Sat 2/hr; Barnstaple to Appledore via Fremington, Instow, East-the-Water & Bideford, Sun 1/hr
85/85C Barnstaple to Holsworthy via Bideford, Mon-Fri 5/day, Sat 2/day, 1-2/day continue to Bude in the afternoon and start in Bude in the morning (see also Jackett's X85)
155 Barnstaple to Exeter via South Molton & Tiverton, Mon-Sat 6/day
308 Croyde to Barnstaple via Saunton, Braunton & Chivenor, Mon-Sat 2/hr, Apr-Oct Sun 5/day
315 Barnstaple to Exeter via Fremington, Instow & Bideford, Mon-Sat 5-6/day
319 Barnstaple to Hartland via Bideford, Clovelly Cross & Clovelly, Mon-Sat 5/day + 1/day Bideford to Hartland; connects with Jackett's 219 service (see above)
910/911 Combe Martin to Ilfracombe, Mon-Fri 1/day college days only.

Turners Tours (☎ 01769-580242, ⌨ www.turnerstours.co.uk)
16   Bideford to Appledore via Westward Ho! (circular route), Mon-Sat 2/day
16A Bideford to Westward Ho! via Appledore (circular route), Mon-Sat 2/day

Webberbus (☎ 0800-096 3039, ⌨ www.webberbus.com)
18   Taunton to Minehead, Mon-Sat 1/hr

Western Greyhound (☎ 01637-871871, ⌨ www.westerngreyhound.com)
576 Plymouth to Bude via Launceston, Mon-Sat 1/day (see also Stagecoach No 76)
595 Bude to Boscastle, Mon-Sat 6/day, Apr-Oct Sun 4/day
599 Bude to Exeter via Holsworthy & Okehampton, daily 2/day

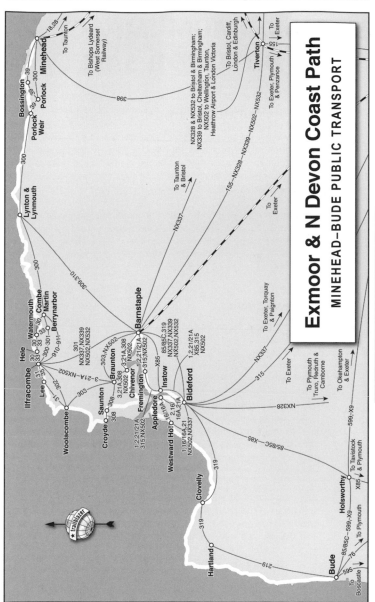

Exmoor & N Devon Coast Path
MINEHEAD–BUDE PUBLIC TRANSPORT

To Taunton

To Bishops Lydeard
(West Somerset
Railway)

To Taunton
& Bristol

To Bristol, Cardiff,
London & Edinburgh

To Exeter

NX328 & NX532 to Bristol & Birmingham;
NX339 to Bristol, Cheltenham & Birmingham;
NX502 to Wellington, Taunton,
Heathrow Airport & London Victoria

To Exeter, Plymouth /
& Penzance

To Exeter, Torquay
& Paignton

To Exeter

To Plymouth,
Truro, Redruth &
Camborne

To Okehampton
& Exeter

To Tavistock
& Plymouth

To Plymouth

To
Boscastle

PLANNING YOUR WALK

MINIMUM IMPACT & OUTDOOR SAFETY

Minimum impact walking

By visiting this rural corner of England you are having a positive impact, not just on your own wellbeing but on local communities as well. Your presence brings money and jobs into the local economy and also pride in, and awareness of, the region's environment and culture.

However, the environment should not just be considered in terms of its value as a tourist asset. Its long-term survival and enjoyment by future generations will only be possible if both visitors and local communities protect it now. The following points are made to help you reduce your impact on the environment, encourage conservation and promote sustainable tourism in the area.

ECONOMIC IMPACT

Support local businesses

Rural businesses and communities in Britain have been hit hard in recent years by a seemingly endless series of crises. Most people are aware of the country code – not dropping litter and closing the gate behind you are still as pertinent as ever – but in light of the economic pressures there is something else you can do: **buy local**.

Look and ask for local produce (see box p22) to buy and eat; not only does this cut down on the amount of pollution and congestion that the transportation of food creates (the so-called 'food miles'), but also ensures that you are supporting local farmers and producers; the very people who have moulded the countryside you have come to see and who are in the best position to protect it. If you can find local food which is also organic so much the better.

It's a fact of life that money spent at local level – perhaps in a market, or at the greengrocer, or in an independent pub – has a far greater impact for good on that community than the equivalent spent in a branch of a national chain store or restaurant. While no-one would advocate that walkers should boycott the larger supermarkets, which after all do provide local employment, it's worth remembering that businesses in rural communities rely heavily on visitors for their very existence. If we want to keep these shops and post offices, we need to use them.

ENVIRONMENTAL IMPACT

A walking holiday in itself is an environmentally friendly approach to tourism. The following are some ideas on how you can go a few steps further in helping to minimise your impact on the environment while walking the South-West Coast Path.

Use public transport whenever possible
While we recognise that public transport along this section of the South-West Coast Path is not ideal, it is preferable to using private cars as it benefits everyone: visitors, locals and the environment.

Never leave litter
Leaving litter shows a total disrespect for the natural world and others coming after you. As well as being unsightly, litter can be harmful to wildlife, pollutes the environment and can be dangerous to farm animals. Please carry a plastic bag so you can dispose of your rubbish in a bin in the next village. It would be very helpful if you could pick up litter left by other people too.

● **Is it OK if it's biodegradable?** Not really. Apple cores, banana skins, orange peel and the like are unsightly, encourage flies, ants and wasps and ruin a picnic spot for others. Using the excuse that they are natural and biodegradable just doesn't cut any ice. When was the last time you saw a banana tree in England?

● **The lasting impact of litter** A piece of orange peel left on the ground takes six months to decompose; silver foil 18 months; a plastic bag 10 years; clothes 15 years; and an aluminium can 85 years.

Respect all wildlife
Care for all wildlife you come across along the path; it has as much right to be there as you. As tempting as it may be to pick wild flowers, leave them in place so the next people who pass can enjoy them too. Don't break branches off or damage trees in any way.

If you come across wildlife, keep your distance and don't watch for too long. Your presence can cause considerable stress, particularly if the adults are with young, or in winter when the weather is harsh and food is scarce. Young animals are rarely abandoned. If you come across young birds, keep away so that their mother can return.

Outdoor toiletry
As more and more people discover the joys of walking in the natural environment issues such as how to go to the loo outdoors rapidly gain importance. How many of us have shaken our heads at the sight of toilet paper strewn beside the path, or even worse, someone's dump left in full view? Human excrement is not only offensive to our senses but, more importantly, can infect water sources.

Where to go The coast path is a high-use area and many habitats will not benefit from your fertilisation. As far as 'number twos' are concerned try whenever possible to use public toilets. There is no shortage of public toilets along the coast path and they are all marked on the trail maps. However, there are those times when the only time is now. If you have to go outdoors help the environment to deal with your deposit in the best possible way by following a few simple guidelines:

● **Choose your site carefully** It should be at least 30 metres away from running water and out of reach of the high tide and not on any site of historical or archaeological interest. Carry a small trowel or use a sturdy stick to dig a small hole about 15cm (6") deep to bury your faeces in. Faeces decompose quicker when in contact with the top layer of soil or leaf mould; by using a stick to stir loose soil into your deposit you will speed decomposition up even more. Do not squash it under rocks as this slows down the decomposition process. If you have to use rocks as a cover make sure they are not in contact with your faeces.

● **Pack out toilet paper and tampons** Toilet paper, tampons and sanitary towels take a long time to decompose whether buried or not. They can easily be dug up by animals and may then blow into water sources or onto the trail. The best method for dealing with these is to pack them out. Put the used item in a paper bag placed inside a plastic bag and then dispose of it at the next toilet.

ACCESS

Britain is a crowded cluster of islands with few places where you can wander as you please. Most of the land is a patchwork of fields and agricultural land and the environment through which the Exmoor and North Devon Coast Path marches is no different. However, there are countless public rights of way (see below), in addition to the main trail, that criss-cross the land.

This is fine, but what happens if you feel a little more adventurous and want to explore the moorland, woodland and hills that can also be found near the walk? Access to the countryside has always been a hot topic in Britain. In the 1940s soldiers coming back from the Second World War were horrified and disgruntled to find that landowners were denying them the right to walk across the moors; ironically the very country that they had been fighting to protect. The battle was finally won in 2005 as new legislation (see opposite) came into force granting public access to thousands of acres of Britain's wildest land.

All those who enjoy access to the countryside must respect the land, its wildlife, the interests of those who live and work there and other users; we all share a common interest in the countryside. Knowing your rights and responsibilities gives you the information you need to act with minimal impact.

Rights of way

As a designated National Trail the coast path is a public right of way. A public right of way is either a footpath, a bridleway or a byway. The SWCP is a footpath for almost all its length which means that anyone has the legal right to use it on foot only.

Rights of way are theoretically established because the owner has dedicated them to public use. However, very few paths are formally dedicated in this way. If members of the public have been using a path without interference for 20 years or more the law assumes the owner has intended to dedicate it as a right of way. If a path has been unused for 20 years it does not cease to exist; the guiding principle is 'once a highway, always a highway'.

On a public right of way you have the right to 'pass and repass along the way' which includes stopping to rest or admire the view, or to consume refreshments. You can also take with you a 'natural accompaniment' (!) which includes a dog, but it must be kept under close control (see pp42-3).

Farmers and land managers must ensure that paths are not blocked by crops or other vegetation, or otherwise obstructed, that the route is identifiable and the surface is restored soon after cultivation. If crops are growing over the path you have every right to walk through them, following the line of the right of way as closely as possible. If you find a path blocked or impassable you should report it to the appropriate highway authority. Highway authorities are responsible for maintaining footpaths. In Somerset and North Devon the highway authorities are Somerset and North Devon county councils respectively. The council is also the surveying authority with responsibility for maintaining the official definitive map of public rights of way.

Wider access

The access situation to land around the coast path is a little more complicated. Trying to unravel and understand the seemingly thousands of different laws and acts is never easy in any legal system. Parliamentary Acts give a right to walk over certain areas of land such as some, but by no means all, common land and some specific places such as Dartmoor and the New Forest. However, in other places, such as Bodmin Moor and many British beaches, right of access is not written in law. It is merely tolerated by the landowner and could be terminated at any time.

Some landowners, such as the Forestry Commission, water companies and the National Trust, are obliged by law to allow some degree of access to their land. Land covered by schemes such as the Environmental Stewardship Scheme, formerly the Countryside Stewardship Scheme, gives landowners a financial incentive to manage their land for conservation and to provide limited public access. There are also a few truly altruistic landowners who have allowed access over their land and these include organisations such as the RSPB, the Woodland Trust, and some local authorities. Overall, however, access to most of Britain's countryside is forbidden to Britain's people, in marked contrast to the general rights of access that prevail in other European countries.

Right to roam

For many years groups such as Ramblers (see box p41) and the British Mountaineering Council (🖥 www.thebmc.co.uk) campaigned for new and wider access legislation. This finally bore fruit in the form of the Countryside and Rights of Way Act of November 2000, colloquially known as the CRoW Act, which granted access for 'recreation on foot' to mountain, moor, heath, down and registered common land in England and Wales. In essence it allows walkers the freedom to roam responsibly away from footpaths, without being accused of trespass, on about four million acres of open, uncultivated land.

❏ **National trails**

There are 15 national trails in England and Wales. According to the National Trail website (🖥 www.nationaltrail.co.uk), the definition of a National Trail 'is a long-distance path [or, in one case, bridleway] for walking, cycling and horse-riding through the finest landscapes in the two countries'. (Scotland, by the way, has its own equivalent, called Long Distance Routes, of which there are four.) In total they cover around 2500 miles (4000km) of pathways, of which the SWCP is the longest by far in the UK; the next longest, the Pennine Way, is a mere 268 miles/429km. The Pennine Way was also the first national trail to be opened, back in 1965.

Each National Trail has been made by linking existing paths together to form one long-distance path, rather than by creating new paths. All of them have a dedicated officer charged with maintaining, improving and promoting the trail. They in turn are helped by the local Highways Authorities, landowners and volunteers who all help in keeping the Trails to a usable standard. Funding for the Trails comes from Natural England and the Countryside Council for Wales, as well as local highway authorities and other funding partners.

On 28 August 2005 the South-West became the sixth region in England/ Wales to be opened up under this act; however, restrictions may still be in place from time to time – check the situation on 🖥 www.openaccess.gov.uk.

Natural England (see p62) has mapped the new agreed areas of open access and they are also clearly marked on all the latest Ordnance Survey Explorer (1:25,000) maps. In the future it is hoped that the legislation can be extended to include other types of land such as cliff, foreshore, woodland, riverside and canal side.

The Countryside Code

The countryside is a fragile place which every visitor should respect. The Countryside Code seems like common sense but sadly some people still seem to have no understanding of how to treat the countryside they walk in. Everyone visiting the countryside has a responsibility to minimise the impact of their visit so that other people can enjoy the same peaceful landscapes. It does not take much effort; it really is common sense.

Below is an expanded version of the Countryside Code, launched under the logo 'Respect, Protect and Enjoy':

● **Be safe – plan ahead and follow any signs** Walking on the Coast path is pretty much hazard free but you're responsible for your own safety so follow the simple guidelines outlined on pp57-60.

● **Leave all gates and property as you find them** Normally a farmer leaves gates closed to keep livestock in but may sometimes leave them open to allow livestock access to food or water. Leave them as you find them and if there is a sign, follow the instructions.

● **Leave livestock, crops and machinery alone** Help farmers by not interfering with their means of livelihood.

● **Take your litter home** See p53.

● **Keep your dog under control** Across farmland dogs should be kept on a lead. During lambing time they should not be taken with you at all; see also pp42-4.

● **Enjoy the countryside and respect its life and work** Access to the countryside depends on being sensitive to the needs and wishes of those who live and work there. Being courteous and friendly to those you meet will ensure a healthy future for all based on partnership and co-operation.

● **Keep to paths across farmland** Stick to the official path across arable or pasture land. Minimise erosion by not cutting corners or widening the path.

● **Use gates and stiles to cross fences, hedges and walls** The path is well supplied with stiles where it crosses field boundaries. If you have to climb over a gate because you can't open it always do so at the hinged end.

● **Help keep all water clean** Leaving litter and going to the toilet near a water source can pollute people's water supplies. See pp53-4 for more advice.

● **Take special care on country roads** Drivers often go dangerously fast on narrow winding lanes. To be safe, walk facing the oncoming traffic and carry a torch or wear highly visible clothing when it's getting dark. If you travel by car drive with care and reduced speed on country roads. Park your car with consideration for others' needs; never block a gateway.

● **Protect wildlife, plants and trees** See p53.

● **Guard against all risk of fire** Accidental fire is a great fear for farmers and foresters. Never make a camp fire: the deep burn damages turf and destroys flora and fauna. Take cigarette butts with you to dispose of safely.

● **Make no unnecessary noise** Stay in small groups and act unobtrusively. Avoid noisy and disruptive behaviour which might annoy residents and other visitors and frighten farm animals and wildlife.

Outdoor safety

AVOIDANCE OF HAZARDS

Swimming

If you are not an experienced swimmer or familiar with the sea, plan ahead and swim only at beaches where there is a lifeguard service, such as Woolacombe, Croyde and Saunton. On such beaches you should swim between the red and yellow flags as this is the patrolled area. Don't swim between black and white chequered flags as these areas are only for surfers. A red flag indicates that it is dangerous to enter the water. If you are not sure about anything ask one of the lifeguards; after all they are there to help you.

If you are going to swim at unsupervised beaches never do so alone and always take care. Some beaches are prone to strong rips. Never swim off headlands or near river mouths as there may be strong currents. Always be aware of changing weather conditions and tidal movement. The South-West has a huge tidal range and it can be very easy to get cut off by the tide.

If you see someone in difficulty do not attempt a rescue until you have contacted the coastguard (see below). Once you know help is on the way try to assist the person by throwing something to help them stay afloat. Many beaches have rescue equipment in red boxes; these are marked on the route maps.

Walking alone
If you are walking alone you must appreciate and be prepared for the increased risk. Take note of the safety guidelines below.

Safety on the Coast Path
Sadly every year people are injured walking along the trail, though usually it's nothing more than a badly twisted ankle. Parts of Exmoor can be pretty remote, however, and it certainly pays to take precautions when walking. Abiding by the following rules should minimise the risks:

● Avoid walking on your own if possible.
● Make sure that somebody knows your plans for every day you are on the trail. This could be the place you plan to stay in at the end of each day's walk or a friend or relative whom you have promised to call every night. That way, if you fail to turn up or call, they can raise the alarm.
● If the weather closes in suddenly and fog or mist descends and you become uncertain of the correct trail, do not be tempted to continue. Just wait where you are and you'll find that mist often clears, at least for long enough to allow you to get your bearings. If you are still uncertain and the weather doesn't look like improving, return the way you came to the nearest point of civilisation and try again another time when conditions have improved.
● Always fill your water bottle or pouch at every available opportunity (don't empty it until you are certain you can fill it again) and ensure you have some food such as high-energy snacks.
● Always carry a torch, compass, map, whistle and wet-weather gear with you; a mobile phone can be useful though you cannot rely on getting good reception (see p38).
● Wear strong sturdy boots with good ankle support and a good grip, not trainers.
● Be extra vigilant with children.

Dealing with an accident
● Use basic first aid to treat the injury to the best of your ability.
● Try to attract the attention of anybody else who may be in the area. The **international distress (emergency) signal** is six blasts on a whistle, or six flashes with a torch.
● If possible leave someone with the casualty while others go to get help. If there are only two people, you have a dilemma. If you decide to get help, leave all spare clothing and food with the casualty.
● In an emergency dial ☎ 999 and ask for the coastguard. They are responsible for dealing with any emergency that occurs on the coast or at sea. Make sure you know exactly where you are before you call.
● Report the exact position of the casualty and their condition.

WEATHER AND WEATHER FORECASTS

The trail suffers from extremes of weather so it's vital that you always try to find out what the weather is going to be like before you set off for the day. It is a good idea to pay attention to **wind and gale warnings**. The wind on any coastline can get very strong and if it is strong it is advisable not to walk, particularly if you are carrying a pack which can act as a sail. If you are on a steep incline or above high cliffs it is also dangerous. Even if the wind direction is inland it can literally blow you right over (unpleasant if there are gorse bushes around!), or if it suddenly stops or eddies (a common phenomenon when strong winds hit cliffs) it can cause you to lose your balance and stagger in the direction in which you have been leaning, ie towards the cliffs!

Another hazard on the coast is **sea mist or fog** which can dramatically decrease visibility. If a coastal fog blows over take extreme care where the path runs close to cliff edges.

Most hotels, some B&Bs and TICs will have pinned up somewhere a summary of the **weather forecast**. Alternatively you can get a forecast through ⌨ www.bbc.co.uk/weather, or ⌨ www.metoffice.gov.uk/weather.

Pay close attention to the weather forecast and alter your plans for the day accordingly. That said, even if the forecast is for a fine sunny day, always assume the worst and pack some wet-weather gear.

BLISTERS

It is important to break in new boots before embarking on a long walk. Make sure the boots are comfortable and try to avoid getting them wet on the inside. Air your feet at every opportunity, keep them clean and change your socks regularly; using talcum powder can help to keep them dry. If you feel any hot spots, stop immediately and apply a few strips of zinc oxide tape and leave on until it is pain free or the tape starts to come off.

If you have left it too late and a blister has developed you should surround it with Compeed or any other blister kit to protect it from abrasion. Popping it can lead to infection. If the skin is broken keep the area clean with antiseptic and cover with a non-adhesive dressing material held in place with tape.

HYPOTHERMIA

Also known as exposure, this occurs when the body can't generate enough heat to maintain its normal temperature, usually as a result of being wet, cold, unprotected from the wind, tired and hungry. It is usually more of a problem in upland areas such as on the moors. Hypothermia is easily avoided by wearing suitable clothing, carrying and eating enough food and drink, being aware of the weather conditions and checking the morale of your companions.

Early signs to watch for are feeling cold and tired with involuntary shivering. Find some shelter as soon as possible and warm the victim up with a hot drink and some chocolate or other high-energy food. If possible give them another warm layer of clothing and allow them to rest until feeling better.

If allowed to worsen, strange behaviour, slurring of speech and poor coordination will become apparent and the victim can quickly progress into unconsciousness, followed by coma and death. Quickly get the victim out of any wind and rain, improvising a shelter if necessary. Rapid restoration of bodily warmth is essential and best achieved by bare-skin contact: someone should get into the same sleeping bag as the patient, both having stripped to their underwear, putting any spare clothing under or over them to build up heat. Send urgently for help.

HYPERTHERMIA

Hyperthermia occurs when the body generates too much heat, eg heat exhaustion and heatstroke. Not ailments that you would normally associate with England, these are serious problems nonetheless.

Symptoms of **heat exhaustion** include thirst, fatigue, giddiness, a rapid pulse, raised body temperature, low urine output and, if not treated, delirium and finally a coma. The best cure is to drink plenty of water. The darker your urine the more you should drink.

Heatstroke is more serious. A high body temperature and an absence of sweating are early indications, followed by symptoms similar to hypothermia (see p59) such as a lack of coordination, convulsions and coma. Death will follow if treatment is not given instantly. Sponge the victim down, wrap them in wet towels, fan them and get help immediately.

SUNBURN

The sun in the South-West can be very strong. The way to avoid sunburn is to stay wrapped up but that's not really an option. What you must do, therefore, is to wear a hat and smother yourself in sunscreen (with a minimum factor of 15); apply it regularly throughout the day.

Don't forget your lips, nose, the back of your neck and even under your chin to protect you against rays reflected from the ground.

THE ENVIRONMENT & NATURE

3

Flora and fauna

With a varied topography that encompasses a full range of land-scapes from windblasted moor to wetland marsh, hogback cliffs to wooded valleys, muddy estuaries to mobile sand dunes, you can begin to appreciate why the South-West can boast such a rich and varied countryside, with several unique species of flora and thriving populations of mammals and birds that, elsewhere in the UK, struggle to survive.

The following is not in any way a comprehensive guide – if it were, you would not have room for anything else in your rucksack – but merely a brief run-down of the more commonly seen flora and fauna on the trail, together with some of the rarer and more spectacular species.

TREES

For a moorland region Exmoor boasts some surprisingly fine patches of woodland. The most interesting species is the **oak** (family name *Quercus*), which was originally planted as coppice or scrub and supports more kinds of insect than any other tree in Britain. Some of these insects affect the oak in interesting ways: the eggs of the gall-fly, for example, cause growths on the leaves, known, appropriately enough, as galls. Each of these growths contains a single insect. In Exmoor the most prolific species of oak is sessile oak (*Quercus petraea*). Oak woodland is a diverse habitat and not exclusively made up of oak. Other trees that flourish here include **downy birch** (*Betula pubescens*), its relative the **silver birch** (*Betula pendula*), **holly** (*Ilex aquifolium*) and **hazel** (*Corylus avellana*) which has traditionally been used for coppicing (the periodic cutting of small trees for harvesting).

In addition to Monterey cypress, Scots and Corsican pine, Sitka spruce and Douglas fir are some of the non-native species that have been planted by the landowners of Exmoor down the centuries. Most of the woodland on Exmoor is owned by the Forestry Commission, the Woodland Trust and the National Trust.

❑ CONSERVATION SCHEMES – WHAT'S AN AONB?

It is perhaps the chief joy of this walk that much of it is spent in either a national park or an Area of Outstanding Natural Beauty (AONB). But what exactly are these designations and what protection do they actually confer?

National Parks

The highest level of landscape protection is the designation of land as a **National Park** (🖳 www.nationalparks.gov.uk). There are 15 in Britain of which nine are in England (including, of course, Exmoor National Park on this trail). This designation recognises the national importance of an area in terms of landscape, biodiversity and as a recreational resource. It does not signify national ownership and these are not uninhabited wildernesses, making conservation a knife-edged balance between protecting the environment and the rights and livelihoods of those living in the park.

Areas of Outstanding Natural Beauty

The second level of protection is **Area of Outstanding Natural Beauty** (AONB; 🖳 www.aonb.org.uk); there are 48 AONBs in the UK; 33 wholly in England. Much of the South-West Coast Path crosses land covered by either this designation or its close relative **Heritage Coasts**, of which there are currently 32 in England. The primary objective of AONBs is conservation of the natural beauty of a landscape. As there is no statutory administrative framework for their management, this is the responsibility of the local authority within whose boundaries they fall. It is of course one of the joys of this part of the South-West Coast Path that much of the last half of the walk is spent in the **North Devon AONB**, which includes the Heritage Coasts of North Devon and Hartland. Out at sea, **Lundy** is also a heritage coast and it is the only Marine Conservation Zone.

National Nature Reserves and Sites of Special Scientific Interest

The next level of protection includes **National Nature Reserves** (NNRs) and **Sites of Special Scientific Interest** (SSSIs). There are 224 NNRs in England of which three are in Exmoor National Park, with Hawkcombe Wood, near Porlock, the closest to the trail (Dunkery Woods and Tarr Steps are the others in the park). Hawkcombe Wood achieved its status largely because of its insect colonies, including fritillary butterflies. Outside the park and east of Bude lies Dunsdon Farm, which achieved its status due to its Culm grassland pasture that's typical of this region.

There are over 4100 **SSSIs** in England. The **Coastal Heaths of Exmoor** cover an area of 1758 hectares (4343 acres) and boast several rare plants including two species of whitebeam. SSSIs are a particularly important designation as they have some legal standing. They are managed in partnership with the owners and occupiers of the land who must give written notice before initiating any operation likely to damage the site and who cannot proceed without consent from **Natural England** (🖳 www.naturalengland.org.uk), the single body responsible for identifying, establishing and managing National Parks, Areas of Outstanding Natural Beauty (both previously managed by the Countryside Agency), National Nature Reserves, Sites of Special Scientific Interest, and Special Areas of Conservation.

Special Area of Conservation (SAC) is an international designation which came into being as a result of the 1992 Earth Summit in Rio de Janeiro, Brazil. This European-wide network of sites is designed to promote the conservation of habitats, wild animals and plants, both on land and at sea. At the time of writing 236 land sites in England had been designated as SACs.

Conservation and campaigning organisations
These voluntary organisations started the conservation movement in the mid-19th century and are still at the forefront of developments. Independent of government and reliant on public support, they can concentrate their resources either on acquiring land which can then be managed purely for conservation purposes, or on influencing political decision-makers by lobbying and campaigning.

Managers and owners of land include well-known bodies such as the **National Trust** (NT; ⌨ www.nationaltrust.org.uk) that owns over 600 miles of coastline including three sites on the Exmoor coastline (Holnicote, Watersmeet, West Exmoor Coast) and other sites on the Devon coast such as Croyde, Woolacombe and Mortehoe, and Bideford Bay and Hartland; the **Royal Society for the Protection of Birds** (RSPB; ⌨ www.rspb.org.uk), and the **Council for the Protection of Rural England** (CPRE; ⌨ www.cpre.org.uk) and **Woodland Trust** (⌨ www.woodland trust.org.uk).

There is also **The Wildlife Trusts** (⌨ www.wildlifetrusts.org), the umbrella organisation for the 47 wildlife trusts in the UK that manage nature reserves and run marine conservation projects.

FLOWERS

There are said to be around 800 species of wild plants within Exmoor National Park. Spring is the time to come and see the spectacular displays of colour on the South-West Coast Path, when most of the flowers are in bloom. Alternatively, arrive in August and you'll see the heathers carpeting patches of the moors in a blaze of purple flowers.

Woodland and hedgerows

From March to May **bluebells** (*Hyacinthoides non-scripta*) proliferate in some of the woods along the trail, providing a wonderful spectacle. The white **wood anemone** (*Anemone nemorosa*) – wide open flowers when sunny, closed and drooping when the weather's dull – and the yellow **primrose** (*Primula vulgaris*) also flower early in spring. **Red campion** (*Silene dioica*), which flowers from late April, can be found in hedgebanks along with **rosebay willowherb** (*Epilobium augustifolium*) which also has the name fireweed due to its habit of colonising burnt areas.

In scrubland and on woodland edges you will find **bramble** (*Rubus fruticosus*), a common vigorous shrub responsible for many a ripped jacket thanks to its sharp thorns and prickles. Blackberry fruits ripen from late summer to autumn. Fairly common in scrubland and on woodland edges is the **dog rose** (*Rosa canina*) which has a large pink flower, the fruits of which are used to make rose-hip syrup.

Look out, too, on the water in streams or rivers for the white-flowered **water crow-foot** (*Ranunculus penicillatus pseudofluitans*) which, because it needs unpolluted, flowing water, is a good indicator of the cleanliness of the stream.

Other flowering plants to look for in wooded areas and in hedgerows include the tall **foxglove** (*Digitalis purpurea*) with its trumpet-like flowers, **forget-me-not** (*Myosotis arvensis*) with tiny, delicate blue flowers, and **cow parsley** (*Anthriscus sylvestris*), a tall member of the carrot family with a large globe of white flowers which often covers roadside verges and hedgebanks.

Heathland and scrubland

There are three species of heather. The most dominant is **ling** (*Calluna vulgaris*) with tiny flowers on delicate upright stems. The other two species are **bell heather** (*Erica cinera*) with deep purple bell-shaped flowers and **cross-leaved heath** (*Erica tetralix*) with similarly shaped flowers of a lighter pink, almost white colour. Cross-leaved heath prefers wet and boggy ground. As a result, it usually grows away from bell heather which prefers well-drained soils.

Heather is an incredibly versatile plant which is put to many uses. It provides fodder for livestock, fuel for fires, an orange dye and material for bedding, thatching, basketwork and brooms. It is still sometimes used in place of hops to flavour beer and the flower heads can be brewed to make good tea. It is also incredibly hardy and thrives on the denuded hills, preventing other species from flourishing. Indeed, at times highland cattle are brought to certain areas of the moors to graze on the heather, allowing other species a chance to grow.

Not a flower but worthy of mention is the less attractive species **bracken** (*Pteridium aquilinum*), a vigorous non-native fern that has invaded many heathland areas to the detriment of native species.

Grassland

There is much overlap between the hedge/woodland-edge habitat and that of pastures and meadows. You will come across **common birdsfoot-trefoil** (*Lotus corniculatus*), **Germander speedwell** (*Veronica chamaedrys*), **tufted** and **bush vetch** (*Vicia cracca* and *V. sepium*) and **meadow vetchling** (*Lathyrus pratensis*) in both. Often the only species you will see in heavily grazed pastures are the most resilient.

Of the thistles, in late summer you should come across the **melancholy thistle** (*Cirsium helenoides*) drooping sadly on roadside verges and hay meadows. Unusually, it has no prickles on its stem. The **yellow rattle** is aptly named as its dry seedpods rattle in the wind; this is a good indication for farmers that it is time to harvest the hay.

Other widespread grassland species include **harebell** (*Campanula rotundifolia*), delicate yellow **tormentil** (*Potentilla erecta*) and **devil's-bit scabious** (*Succisa pratensis*). Also keep an eye out for orchids such as the **fragrant orchid** (*Gymnaadenia conopsea*) and **early purple orchid** (*Orchis mascula*).

Dunes

Dunes are formed by wind action creating a fragile, unstable environment. Among the first colonisers is **marram grass** (*Ammophila arenaria*) which is able to withstand drought, exposure to wind and salt spray and has an ability to grow up through new layers of sand that cover it. Other specialist plants are **sea holly** (*Eryngium maritimum*), **sea spurge** (*Euphorbia paralias*) and **sea**

Bell Heather
Erica cinerea

Heather (Ling)
Calluna vulgaris

Thrift (Sea Pink)
Armeria maritima

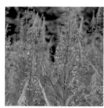

Rosebay Willowherb
Epilobium angustifolium

Common Vetch
Vicia sativa

Forget-me-not
Myosotis arvensis

Rowan (tree)
Sorbus aucuparia

Spear Thistle
Cirsium vulgare

Red Campion
Silene dioica

Early Purple Orchid
Orchis mascula

Foxglove
Digitalis purpurea

Sea Holly
Eryngium maritimum

Common Dog Violet
Viola riviniana

Common Centaury
Centaurium erythraea

Honeysuckle
Lonicera periclymemum

Ramsons (Wild Garlic)
Allium ursinum

Germander Speedwell
Veronica chamaedrys

Herb-Robert
Geranium robertianum

Lousewort
Pedicularis sylvatica

Self-heal
Prunella vulgaris

Scarlet Pimpernel
Anagallis arvensis

Sea Campion
Silene maritima

Bluebell
Hyacinthoides non-scripta

Hogweed
Heracleum sphondylium

Dog Rose
Rosa canina

Meadow Buttercup
Ranunculis acris

Gorse
Ulex europaeus

Tormentil
Potentilla erecta

Birdsfoot-trefoil
Lotus corniculatus

Ox-eye Daisy
Leucanthemum vulgare

Common Ragwort
Senecio jacobaea

Primrose
Primula vulgaris

Cowslip
Primula veris

Colour photos (following pages)

● **C4 Top left**: The route is well signposted so you shouldn't get lost; look for the acorn logo. **Middle left**: The riverbank at Lynmouth (see pp98-102). **Bottom left**: Sparkhayes Farm Campsite, Porlock (p88). **Right**: Strolling past the thatched cottages of Bossington (p84).
● **C5 Top left**: Heading towards Morte Point and Woolacombe (see p128). **Main picture**: Enjoying the views on the way to Heddon's Mouth (p110). **Bottom**: The attractive harbour at Ilfracombe (pp120-6) is the largest in North Devon. The *MS Oldenburg* makes the two-hour voyage to Lundy Island from here, up to five times a week in summer.
● **C6 Top**: The beautiful sweep of sand at Woolacombe (see p130) stretches for almost two miles. **Bottom left**: Saunton Court, visible from the alternative route out of Saunton Sands. **Bottom right**: Pub sign, Appledore. Hartland Lighthouse, on Hartland Point (p185).
● **C7 Top left**: Fishing boats at Bude (see pp196-203). **Bottom left & centre**: Steep, cobbled Up-a-Long and Down-a-Long St in picturesque Clovelly (p177). Waterfall at Speke's Mill Mouth (p187). **Right**: The view towards Blackchurch Rock (p181), west of Clovelly.

COAST PATH
OLLOW THE 🔔 SIGNS 👉

C5

bindweed (*Calystegia soldanella*). The one thing that these seemingly indomitable plants can't tolerate is trampling by human feet; stay on the path which is nearly always well marked through dunes.

MAMMALS

The South-West is blessed with wildlife and three species of mammals are particularly associated with the region. The largest population of **red deer**, *Cervus Elaphus*, lives on Exmoor – one of only three places where the herds are resident in England. Red deer, Britain's biggest wild animal, are nevertheless shy by nature and tend to flee at the approach of people. There is a very slim chance that a stag may charge during the rutting (mating) season when their behaviour can be unpredictable, though there is no record of this ever happening on Exmoor. They are largely nocturnal and your best chance of seeing them is at dusk when they move out of their woodland coverts to feed. Stags and hinds live separately for most of the year, mingling properly only during the mating season of October and November.

Also at home on the moor are the famous **Exmoor ponies**, a very ancient breed that resembles the miniature breeds of Asia more than any other native British horse. These ponies are hardy and also largely wild or feral, though in the past they have been trained to work in mines, on farms or for shepherding. There have never been many of them and during WWII their numbers collapsed to around 50. Today there are more than 500 adult breeding females (most on Exmoor), though a relatively small gene pool – after all, all today's ponies are descended from those 50 – means that they are still on the endangered list.

The third species for which the South-West is renowned is the **otter** (*Lutra lutra*). With Devon the home of the author Henry Williamson – author of *Tarka the Otter* – the county is proud to be associated with this most graceful of British carnivores and even has a Tarka Trail (see p34). It wasn't always like this, however, and for much of the 20th century (and before) the otter was persecuted because it was (wrongly) believed to have an enormously detrimental effect on fish stocks. Indeed, the otter was hunted with dogs up until 1977 and the Culmstock Otter Hounds were a regular sight in Exmoor National Park, particularly in the Exe and Barle valleys. Thankfully, today the otter is enjoying something of a renaissance due to some concerted conservation efforts. At home both in saltwater and freshwater, they are a good indicator of an unpolluted environment and Exmoor in particular is enjoying a resurgence in otter numbers, with at least 23 recorded in 2009 – a healthy number, given the size of the territory an otter requires. (Trivia fans may like to know that the final, climactic scene of the 1979 film version of *Tarka* was set on Instow Beach in North

---

(Opposite) Top: The feral goats that inhabit the Valley of the Rocks (see p106), near Lynmouth, have been here for many centuries and are now a mix of breeds including the Cheviot (an ancient British breed) and the Swiss Saanen. **Middle**: Great views but no meat on the bones atop the summit of Great Hangman (see p112), at 318m/1043ft the highest point on the entire South-West Coast Path. **Bottom**: Springtime in Exmoor.

Devon. The author Henry Williamson was actually taken seriously ill during filming and is said to have died during the filming of the last scene.)

Seeing any of these animals requires patience and no little amount of luck. One creature that you will definitely see along the walk, however, is the **rabbit**

❏ The Beast of Exmoor

Red deer, ponies, otters, badgers... Exmoor isn't short of wildlife to observe and admire. Ask the people of Britain, however, what animal they most associate with the park and the chances are many will mention a creature that only a handful of people have ever seen – and which, officially at least, doesn't even exist.

That creature is the Beast of Exmoor. Sightings of a large, panther-like animal roaming the moors of North Devon were first reported back in the 1970s and reached their peak in 1983 when a sheep farmer in South Molton claimed that over 100 of his herd had been killed in the space of just three months, their throats in each case having savagely been ripped from them. As speculation about the nature of the beast reached fever-pitch, there were reports of 'copycat' (!) sightings of similar creatures from as far away as Kent and Scotland.

At first the authorities were inclined to take the reports seriously and in response to the attacks on livestock, the Ministry of Agriculture sent in a troop of marines with high-powered rifles to hunt and kill any animal that fitted the description of a large cat between four and eight feet from nose to tail, that tended to crouch low to the ground but which had the ability to leap over six-foot-tall fences, and which was either black, tan or dark grey in colour.

Their mission proved unsuccessful, however, and the commanding officer – possibly with his tongue lodged in his cheek at the time – asserted that, if the creature did exist, it used the surrounding cover of hedges and woods with an almost 'human-like intelligence'.

News that the marines had returned back to their barracks clearly reached the creature, for reports of sheep deaths on the moor continued to rise, with 200 sheep killings attributed to the beast in 1987. There was even more good news for the Beast in the mid-1990s when the authorities, growing ever-more sceptical at the lack of any hard evidence of its existence, concluded that there was, in fact, no Beast of Exmoor. In their opinion, all alleged sightings were either the product of mistaken identifications of the more 'mundane' members of Exmoor's animal kingdom (eg domestic cats, dogs and even sheep), or deliberate hoaxes. It was a point of view that was given added credence in 2009 when a carcass washed up on North Devon turned out not to be the body of the beast, but a badly decomposed seal; and again in 2010 when photos of the beast appeared on the front pages of various tabloids – before it was discovered that the photographer had been doctoring his pictures using Photoshop.

Today, the more sober followers of the story have concluded that, if there ever was a Beast of Exmoor, there isn't one now (panthers live for only about 15 years on average). But there remains the distinct possibility that such a creature did once prowl the moors. Experts of 'phantom' or cryptozoological cats (to give them their proper title) point to a fad in the 1960s and 1970s to keep wild cats as pets. Given that in 1976 the Dangerous Wild Animals Act effectively outlawed this practice, it is highly possible that one of these large cats either escaped – or was deliberately released – by its owner into the wild.

But while the creature may not exist any more, it does, of course, live on in popular memory, folklore – and as a particularly potent concoction of Exmoor Ales Brewery whose Beast of Exmoor Ale weighs in at an impressive 6.6% ABV!

(*Oryctolagus cuniculus*). Timid by nature, most of the time you'll have to make do with nothing more than a brief and distant glimpse of their white tails as they race for the nearest warren at the sound of your footfall. Because they are so numerous, however, the laws of probability dictate that you will at some stage during your walk get close enough to observe them without being spotted; trying to take a decent photo of one, however, is a different matter.

If you're lucky you may also come across **hares** (*Lepus europaeus*), often mistaken for rabbits but much larger, more elongated and with longer ears and back legs. There are populations of hares all over the arable parts of Exmoor, though nowhere is it common.

Like the otter, the **water vole** (*Arvicola terrestris*) has both been a major character in a well-known work of fiction (in this case 'Ratty' from Kenneth Grahame's classic children's story *Wind in the Willows*), and has suffered a devastating drop in its population. Their numbers had originally declined due to the arrival in the UK countryside of the mink from North America, which successfully adapted to living in the wild after escaping from local fur farms. Unfortunately, the mink not only hunts water voles but is small enough to slip inside their burrows. Thus, with the voles afforded no protection, the mink was able to wipe out an entire riverbank's population in a matter of months. (Incidentally, this is another reason why protecting the otter is important: they kill mink.) A programme is now in place in which the water vole and its habitat is not only protected but the mink are being trapped and killed.

Another native British species that has suffered at the hands of a foreign invader – and indeed has now disappeared altogether from Exmoor and this part of the South-West – is the red squirrel (*Sciurus vulgaris*), a small, tufty-eared native that has been usurped by its larger cousin from North America, the **grey squirrel** (*Sciurus carolinensis*). The nearest place to see the red squirrel is at Poole Harbour – at the very end of the South-West Coast Path!

Other creatures you might see include the ubiquitous **fox** (*Vulpes vulpes*), now just as at home in the city as it is in the countryside. While generally considered nocturnal, it's not unusual to encounter a fox during the day too, often lounging in the sun near its den.

Another creature of the night you may *occasionally* see in the late afternoon is the **badger** (*Meles meles*). Relatively common throughout the British Isles, these sociable mammals with their distinctive black-and-white striped muzzles live in large underground burrows called setts, appearing around sunset to root for worms and slugs.

One creature that is strictly nocturnal, however, is the **bat**, of which there are 17 species in Britain, all protected by law. Your best chance of spotting one is at dusk while there's still enough light in the sky to make out their flitting forms as they fly along hedgerows, over rivers and streams and around street lamps in their quest for moths and insects. The commonest species in Britain is the **pipistrelle** (*Pipistrellus pipistrellus*).

In addition to the above, keep a look out for other fairly common but little seen species such as the carnivorous **stoat** (*Mustela erminea*), its diminutive cousin the **weasel** (*Mustela nivalis*), the **hedgehog** (*Erinaceus europaeus*) – these days, alas, most commonly seen as roadkill – and any number of species of **voles**, **mice** and **shrews**.

REPTILES

The **adder** (*Vipera berus*) is the only poisonous snake of the three species found in Britain. They pose very little risk to walkers – indeed, you should consider yourself extremely fortunate to see one, providing you're a safe distance away. They bite only when provoked, preferring to hide instead. The venom is designed to kill small mammals such as mice, voles and shrews, so deaths in humans are very rare but a bite can be extremely unpleasant and occasionally dangerous to children or the elderly. You are most likely to encounter them in spring when they come out of hibernation and during the summer when pregnant females warm themselves in the sun. They are easily identified by the striking zigzag pattern on their back. Should you be lucky enough to encounter one, (they enjoy basking on clifftops and on the moors) enjoy it but leave it undisturbed. The **grass snake** (*Natrix natrix*) is the largest British species, growing up to four feet in length. Olive-grey in colour with short black bars down each side and orange or yellow patches just below the head, they are harmless, relying not on venom or biting for defence but instead give off a foul odour if disturbed. It is pretty scarce in the South-West but can be found in damp places on Exmoor.

The **slow-worm** (*Anguis fragilis*) must be one of the more unusual creatures in the British Isles – a reptile that is called a worm, looks like a snake but is actually a legless lizard! Silver-grey with a dark line down the centre of the back and along each side, it is common on Exmoor and in North Devon in general, where it feeds on slugs, worms and insects.

SEA LIFE

The high cliffs are also a great place from which to look out over the sea. Searching for seals is an enjoyable and essential part of cliff walking. You'll spot lots of grey lobster-pot buoys before your first seal, but it's worth the effort. **Atlantic grey seals** (*Halichoerus grypus*) relax in the water, looking

---

❏ **Reporting wildlife sightings**
Report basking shark sightings to the website of the Marine Conservation Society (🖳 www.mcsuk.org). Remember to note any tags you've spotted. Reports are greatly appreciated.

If you see any of the other larger marine creatures such as dolphins, whales or seals you can report them online through Seaquest Southwest, part of the Devon Biodiversity Records Centre (🖳 www.dbrc.org.uk). With any report give the location, number and the direction they were heading in.

If you come across a stranded marine animal like a dolphin or porpoise, don't approach it but contact either British Divers' Marine Life Rescue (☎ 01825-765546) or the RSPCA hotline (☎ 0300-123 4999).

over their big Roman noses with doggy eyes, as interested in you as you are in them. Twice the weight of a red deer, a big bull can be over 200kg. On calm sunny days it's possible to follow them down through the clear water as they dive, as elegant in their element as they are clumsy on land. Seals generally come ashore only to rest, moult their fur, or to breed. The main centre where seals 'haul out' – come up on the rocks – is Lundy Island (see box p121). Indeed, Devon is a sort of frontier for the seals, as they rarely haul out east of here until you reach Norfolk.

A cliff-top sighting of Britain's largest fish is also a real possibility, but is more chilling than endearing! **Basking sharks** (*Cetorhinus maximus*) can grow to a massive eleven metres and weigh seven tonnes, and their two fins, a large shark-like dorsal fin followed by a notched tail fin, are so far apart it takes a second look to be convinced it's one fish. But these are gentle giants, cruising slowly with open jaws, filtering microscopic plankton from the sea. You are most likely to see one during late spring and summer when they feed at the surface during calm, warm weather. Look out for the coloured or numbered tags, which have been put on for research into this sadly declining species, and report them to the address given in the box opposite.

Taking a longer view and with some good luck, you may see **harbour porpoises** (*Phocoena phocoena*) and **bottlenose dolphins** (*Tursiops truncatus*); the former are particularly prevalent in Ilfracombe. Other cetaceans you may catch a glimpse of are: **Risso's dolphins** (*Grampus griseus*), **common dolphins** (*Delphinus delphis*), **striped dolphins** (*Stenella coeruleoalba*), **orcas** or **killer whales** (*Orcinus orca*) and **pilot whales** (*Globicephala melaena*). However, be warned, they are fiendishly difficult to tell apart: a brief glimpse of a fin is nothing like the 'whole animal' pictures shown in field guides.

BIRDS

In and around the fishing villages

The wild laugh of the **herring gull** (*Larus argentatus*) is the wake-up call of the coast path. Perched on the rooftops of the stone villages, they are a reminder of the link between people and wildlife, the rocky coast and our stone and concrete towns and cities. Shoreline scavengers, they've adapted to the increasing waste thrown out by human society. Despite their bad reputation it's worth taking a closer look at these fascinating, ubiquitous birds. How do they keep their pale grey and white plumage so beautiful feeding on rubbish?

Nobel-prize-winning animal behaviourist Nikko Tinbergen showed how the young pecking at the red dot on their bright yellow bills triggers the adult to regurgitate food. In August the newly fledged brown young follow their parents begging for food. Over the next three years they'll go through a motley range of plumages, more grey and less brown each year till they reach adulthood. But please don't feed them and do watch your sandwiches and fish and chips – they are quite capable of grabbing food from your hand.

The village harbours are a good place for lunch or an evening drink after a hard day on the cliffs. Look out for the birds which are equally at home on a rocky shore or in villages, such as the beautiful little black-and-white **pied wagtail** (*Motacilla alba*) with its long, bobbing tail.

Also looking black from a distance as they strut the beach are **jackdaws** (*Corvus monedula*). Close up, however, they are beautiful with a grey nape giving them a hooded look and shining blue eyes. They are very sociable: you will often see them high up in the air in pairs or flocks playing tag or performing acrobatic tricks.

Small, dark brown and easy to miss, the **rock pipit** (*Anthus petrosus*) is one of our toughest birds, as it feeds whilst walking on the rocks between the land and the sea. They nest in crevices and caves along the rocky coastline.

Seen on or from the sea cliffs

Walking on the coastal path leads you into a world of rock and sea, high cliffs with bracken-clad slopes, exposed green pasture, dramatic drops and headlands, sweeping sandy beaches and softer country around the estuaries. Stunning **stonechats** (*Saxicola torquata*) with black, white and orange colouring are common on heath and grassy plains where you may hear their distinctive song, which is not dissimilar to two stones being clacked together. Twittering **linnets** (*Carduelis cannabina*) with their bright red breasts and grey heads fly ahead and perch on gorse and fences. The vertiginous swoops of the path mean it's often possible to be at eye level or even look down on birds and mammals. Watch for **kestrels** (*Falco tinnunculus*), hovering on sharp brown wings, before plummeting onto their prey.

At eye level the black 'moustache' of the powerful slate-grey-backed **peregrine** (*Falco peregrinus*) is sometimes visible. At a glance it can be mistaken for a pigeon, its main prey. But the power and speed of this, the world's fastest bird, soon sets it apart. In the late summer whole families fly over the cliffs. In mid winter look for them over estuaries where they hunt ducks and waders. Despite the remote fastness of the cliffs, peregrine have suffered terribly. Accidental poisoning by the pesticide DDT succeeded where WWII persecution for fear they would kill carrier pigeons failed, and they were almost extinct in this region by the end of the 1960s. Its triumphant return means not only a thriving population on its traditional sea cliffs, but more and more nesting in our cities on man-made cliffs, such as tower blocks and cathedrals.

Cliff ledges, a kind of multi-storey block of flats for birds, provide nesting places safe from marauding land predators such as foxes and rats. It's surprising just how close it's possible to get to **fulmars** (*Fulmarus glacialis*), which return to their nesting ledges in February for the start of the long breeding season that goes on into the autumn. Only in the depth of winter are the cliffs quiet. Fulmars are related to albatrosses and like them are masters of the air. You can distinguish them from gulls by their ridged, flat wings as they sail the wind close to the waves with the occasional burst of fast flapping. Fulmars are incredibly tenacious at holding their nesting sites and vomit a stinking oily secretion over any intruders, including rock-climbers! The elegant **kittiwake** (*Rissa tridactyla*), the one true seagull that never feeds on land, is another cliff nester, identified by its 'dipped in ink' black wingtips.

Black above, white below, **manx shearwaters** (*Puffinus puffinus*) make globe-encircling journeys as they sail effortlessly just above even the wildest sea. Small and fast on hard-beating wings black and white **guillemots** (*Uria troile*) and **razorbills** (*Alca torda*) shoot out from their nesting ledges hidden in the cliffs. Guillemot have a long thin bill, razorbill a heavy half circle. There are large colonies of auks, razorbills and guillemots around the Highveer-Lynmouth area. **Puffins** (*Fratercula arctica*) with their unmistakable parrot-shaped bills are a rare prize round these coasts. Lundy, once again, is the best place to see these lovely birds.

Less lovely in most people's eyes, though undeniably magnificent, the big, rapacious **great black-backed gulls** (*Larus marinus*) cruise the nesting colonies for prey. Star of the sea show, however, has to be the big, sharp-winged, Persil-white **gannets** (*Morus bassanus*) cruising slowly for fish, then suddenly plunging with folded wings into the sea. Their strengthened skulls protect them from the huge force of the impact with the water.

Two birds more familiar from the artificial cliffs of our cities can be seen here in their natural habitat – **house martins** (*Delichon urbica*), steely-blue backed like a **swallow** (*Hirundo rustica*), but with more V-shaped wings and a distinctive white rump, and **rock doves** (*Columba livia*). These are so mixed with **town pigeons** (*Columba livia domest.*) it's hard to say if any 'pure' wild birds remain, but many individuals with the characteristic grey back, small white rump and two black wing bars can be seen.

Where the path drops steeply to a rocky bay, **oystercatchers** (*Haematopus ostralegus*), with their black and white plumage and spectacular carrot-coloured bill, pipe in panic when they fly off. This is also a good spot to get close to **shags** (*Phalacrocorax aristotelis*) and **cormorants** (*Phalacrocorax pygmeus*), common all round the coast, swimming low and black in the water. Shags are smaller and are always seen on the sea – cormorants are also on rivers and estuaries – and in the summer have a crest whilst cormorant have a white patch near their tail and white face. Close up, these oily birds shine iridescently; shags are green, cormorants are purple. They are a primitive species and since their feathers are not completely waterproof both have to dry their bodies after time in the sea; their heraldic pose, standing upright with half-spread wings on drying rocks is one of the special sights of the coast path.

In pastures, combes and woods

The path rises up onto rich green pasture. **Skylark** (*Alauda arvensis*) soar tunefully – almost disappearing into the spring sky, while in winter small green-brown **meadow pipits** (*Anthus pratensis*) flit weakly, giving a small high-pitched call. Spring also brings migrant **wheatears** (*Oenanthe oenanthe*): they are beautiful with their grey and black feathers above, buff and white below, and unmistakable when they fly and show their distinctive white rump. **Buzzard** (*Buteo buteo*) soar up with their tilted, broad round wings, giving their high, wild Ke-oow cry. **Ravens** (*Corvus corax*) cronk-cronk over the cliffs and are distinguished from more common **carrion crows** (*Corvus corone*) by their huge size and wedge-shaped tail. In the woods you'll find all three native species of

woodpecker – **green**, **great** and **lesser spotted** (*Picus viridis* and *Dendrocopos major* and *minor* respectively); the latter two are very much wedded to the woods, while the former, with its laughing call, can often be seen on the moors looking for insects.

In spring familiar birds such as **robins** (*Erithacus rubecula*), **blackbirds** (*Turdus merula*), **blue** and **great tits** (*Parus major* & *caeruleus*), **chaffinches** (*Fringila coelebs*) and **dunnocks** (*Prunella modularis*) are joined by the small green **chiffchaff** (*Phylloscopus collybita*); it's not much to look at but is one of the earliest returning migrants and unmistakably calls its own name in two repeated notes.

In and around estuaries

Descending to the long walk round the estuaries is moving into a different, softer world of shelter and rich farmland. Best for birds in winter, they are a welcome refuge from the ferocity of the worst weather for wildlife and people. There are large flocks of ducks – whistling **wigeon** (*Anas penelope*), a combination of grey and pinky brown, with big white wing patches in flight – and waders like the brown **curlew** (*Numenius arquata*) with its impossibly long, down-curved beak and beautiful sad fluting call, evocative of summer moors. The **redshank** (*Tringa totanus*), **greenshank** (*Tringa nebularia*), golden and grey **plover** (*Pluvialis sp.*) and black-tailed and bar-tailed **godwit** (*Limosa sp.*) can also be seen in winter.

Look out for the big black, white and chestnut **shelduck** (*Tadorna tadorna*), and for the tall grey **heron** (*Ardea cinerea*), hunched at rest or extended to its full 175cm as it slowly, patiently stalks fish in the shallows. A real rarity 10 years ago, another species of heron, the stunning white **little egret** (*Egretta garzetta*) is now unmissable on estuaries. Here the more common gull is the nimble **black-headed gull** (*Larus ridibundus*), with its elegant cap, dark in summer but pale in winter. In summer, terns come: the big **sandwich tern** (*Sterna sandvicensis*) with its shaggy black cap and loud rasping call, and the smaller sleeker aerobatic **common tern** (*Sterna hirundo*).

BUTTERFLIES AND MOTHS

Butterflies are an unexpected treat on the SWCP. Not only are they numerous, but there are several different varieties too. Braunton Burrows plays host to several species including marbled whites, graylings, ringlets and skippers, as well as to **moths**, including ghost, common swift, diamond-back, garden grass veneer and small China mark moths. Butterflies and moths aren't confined to the burrows, however.

The most famous butterfly in the region is the orange and brown heath fritillary, which has declined rapidly over the last 30 years in the UK, but which is thriving in the combes of Exmoor (indeed, Exmoor is one of only four places where they still live, and there are now 15 colonies in the national park).

ROUTE GUIDE & MAPS

Using this guide

The route guide has been described from east to west and divided into ten stages. Though each of these roughly corresponds to a day's walk, do not assume that this is the only way to plan your walk. There are so many places to stay en route that you can pretty much divide up the walk wherever you want. However, see pp29-30 for some suggested itineraries.

To provide further help, practical information is presented on the trail maps, including walking times, places to stay, camp and eat, as well as shops where you can buy supplies, and public toilets. Further service details are given in the text under the entry for each settlement.

For a condensed overview of this information see the village and town facilities table on pp32-3.

TRAIL MAPS
Scale and walking times
The trail maps are to a scale of 1:20,000 (1cm = 200m; $3^{1}/_{8}$ inches = one mile). Walking times are given along the side of each map and the arrow shows the direction to which the time refers. Black triangles indicate the points between which the times have been taken. **See note in box on p74 on walking times**.

The time-bars are a tool and are not there to judge your walking ability. There are so many variables that affect walking speed, from the weather conditions to how many beers you drank the previous evening. After the first hour or two of walking you will be able to see how your speed relates to the timings on the maps.

Up or down?
Other than when on a track or bridleway the trail is shown as a dotted line. An arrow across the trail indicates the slope; two arrows show that it is steep. Note that the arrow points towards the higher part of the trail. If, for example, you are walking from A (at 80m) to B (at 200m) and the trail between the two is short and steep it would be shown thus: A— — — >> — — – B. Reversed arrow heads indicate downward gradient.

GPS waypoints
The numbered GPS waypoints refer to the list on pp204-5.

> **❑ Where to stay: the details**
> Unless specified, B&B-style accommodation is either **en suite** or has **private facilities**; 🛁 means at least one room has a bath; 🐕 signifies that dogs are welcome in at least one room but always by prior arrangement, an additional charge may also be payable; WI-FI means wi-fi is available.

Accommodation

Apart from in large towns where some selection of places has been necessary, almost every place to stay that is within easy reach of the trail is marked. Details of each place are given in the accompanying text.

For B&B-style accommodation the number and type of rooms is given after each entry: S = single room, T = twin room, D = double room, F = triple or family room (usually either three single beds, a double and bunk beds, or a double and two singles). Family rooms can therefore almost always also be used as a double or twin.

Rates quoted are **per person** (pp) based on two people sharing a room for a one-night stay; rates are usually discounted for longer stays. Where a single room is available the rate for that is quoted if different from the per person rate. The rate for single occupancy of a double/twin may be higher, and the rate for three or more sharing a family room may be lower. Single room (sgl) and where relevant single occupancy (sgl occ) rates are also provided. Unless specified rates are for B&B. At some places the only option is a room rate; this will be based on two people sharing. Many places either do not accept single-night bookings at peak times or they charge extra for them. Most B&Bs don't accept credit/debit cards but hotels usually do.

The text also mentions whether the premises have **wi-fi** (WI-FI); if a **bath** is available (🛁) in at least one room; and whether **dogs** (🐕) are welcome. Most places will not take more than one dog in a room and also accept them subject to prior arrangement. Some make an additional charge (usually per night but occasionally per stay) while others may require a deposit which is refundable if the dog doesn't make a mess.

Booking is essential for all **campsites** in school holidays but is usually not necessary at other times.

Other features

Features are marked on the map when pertinent to navigation. In order to avoid cluttering the maps and making them unusable not all features have been marked each time they occur.

> **❑ Important note – walking times**
> Unless otherwise specified, **all times in this book refer only to the time spent walking**. You will need to add 20-30% to allow for rests, photography, checking the map, drinking water etc. When planning the day's hike count on 5-7 hours' actual walking.

The route guide

MINEHEAD   [MAP 1, p77]

*Some towns inspire. They have an air of
adventure and a sense of urgency. They are
mysterious and just a little frightening. You
know as soon as you walk into them they are
special places. Minehead isn't one of them.*
        Mark Wallington, *500 Mile Walkies*

Minehead may not be quite as bad as Mr
Wallington would have you believe but
there's not much to delay you here. The
town's major draw, the huge Butlin's holiday camp on Minehead's eastern fringes,
will probably hold little appeal to the average walker. Indeed, Minehead doesn't even
have a mine – the name actually derives
from the Celtic word, Mynedd, meaning
'hill'.

Nevertheless, Minehead's location,
where the flat, former marshlands of
Somerset collide with the rolling hills of
Exmoor, is a good one, and the town's port
was once, during Elizabethan times, a thriving place, built on foundations that date
back to Saxon times. Today, however, the
place is much sleepier, the biggest thrill in
town being the intermittent arrival of the
steam trains of the **West Somerset
Railway** (see box p45) as they puff and
chuff into Minehead's centre.

Despite its lack of thrills, as a place to
begin a 630-mile adventure Minehead is
pretty good: there are reasonable transport
connections (by the standards of the South-
West, anyway); plenty of places to stay and
eat, should you require them; and with no
'must-sees' in town that demand to be visited, there's little to delay you should you
wish to push on with your walking as soon
as you arrive.

Services

At the time of research the tourist office on
the seafront had closed and it was uncertain
whether it would open again. The staff at
Porlock Visitor Centre (☎ 01643 702624;

see p87) are happy to answer questions
about Minehead; alternatively visit ⌨ www
.minehead.co.uk.

For supplies the most central **supermarket** is the Co-op (Mon-Sat 8am-10pm,
Sun 10am-4pm), on The Avenue, at the
back of which you'll find the **post office**
(Mon-Fri 9am-5.30pm, Sat 9am-12.30pm).

The library (☎ 0845-345 9177, ⌨
www.librarieswest.org.uk; Mon, Tue, Thur
& Fri 9.30am-5pm, Sat 9.30am-1pm) has a
few terminals dedicated to **internet access**
(non members first 30 mins free then
£1.20/20 mins). An alternative is Exmoor
Printers (☎ 01643-704799; Mon-Fri
9.30am-5pm; £1 for 15 mins, rate reduced
for longer usage). **Minehead Eye** (☎
01643-703155; Tue-Sat 10am-10pm, Sun
10am-8pm) also offers internet access (free
as long as you buy something in the café),
and there is a small gallery and a *café* here
too. If on the journey here you've already
managed to acquire blisters or other ailments, Boots the **Chemist** (Mon-Sat
8.30am-5.30pm, Sun 10am-4pm) has a
branch on the main drag of The Parade and
there are several **banks** with ATMs scattered along it, including HSBC by The
Duke of Wellington.

Where to stay

For **campers**, the nearest site lies about a
mile from Minehead. *Minehead Camping
and Caravanning Club* (☎ 01643-704138,
out of season ☎ 0845-130 7633, ⌨ www
.campingandcaravanningclub.co.uk; late
Apr to late Sep; 🐾; WI-FI) is on Hill Rd on
North Hill. It's a well-equipped place
which boasts wonderful views over the
town to the sea. It's good value, too, at
£4.65-6.60pp; the only problem is getting
to the place, which involves a 30-minute
walk up a steep hill (though you can cut in
from the coast path).

YHA Minehead (☎ 0845-371 9033; 🖳 www.yha.org.uk; 35 beds; £18.40pp) is actually a little way out of town at Alcombe Combe – and far from the coast path too – so is not really practical for most people. It doesn't particularly matter, however, for there is the always popular *Base Lodge* (☎ 01643-703520; 2T/two 5-bed rooms/one 6-bed room; WI-FI; quiet 🐾; £15-20pp), at 16 The Parks, one of several independent hostels on this path and smarter than most, a Grade-II listed Victorian building just west of the town centre. The genial host is a qualified mountain guide and a mine of information, the rooms are clean, basic and pleasant and the kitchen is well equipped.

Just up the road at No 26 is one of the finest **B&Bs** in town: *The Parks* (☎ 01643-703547, 🖳 www.parksguesthouse.co.uk; 4D/1T/2F; WI-FI; 🐾; £31.25-36pp, sgl occ £50) is an elegant Georgian property in a leafy part of town and it has immaculately maintained rooms.

Most B&Bs, however, tend to be at the eastern side of town. The first place to look is Tregonwell Rd, where a string of guesthouses & B&Bs stand cheek-by-jowl. *Tregonwell House* (☎ 01643-709287, 🖳 www.tregonwellhouse.co.uk; 1S/5D/2T; £30-34.50pp, £28 sgl), at No 1, is fairly typical – it's an unassuming B&B with comfy rooms and amiable owners. Heading south along the road, next door is *Lyn Valley* (☎ 01643-703748, 🖳 www.lynvalleyminehead.co.uk; 1S/3D/1T/1F; 🐾; WI-FI; £30pp, £40sgl). *Kenella House* (☎ 01643-703128, 🖳 www.kenellahouse.co.uk; 4D/ 2T; WI-FI; £32.50-35pp, £55-60 sgl occ), at No 7, is slightly smarter than most on this street and the landlady has been a finalist in a Landlady of the Year competition; while across the road at No 14 is *Montrose Guesthouse* (☎ 01643-706473, 🖳 www.montroseminehead.co.uk; 3D/2D or T; £29-36pp, sgl occ £48-60).

Still on Tregonwell Rd, there is *The Bactonleigh* (☎ 01643-702147, 🖳 www.bactonleigh.co.uk; 1S/3D/3D or T/2T/2F; 🐾; WI-FI; small 🐾; £26-31pp). *Tranmere Guesthouse* (☎ 01643-702647, 🖳 www.tranmereguesthouse.co.uk; 3D/1T/2F;

£28pp, sgl occ £45-50) is another smart place and good value; *Lorna Doone* (☎ 01643-702540, 🖳 www.lornadooneguesthouse.co.uk; 2S/1T/2D/1F; WI-FI; from £27pp) at No 26, has been recommended by more than one coastal walker. *Farlands House* (☎ 01643-702975, 🖳 www.farlands-house.co.uk; 2D/1D or T; 🐾; WI-FI; 🐾 about £4; from £30pp, sgl occ £40) is my favourite, less 'chintz-tastic' than some and with a very amiable host who is trying, in his own lethargic way, to complete the whole of the SWCP (he thinks he'll have it done by the time he's 85). And finally on this strip there's *Glendower House* (☎ 01643-707144, 🖳 www.glendower-house.co.uk; 3S/5D/3T; WI-FI; £35-40pp, sgl £45), another large Edwardian place.

Sunfield (☎ 01643-703565, 🖳 www.sunfieldminehead.co.uk; 1S/4D/3D or T; 🐾; 🐾; £32pp, sgl £32), at 83 Summerland Ave, has also been recommended by walkers.

Gascony Hotel (☎ 01643-705939, 🖳 www.gasconyhotel.co.uk; 3S/13D or T/4F; 🐾; WI-FI; from £38pp, sgl from £45), 50 The Avenue, at the junction with Tregonwell Rd, is a traditional hotel with huge lounges set in an old Victorian house.

There are some pubs with rooms and real character on Quay St, which conveniently is also the street where the SWCP starts. *The Quay Inn* (☎ 01643-707323, 🖳 www.quay-inn.co.uk; 2D/2F; 🐾; WI-FI; small 🐾; £40-55pp, sgl occ from £50), the first you come to, is a smart and modern affair with a good kitchen (see Where to eat). At the very northern edge of town, and right on the trail, *The Old Ship Aground* (☎ 01643-702087, 🖳 www.theoldshipaground.co.uk; 2S/4D/4T/2F; £27.50-35pp, sgl £40) is not actually as old as it looks, having been built in the 1900s, though it's still got a certain charm, pleasant rooms and, best of all, the finest views in Minehead over the harbour. Do note, however, that dogs, though welcome in the bar, can't stay the night.

Another pub, and one whose origins are significantly older, is *The Duke of Wellington* (☎ 01643-701910, 🖳 www.jdwetherspoon.co.uk; 6S/1T/17D/5F; 🐾; WI-FI in the bar; £27pp, sgl £44), built in 1820

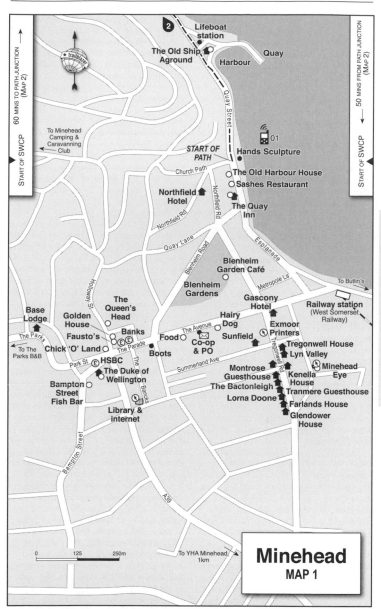

ROUTE GUIDE AND MAPS

Minehead
MAP 1

as a coaching inn but now a Wetherspoons-owned place and thus typical of the chain, being functional, central and fair value. More tranquil, *Northfield Hotel* (☎ 01643-705155, 🖥 www.northfield-hotel.co.uk; 4S/11D/2T/13D or T; 🛥; WI-FI; 🐕 £8; £74.50-84.50pp inc afternoon tea, supper, bed & breakfast), on the road of the same name and part of the Best Western group, has a pool, Jacuzzi and some pleasant gardens.

Where to eat and drink

The nicest place to sit down during the day is *Blenheim Garden Café* (daily 10am-5pm; WI-FI), situated in the eponymous gardens. They don't do breakfasts – and the park doesn't allow dogs – but they do have a good lunch menu including fish 'n' chips for £4.95.

The main drag in Minehead, The Avenue, is the first place to look for food. And where better to begin your search than *Food* (☎ 01643-702010; Mon-Sat 8am-4pm), at No 10, a modern sandwich take-away and coffee bar selling sticky pastry products, all baked on the premises. A bit further down at No 32, *The Hairy Dog* (☎ 01643-706317, 🖥 www.thehairydog.co.uk; food served daily 11.30am-9pm) dominates one end of the road. A former 'UK Family Pub of the Year' winner, it's been well run by the same family for over 25 years and is full of features such as large gardens, a conservatory, play area and pool table. The menu includes fairly standard pub fare (eg jacket potatoes £6.95), but the portions are large and the steaks (rump £12.95, sirloin £14.95) are good.

For fast food, there are several options: *Chick 'O' Land* (☎ 01643-703036; daily noon-midnight) is a standard fast-food out-let with a cholesterol-heavy menu including pizzas and, of course, fried chicken. *Bampton Street Fish Bar* (☎ 01643-702968; Mon 5-8.30pm, Tue-Sat 11.45am-1.45pm & 4.45-9.30pm, to 8pm/9pm in the winter) is a superlative award-winning fish bar, unpretentious but very friendly and deserving of all the plaudits it has garnered.

For more formal (ie sit-down) dining, Holloway St has a few options. *Fausto's* (☎ 01643-706372; Mon-Sat 11.30am-3pm, 5pm to late), at No 4, is a reasonably priced Italian, with pizzas starting at only £3.50, though the reviews are mixed; while *The Queen's Head* (☎ 01643-702940; food served Tue-Sat noon-2pm & 6-9pm, Sun noon-2pm) serves real ales including their own Queen's Head Ale and has reasonably priced meals, most for under £10. Between the two, *Golden House* (☎ 01643-702723; mid Feb to mid Jan Mon-Sat noon-2pm, daily 5.30-10.30pm), offers a fairly stan-dard Chinese menu, with huge set meals (around £18) or individual mains for £6.80-8. Nearby, *The Duke of Wellington* (see Where to stay; daily 7am-10pm) boasts a typical, very reasonably priced Wetherspoons' menu.

The Quay is also a good area for food, with two decent pubs: *The Quay Inn* (see Where to stay; food served May-Oct noon-8.45pm, Nov-Apr Mon-Fri noon-2pm & 6-8.45pm, Sat noon-8.45pm), just a walking-pole's throw from the start of the coast path, is a smart, well-furnished pub with a large multi-tiered garden and skittle alley. It has a reasonably priced menu including a 'Build your own burger' and also serves real ales. *The Old Ship Aground* (see Where to stay; food served Feb-Dec Mon-Sat noon-9pm, Sun noon-8pm; Jan daily noon-3pm & 5-8pm) serves locally sourced and reasonably priced food.

There are some good restaurants on The Quay too. *The Old Harbour House* (☎ 01643-705917, 🖥 www.theoldharbour houserestaurant.co.uk; Mon-Sat 7-8pm, Sun noon-2.30pm) offers some great set menus (£22.75-24.75) or you can feast on one of their à la carte mains such as beef en croûte (steak and pâté wrapped in puff pas-try) for £16.50. Note: booking is preferred and when you book you are given or sent a menu so that you can choose what you would like to eat and be certain of getting it; also credit cards are not accepted here.

Sashes Restaurant (☎ 01643-709890, 🖥 www.sashesgoodfood.co.uk; Tue-Sat 7-8.30pm), at 11a, boasts an extensive menu including a fish of the day, with main cours-es for £14.95-19.95.

Transport

For details on **getting to Minehead**, see p45. For destinations further along the path, Quantock Motor Services operates: No 39 to Porlock/Porlock Weir via Bossington; and a seasonal open-top bus service – No 300 (to Lynmouth via Porlock). See pp49-51 for further details. Most services drive down The Avenue.

MINEHEAD TO PORLOCK WEIR [MAPS 1-7]

This **9-mile (14.5km; 3hrs 50 mins, 5hrs 20 mins if taking the rugged alternative route)** first stage of the SWCP offers a taster of much that is wonderful about the Exmoor coast. Beginning with a stroll through ancient, ivy-strangled woodland (Exmoor can, after all, boast some of the most extensive broadleaved coastal woods in Britain), you emerge eventually at North Hill, whereafter the route offers you two choices: a gentle pastoral stroll by fields of livestock or a more rugged alternative that offers a wilder, longer and more remote experience (and, so it is said, a greater chance of spotting native Exmoor wildlife such as red deer) as you contour the coastline on a narrow trail.

The two paths then reunite just before the descent to the cream-tea cosiness of Bossington, from where a flat track takes you across farmland, via a turn-off to nearby Porlock and a submerged forest, to the village of Porlock Weir, home to a thousand-year-old port, several thatched grade-II listed cottages – and a fabulously eccentric hotel.

The route

The South-West Coast Path begins by what has become popularly known either as the '**Hands Sculpture**' or the '**Map Sculpture**', sculpted in bronze by Owen Cunningham and erected in 2001; it is, of course, pretty much obligatory to have your photo taken next to it. Photographed, fed, backpacked and booted, it's now time for you to begin. Ignore the acorn symbols on the tarmac that suggest there's an alternative inland route (that route is no longer in use) and instead stick to the waterfront as it takes you towards and beyond The Old Ship Aground and its neighbouring **lifeboat station**.

Leaving the last vestiges of Minehead behind, the trail enters some deep, dark woods scored with numerous paths and bridleways before emerging above the trees below the summit of **North Hill**. (A diversion off the path here takes you down the steep slope to the ruined **Burgundy Chapel** and its accompanying hermitage, a medieval two-roomed construction that dates back over 600 years.) Look out for nightjars and the rare Dartford warbler flitting amongst the western gorse, which itself is a plant that's a bit of a rarity, found only in the West Country and southern Wales.

The path continues westwards a short distance before dividing; the northern path is known as 'the rugged alternative' (see p82). Meanwhile the main

ROUTE GUIDE AND MAPS

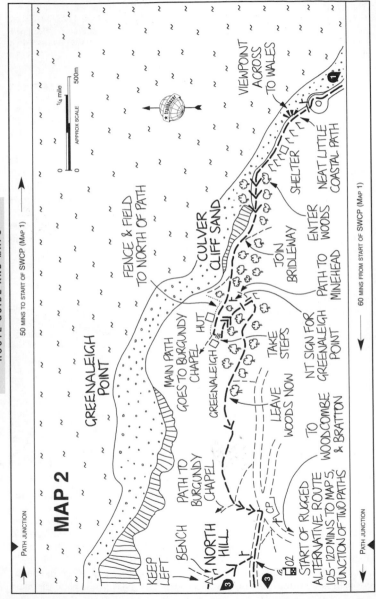

50 MINS TO START OF SWCP (MAP 1)

PATH JUNCTION

MAP 2

GREENALEIGH POINT

KEEP LEFT

BENCH

NORTH HILL

PATH TO BURGUNDY CHAPEL

MAIN PATH GOES TO BURGUNDY CHAPEL

HUT

CREENALEIGH

LEAVE WOODS NOW

TAKE STEPS

NT SIGN FOR GREENALEIGH POINT

CP

START OF RUGGED ALTERNATIVE ROUTE 105-120MINS TO MAP 5, JUNCTION OF TWO PATHS

TO WOODCOMBE & BRATTON

FENCE & FIELD TO NORTH OF PATH

CULVER CLIFF SAND

JOIN BRIDLEWAY

ENTER WOODS

PATH TO MINEHEAD

VIEWPOINT ACROSS TO WALES

SHELTER

NEAT LITTLE COASTAL PATH

APPROX SCALE

0   500m

0   ¼ mile

60 MINS FROM START OF SWCP (MAP 1)

PATH JUNCTION

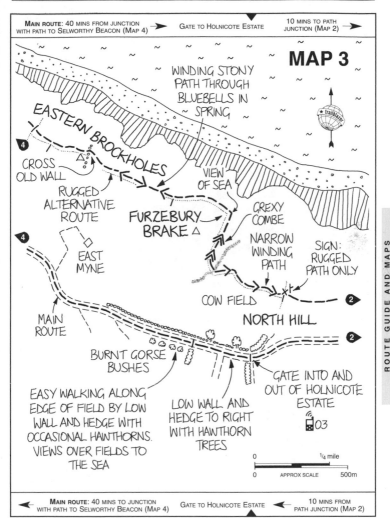

MAP 3

WINDING STONY PATH THROUGH BLUEBELLS IN SPRING

EASTERN BROCKHOLES

CROSS OLD WALL

RUGGED ALTERNATIVE ROUTE

FURZEBURY BRAKE △

VIEW OF SEA

GREXY COMBE

NARROW WINDING PATH

SIGN: RUGGED PATH ONLY

EAST MYNE

COW FIELD

NORTH HILL

MAIN ROUTE

BURNT GORSE BUSHES

GATE INTO AND OUT OF HOLNICOTE ESTATE

EASY WALKING ALONG EDGE OF FIELD BY LOW WALL AND HEDGE WITH OCCASIONAL HAWTHORNS. VIEWS OVER FIELDS TO THE SEA

LOW WALL AND HEDGE TO RIGHT WITH HAWTHORN TREES

0   ¼ mile

0   APPROX SCALE   500m

ROUTE GUIDE AND MAPS

trail meanders gently, scarcely rising or falling, past fields and flocks, with unbroken views over the sheep to the sea. Wales winks at you across the waves to the north, while Dunkery Beacon – the highest point on Exmoor – glimpses your progress from the south. Passing **Selworthy Beacon** (309m/1013ft), the path descends to a reunion with the alternative trail before descending steeply through **Hurlstone Combe** and on to Bossington.

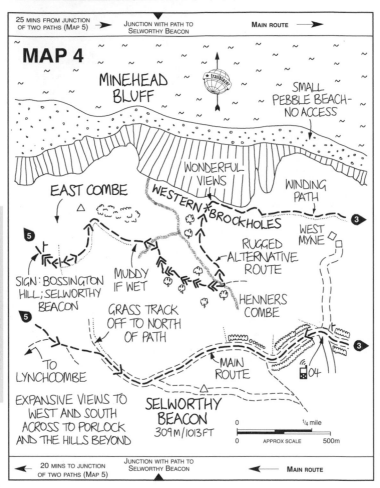

MAP 4

MINEHEAD BLUFF

★ trailblazer

SMALL PEBBLE BEACH- NO ACCESS

WONDERFUL VIEWS

WINDING PATH

EAST COMBE

WESTERN BROCKHOLES

WEST MYNE

RUGGED ALTERNATIVE ROUTE

5

SIGN: BOSSINGTON HILL; SELWORTHY BEACON

MUDDY IF WET

HENNERS COMBE

GRASS TRACK OFF TO NORTH OF PATH

5

TO LYNCHCOMBE

MAIN ROUTE

04

EXPANSIVE VIEWS TO WEST AND SOUTH ACROSS TO PORLOCK AND THE HILLS BEYOND

SELWORTHY BEACON
309M/1013FT

0   ¼ mile
0   APPROX SCALE   500m

3

3

The rugged alternative route

Do not be put off by the name of this alternative trail – though more testing than the official path this route is not overly difficult and is well worth the extra 90 minutes that it takes to walk it. **Note that dogs are not allowed on this path**.

    The trail runs along a thin and winding path, intermittently following field boundaries and keeping close to the sea, occasionally dipping into miniature combes and crossing streams. The views are tremendous, the path is wilder than the official route and you are less likely to see other people too – and far

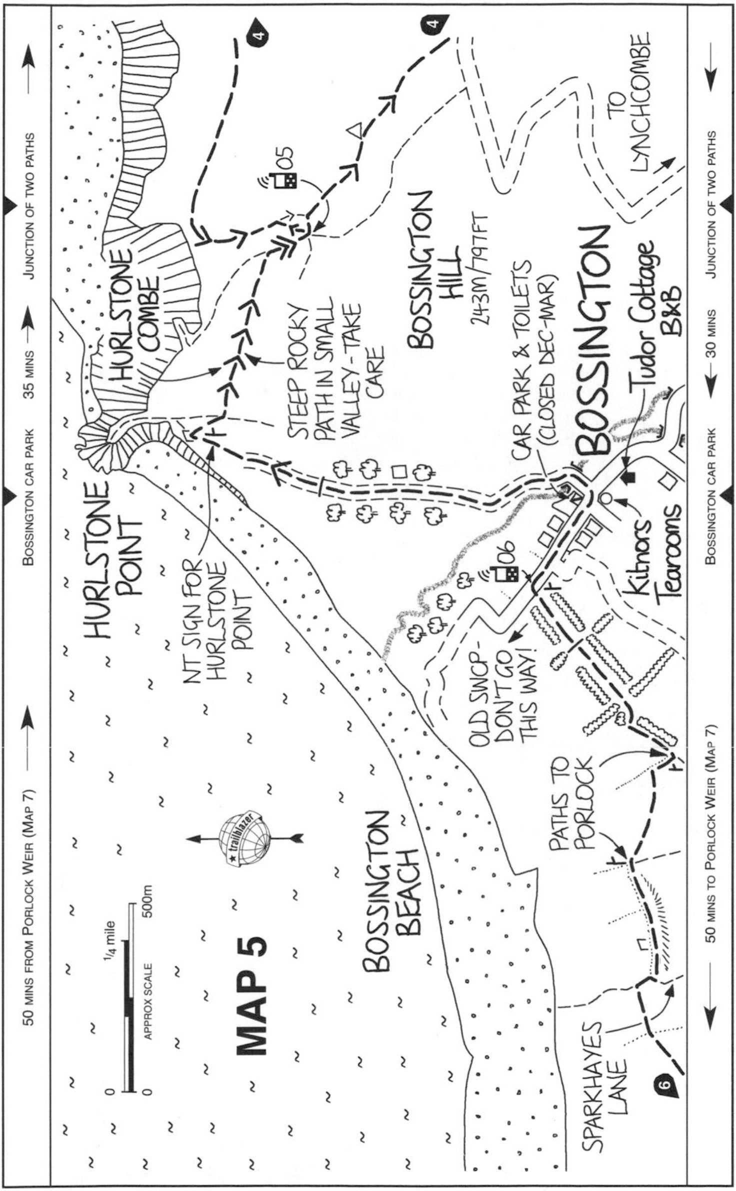

MAP 5

50 MINS FROM PORLOCK WEIR (MAP 7)

HURLSTONE POINT

NT SIGN FOR HURLSTONE POINT

BOSSINGTON BEACH

SPARKHAYES LANE

PATHS TO PORLOCK

OLD SWCP— DON'T GO THIS WAY!

BOSSINGTON

Tudor Cottage B&B

Kitnors Tearooms

CAR PARK & TOILETS (CLOSED DEC-MAR)

BOSSINGTON HILL 243M/797FT

STEEP ROCKY PATH IN SMALL VALLEY—TAKE CARE

HURLSTONE COMBE

TO LYNCHCOMBE

¼ mile
500m
0
0
APPROX SCALE

BOSSINGTON CAR PARK ◀ 35 MINS ▶ JUNCTION OF TWO PATHS

BOSSINGTON CAR PARK ◀ 30 MINS ▶ JUNCTION OF TWO PATHS

50 MINS TO PORLOCK WEIR (MAP 7)

ROUTE GUIDE AND MAPS

more likely to see red deer. Throughout much of it you are surrounded by gorse although bluebells make for a spectacular display in spring.

Where the regular trail passes near the summit of Selworthy Beacon, the alternative path goes around its lower slopes. Having crossed the upper reaches of **Grexy Combe**, on your left but not visible is the Iron-Age hill fort of **Furzebury Brake**. Further archaeology lies ahead on the path with two medieval settlements, **East** and **West Myne**, while to your right are the **Eastern Brockholes**, which along with the Western Brockholes are considered to be the places where the stone was quarried to build the two settlements.

At **East Combe** you can turn left and climb to the top of Selworthy Beacon, or you can keep on and rejoin the official path after **Hurlstone Combe**.

BOSSINGTON [MAP 5, p83]

Bossington is the kind of blink-and-you-miss-it village that people come to Devon specifically to see: ancient, cosy, with a gorgeous tearoom and picture-perfect cottages scattered willy-nilly along a single track lane. With its thatched roofs and lack of telegraph wires, it can feel like you've wandered onto the set of a BBC period drama.

Kitnors Tearooms (☎ 01643-862643; Easter to Oct daily 11am-5pm, Mar & Nov-Dec Fri-Sun), situated right on the path, has a splendid little garden at the rear where one can relax to a gentle cacophony

---

❏ Porlock Beach

The beach at Porlock Vale is a very dynamic environment. The **shingle bank** that protects the vale from flooding at high tide – and which looks for all the world like a man-made defensive barrier – was actually established about 8000 years ago at the end of the last Ice Age, the rising sea levels piling up the rocks and shingle that had fallen from the nearby cliffs.

Though man may not have built it he has certainly done his best to repair it down the centuries in order to protect the valuable farmland behind, with the last major rebuild occurring in 1990. Man is also responsible for building the WWII **pillboxes** (a type of defensive bunker, usually made from concrete) and the now-ruined **lime kiln** along the beach. Yet in spite of these efforts at preservation, a further breach to the shingle bank in 1996 forced the authorities to rethink their policy and as a result it was decided to allow nature to take its course – meaning that, in years to come, Porlock Vale may well become a lagoon, just as it was around 200 years ago.

The ever-changing landscape of Porlock Vale has exposed some interesting sites and artefacts that had previously lain hidden beneath the seabed. The **submerged forest** that you walk past on the way to Porlock Weir is actually around five or six thousand years old and was first observed only in 1890. In 1998 part of a skeleton of an **auroch**, a giant precursor to modern cattle that roamed these parts about 3500 years ago, was found in the exposed blue clay of an old riverbed. The bones are now on display in Porlock Visitor Centre (see p87). A piece of worked timber from 900AD has also been unearthed embedded in beach clay near the shingle ridge, as have numerous flints.

Perhaps unsurprisingly, the entire beach has been declared a **Site of Special Scientific Interest** (SSSI; see p62) as it allows scientists to study how such a landscape will develop if left to its own devices, as well as the effect this will have on the flora and fauna of the area, with lapwings, herons, teal, shelduck and egret regular visitors to this rare salt marsh environment.

of birdsong (the robins are particularly friendly). It's a lovely place to stop and they serve sandwiches, light lunches and cream teas (from £3.50). As for a place to stay, just up the road is *Tudor Cottage* (☎ 01643- 862255, 🖳 www.tudorcottage.net; 2D/1T; ☎; WI-FI; from £35pp, £50 sgl occ), a 15th-century cottage with a splendid garden and wonderful views across to Porlock Weir.

Bossington sits at the eastern extremity of the wide **Porlock Vale**, an unusually wide, flat valley in comparison with the narrow combes typical of Exmoor. Standing between it and the sea is a natural shingle ridge – a ridge that was breached in 1996 (see box opposite), causing the farmland to turn into a salt marsh that receives a fresh inundation of salt every high tide. It also led to a rerouting of the SWCP that once followed this ridge but which now takes a more inland course, around the back of the beach. This does mean that the sea will be out of sight for the next few miles – but also that it is much less of a detour to visit the charming village of Porlock.

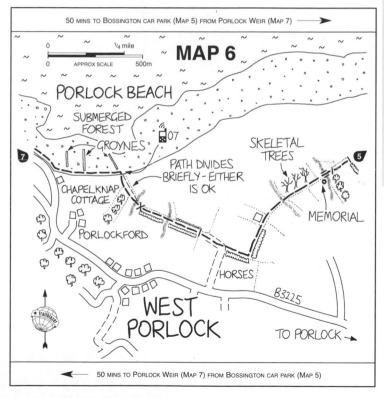

50 MINS TO BOSSINGTON CAR PARK (MAP 5) FROM PORLOCK WEIR (MAP 7) ⟶

MAP 6

PORLOCK BEACH

SUBMERGED FOREST

GROYNES

07

SKELETAL TREES

PATH DIVIDES BRIEFLY - EITHER IS OK

CHAPEL KNAP COTTAGE

PORLOCKFORD

MEMORIAL

HORSES

B3225

WEST PORLOCK

TO PORLOCK ⟶

⟵ 50 MINS TO PORLOCK WEIR (MAP 7) FROM BOSSINGTON CAR PARK (MAP 5)

PORLOCK

Though 15 minutes from the path, Porlock remains a popular stopover on the SWCP. The plentiful accommodation, amenities, attractions and ancient architecture are enough to tempt the tiring walker off the trail.

A survey of 2010 based on data from the Office of National Statistics found the village to have the oldest average population in the UK, with over 40% above pensionable age – and indeed the village is venerable in many ways. The place was mentioned in the Domesday Book of 1086 (as 'Portloc') and several of the village's buildings are only slightly younger. The oldest, **The Chantry**, has parts dating back to the 12th century. The truncated tower on the neighbouring **Church of St Dubricius** (named after a 6th-century Welsh saint who, according to legend, crowned King Arthur and later married him to Guinevere) was built only a few decades later; while, inside the church, you'll find fragments of a cross that date back to pre-Norman times.

The main street is also scattered with more old thatched cottages than you can shake a sheaf of straw at, from The Old Rose and Crown Cottage (formerly a pub), opposite the church, to the 13th-century Ship Inn at the western end of the village.

For a more intimate look at one of Porlock's hoary homes, **Dovery Manor Museum** (🖳 www.doverymanormuseum .org.uk; Mon-Fri 10am-1pm & 2-5pm, Sat

❏ The poets of Porlock

Porlock has long been a favourite place of poets, romantics and dreamers. Robert Southey's friends Samuel Taylor Coleridge and William Wordsworth (who both lived nearby at Nether Stowey and Alfoxden respectively) were frequent visitors and often wandered (as lonely as clouds, presumably) the hills and beaches surrounding the village. Indeed, the regularity of their perambulations and the fact that many of them were undertaken at night aroused suspicions in the locals and rumours began to circulate that they were actually French spies. A government agent sent to investigate however, witheringly concluded that they were 'mere poets' and thus no threat to the Crown.

Porlock! thy verdant vale so fair to sight,
Thy lofty hills which fern and furze imbrown,
The waters that roll musically down
Thy woody glens, the traveller with delight
Recalls to memory, and the channel grey
Circling its surges in thy level bay.
Porlock! I shall forget thee not,
Here by the unwelcome summer rain confined;
But often shall hereafter call to mind
How here, a patient prisoner, 'twas my lot
To wear the lonely, lingering close of day,
Making my sonnet by the alehouse fire,
Whilst Idleness and Solitude inspire
Dull rhymes to pass the duller hours away.
Robert Southey (1774-1843)

Today, of course, many hikers walk in the footsteps of the Romantic poets along the Coleridge Way (see box p34) which ends in the village; a walk that both celebrates the area's associations with the Romantic poets and the wonderful countryside of this part of the world. Yet, ironically, Porlock is perhaps best known not for a poem that it inspired, but one that it prevented: Samuel Coleridge was famously interrupted during the composition of his epic *Kubla Khan* by 'a person on business from Porlock', with the result that he forgot the details of the dream on which his poem was to be based and thus never completed the work! The phrase 'a person from Porlock' has since become a synonym for an unwanted visitor; characters named Porlock crop up in works by Arthur Conan Doyle and Alan Bennett amongst others – usually as somebody who arrives unannounced and interrupts the business of others.

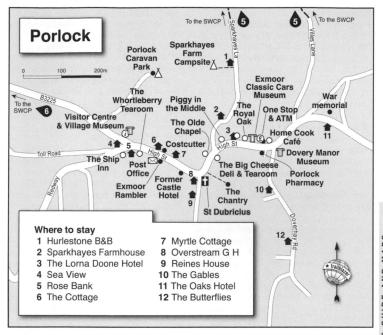

Porlock

0   100   200m

To the SWCP 5
To the SWCP 5
To the SWCP 6

Porlock Caravan Park
Sparkhayes Farm Campsite
The Whortleberry Tearoom
Piggy in the Middle
Exmoor Classic Cars Museum
War memorial
Visitor Centre & Village Museum
The Olde Chapel
The Royal Oak
One Stop & ATM
Home Cook Café
Costcutter
The Ship Inn
Post Office
Exmoor Rambler
Former Castle Hotel
The Big Cheese Deli & Tearoom
Porlock Pharmacy
Dovery Manor Museum
The Chantry
St Dubricius
B3225
Toll Road
Redway
High St
Villes Lane
Sparkhayes La
Dovehay Rd

Where to stay

1 Hurlestone B&B	7 Myrtle Cottage
2 Sparkhayes Farmhouse	8 Overstream G H
3 The Lorna Doone Hotel	9 Reines House
4 Sea View	10 The Gables
5 Rose Bank	11 The Oaks Hotel
6 The Cottage	12 The Butterflies

trailblazer

ROUTE GUIDE AND MAPS

10.30am-12.30pm & 2-4pm; free admission) is housed in a 15th-century manor house and has a physic garden based on designs from medieval times.

A few steps away, **Exmoor Classic Cars** (☎ 01643-841476; Easter to end Sep, Fri-Sun & Bank Hols 11am-4pm; £3) is a wonderful little collection of gleaming vintage cars and bikes, some of which are as old as the inhabitants of Porlock themselves. While at the other end of the village, the Visitor Centre (see below) boasts a small **village museum** including many of the items discovered on the beach that predate even Porlock (see box p84).

See p16 for details of the Porlock Arts Festival.

Services

The **Visitor Centre** (☎ 01643-863150, 🖳 www.porlock.co.uk; Easter to end Oct Mon-Fri 10am-12.30pm & 2-5pm, Sat 10am-5pm, Sun 10am-1pm; Nov to Easter Mon-Fri 10am-12.30pm, Sat 10am-1pm) lies at the far western end of Porlock and claims to be the friendliest in the entire South-West.

The village is big enough for two small **supermarkets**, Costcutter (Mon-Thur 7.30am-8pm, Fri & Sat 7.30am-9pm, Sun 7.30am-6pm) towards the western end of town and One Stop Local Stores (daily 7am-10pm), which has an **ATM** (free), at the eastern end.

Opposite the Costcutter is a shop, Exmoor Rambler, selling **walking gear**, and the **post office** (Mon-Fri 9am-5.30pm, Sat 9am-12.30pm). Nearby on the High St, **Porlock Hardware** (Mon-Sat 8.30am-5.30pm) also has some camping gear.

Porlock Pharmacy (Mon-Fri 8.30am-6pm, Sat 9am-1pm) is opposite the One Stop.

Where to stay

For **campers**, *Sparkhayes Farm Campsite* (☎ 01643-862470; open all year; £7pp; 🐕 50p) is on Sparkhayes Lane just on the edge of the village. There are plenty of pitches as well as laundry and hot shower facilities and a fridge freezer. *Porlock Caravan Park* (☎ 01643-862269, 🖥 www.porlockcaravanpark.co.uk; mid Mar to end Oct; 🐕 £1), at the High Bank end of the village, charges £6-8/13-15 for a hiker/two people and tent including use of toilet/shower facilities.

B&B-wise, few places here take bookings for only one night in summer, especially at weekends – but once again it's always worth asking as they won't turn custom away if they've got rooms free.

Two places that *don't* mind people staying for one night only – and which provide some of the cheapest accommodation in the village – are *Reines House* (☎ 01643-862913, 🖥 www.reineshouse.co.uk; 1S or D/1D/2D, T or F; 👄; WI-FI; £5; from £29pp), near the church; and, on Doverhay, unfussy, amiable *The Butterflies* (☎ 01643-862695, 🖥 www.butterfliesporlock.co.uk; 1D/1D or T; 👄; WI-FI; £27.50pp, £35 sgl occ).

In a village with so much thatch it's possible that you'll end up sleeping under a roof of straw, such as at *The Gables* (☎ 01643-863432, 🖥 www.thegablesporlock.co.uk; 1D or T/2D/1F; 👄; 🐕; WI-FI in public areas; no one-night bookings Easter to end Sep on Fri or Sat; £32.50pp, £45 sgl occ), a gorgeous 17th-century country home on Doverhay Rd, its ancient exterior belying the modern facilities on offer including DVDs and games rental.

A more humble straw-topped 17th-century dwelling, *Myrtle Cottage* (☎ 01643-862978, 🖥 www.myrtleporlock.co.uk; 2D/1T/1F; 👄; 🐕; WI-FI; £27.50pp, £30 sgl occ) advertises B&BB (bed and big breakfast) in addition to providing timber-beamed rooms in a central location. One-night stays are fine here.

Further ancient accommodation (though this time thatch-free) can be had at the fairly grand 17th-century *Sparkhayes Farmhouse* (☎ 01643-862765; 1D/1T or F; 👄; £30pp, sgl occ £35), on the lane of the

same name, and *The Cottage* (☎ 01643-862996, 🖥 www.cottageporlock.co.uk; 2D/2D or T; 👄; WI-FI in public areas; £27.50-35pp, £37.50 sgl occ), another gorgeous little place, this time on the High St. Moving forward a century or two, the large and impressive Victorian *Rose Bank Guest House* (☎ 01643-862728, 🖥 www.rosebankguesthouse.co.uk; 1S/1D/3D or T/1F; 🐕 £5; WI-FI; £25-35pp, sgl £35) has a great reputation. Nearby, opposite the Visitor Centre, *Sea View* (☎ 01643-863456, 🖥 www.seaviewporlock.co.uk; 1S/2D/1T; 👄; WI-FI; £25-27pp, sgl £50) lives up to its name.

Sea views are also available from the rooms at *Hurlestone B&B* (☎ 01643-862589, 🖥 www.hurlestonebandb.co.uk; 3D; WI-FI; 🐕 £5 (bring bedding); £30-40pp, sgl occ £50), by the entrance to Sparkhayes Farm Campsite.

Overstream Guest House (☎ 01643-862421, 🖥 www.overstreamhotel.co.uk; 1S or D/3D/2D or T/1F; 👄; WI-FI; £27-30pp, £35 sgl), a sunny, pleasant and friendly place built opposite the church. Overstream is licensed and their bar is open for guests.

Finally, there are some **hotels**: *The Lorna Doone* (☎ 01643-862404, 🖥 www.lornadoonehotel.co.uk; 9S or D/2D or T/2D or F; 👄; 🐕 £5; WI-FI; £25-42.50pp, sgl occ £40), slightly more salubrious and superior and with very flexible rooms; and *The Oaks Hotel* (☎ 01643-862265, 🖥 www.oakshotel.co.uk; 8D or T; WI-FI; from £75pp, sgl occ rates on request; Easter-Oct), which is slightly grander and on the edge of the village, with great views across to the sea from some rooms.

At the time of research The Castle Hotel was on the market. However, by the time you are here it may have been bought and be providing accommodation again.

Where to eat and drink

You certainly won't starve in Porlock, with plenty of tearooms, cafés and restaurants all along the main street.

During the day the pick of the traditional tearooms are *The Whortleberry Tearoom* (☎ 01643-862337, 🖥 www.whortleberry.co.uk; Easter to Oct Tue-Sat 9.30am-5pm, Oct to Easter Wed-Sat

9.30am-5pm), which is named after the local blueberry (see box p22); *The Olde Chapel* (☎ 01643-862241; Feb to early Dec daily 10am-8pm), a large establishment that was formerly a Methodist chapel, with tables outside on the street where you can tuck into homemade soups, freshly ground coffee and fresh crab sandwiches (£6.95); and *Home Cook Café* (☎ 07790-725357; Easter to Oct Mon-Fri 9.30am-5pm, Sat to 5.30pm, Sun 10.30am-5pm; Nov to Easter Mon-Sat 10am-4pm, Sun 11am-4pm but hours depend on demand) which lives up to its name by making their own soups, cakes and scones. Even if you don't fancy eating there, do take time to visit *The Big Cheese Deli and Tearoom* (☎ 01643-862773, 🖳 www.thebigcheeseporlock.co .uk; Mar-Dec daily 9am-5pm, Sun 10am-4pm; Jan & Feb Tue-Sat 9am-5pm, Sun 10am-4pm), the local champions of cheese (they usually have at least 50 on sale) as well as other locally produced comestibles including wines, jams and vinegars.

There's a surprisingly good choice of places to eat in the evening too. For cheap eats, there's a **pizza wagon** that pulls up outside the Visitor Centre on Thursday nights, with a **fish and chip van** that calls in at the same place on Wednesdays.

Piggy in the Middle (☎ 01643-862647; mid Feb to Dec Mon-Sat 7-10pm) is a restaurant which may also serve take-away pizzas or fish & chips (5-6.45pm) before the restaurant opens. Nearby, *Doone's Restaurant* (see Where to stay), in The Lorna Doone, is open throughout the day, serving breakfast (daily 8-10am) to both residents and non-residents, before converting to a coffee-shop during the day (cream tea £4.95), then transforming itself into a restaurant from 5.30pm with hearty dishes such as venison pie with sautéed potatoes & vegetables (£16.50).

The Royal Oak (food served daily noon-2.30pm & 6.30-9.15pm) is a pub with traditional pub grub including a great steak-and-ale pie. Its status as the most popular place in town is rivalled only by the ancient *Ship Inn*, a cosy, fascinating, slightly eccentric pub (check out the displays of battle helmets, gas masks, and even a 'German officer's uniform', as worn by an extra in the film *The Great Escape*) with local ales (and even local crisps) including the potent 6.6% Exmoor Beast (see box p23).

Transport
[See also pp49-51] **Bus**-wise, there's Quantock's No 39 service running from Minehead to Porlock Weir and back. Their open-top No 300 (seasonal) calls in on its way between Minehead and Lynmouth. Buses stop at the Visitor Centre.

For a **taxi** try Colin Strange at Porlock Taxis (☎ 01643-862739).

ROUTE GUIDE AND MAPS

Continuing on the SWCP, the path plots a flat course between the back of the beach and the farmland before turning sharp right to rejoin the shoreline to Porlock Weir.

PORLOCK WEIR   [Map p91]
Peaceful Porlock Weir feels like the type of place where you could quite easily sit back and forget that you're supposed to be walking, as you opt instead to while away your time listening to the sea and staring wearily out towards Wales. The boats rock lazily in the hamlet's small port and the waves lap somnolently onto the pebbles and shingle of the millennia-old harbour arm.

Porlock Weir Marine Aquarium (☎ 01643-863540, 🖳 porlockweiraquarium .moonfruit.com; opening times vary but generally Easter to Oct daily 10am-5pm; £3) displays some of the hundred or so fish which inhabit the Bristol Channel throughout the year. There's also the single-room **Boatshed Museum** (☎ 01643-862674; Easter to Oct daily 10am-5pm, winter opening times vary; free) with some interesting displays about the village's seafaring heritage.

Facility-wise, there's no tourist **information** but the harbour master is an amiable chap, often seen pottering around the

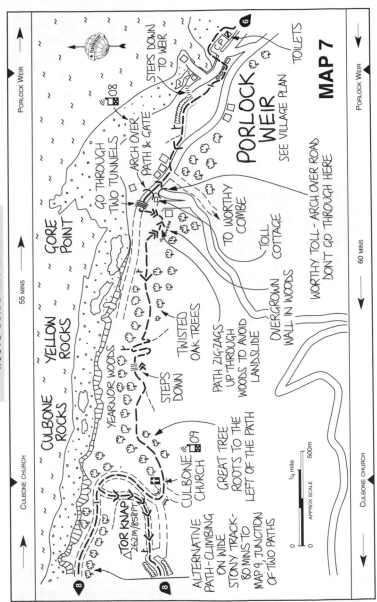

MAP 7

PORLOCK WEIR

SEE VILLAGE PLAN

TOILETS

PORLOCK WEIR

60 MINS

WORTHY TOLL - ARCH OVER ROAD DON'T GO THROUGH HERE

OVERGROWN WALL IN WOODS

TOLL COTTAGE

TO WORTHY COMBE

Overbridge

PATH ZIG-ZAGS UP THROUGH WOODS TO AVOID LANDSLIDE

STEPS DOWN

TWISTED OAK TREES

GREAT TREE ROOTS TO THE LEFT OF THE PATH

CULBONE CHURCH ⌂09

GO THROUGH TWO TUNNELS

STEPS DOWN TO WEIR

ARCH OVER PATH & GATE

⌂08

trailblazer

GORE POINT

YEARNOR WOODS

CULBONE ROCKS   YELLOW ROCKS

55 MINS

CULBONE CHURCH

△TOR KNAP 262M (858 FT)

ALTERNATIVE PATH-CLIMBING ON WIDE STONY TRACK- 80 MINS TO MAP 9, JUNCTION OF TWO PATHS

8

8

6

CP

0   500m
     ¼ mile
APPROX SCALE
0

CULBONE CHURCH

60 MINS

PORLOCK WEIR

harbour wall, who can point you in the right direction. Fittingly, for such a languid spot, some of the businesses open on an as-and-when-required basis. **Harbour Stores** (☎ 01643-862379) selling essentials (including takeaway tea) is one of these; it has no set hours but between Easter and October endeavours to open daily by 9.30am and, if busy, will close as late as 5pm. In the winter months the hours are very variable and depend partly on the weather.

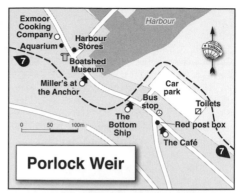

Porlock Weir

If it's a takeaway that you're after, tucked away at the end of Harbour Studios is *Exmoor Cooking Company* (☎ 01643-862117, 🖳 www .exmoorcookingcompany.co.uk; summer Wed-Sun 10.30am-8pm, winter Tue-Sat 5-8pm) which sells baguettes (£3.80-6) and noodles (£5.50) for lunch and has themed meals (noon-8pm) such as fish'n'chips (Wed & Fri) and oriental food (Tue, Thur & Sat).

There are three **B&Bs** in Porlock Weir, all with restaurants. *Miller's at The Anchor* (☎ 01643-862753, 🖳 www.millersatthean chor.co.uk; 14D or T; ➥; 🐾 £5; WI-FI; £42.50-67.50pp, £65-95 sgl occ) is as much a museum and gallery as it is a hotel. The interior is fabulous, with paintings, busts and antiquities crammed into every spare space. The walls are lined with books, including some written by the owner himself; everywhere you look there is something to catch the eye. There's also a billiards room, a small cinema (offering a £12 'Movie and Meal' deal on Sun & Wed eves) and even an honesty bar providing drinks on the basis of trust – definitely a novelty in this day and age! Lunch (daily noon-3pm,

from £4.95) and cream teas (available all day) are served, with an à la carte menu (Wed-Sun; £25-29) in the evenings; packed lunches can also be provided. One tip: this is not a place to come with a full rucksack on your back – just turn up with an empty belly and a thirst for the obscure!

The Bottom Ship (☎ 01643-863288, 🖳 www.shipinnporlockweir.co.uk; 2D/1T; ➥; 🐾; £30-32.50pp, sgl occ £35-40) is a simpler place with far fewer distractions. Amongst the food (Easter to Oct Mon-Fri noon-3pm & 6-8.30pm, Sat & Sun noon-8pm; Nov-Easter Mon-Thur & Sun noon-3pm, Fri & Sat noon-3pm & 6-8.30pm) on offer is an Exmoor steak and ale pie for £8.75 (small portion £7.15).

The Café (☎ 01643-863300, 🖳 www.thecafeatporlockweir.co.uk; 4D/1D or T; ➥; 🐾; £44-68.75pp; Wed-Sun) sits in a slightly elevated position with good views across the harbour and beyond and serves (Wed-Sun noon-8pm) such treats as a delicious fish soup for £5.95, or a cheese ploughman's for £8.50.

Quantock's No 39 **bus** passes through on its way to either Lynmouth or Minehead.

ROUTE GUIDE AND MAPS

PORLOCK WEIR TO LYNTON   [MAPS 7-12]

This **12¹/₂-mile (20.1km; 4¹/₂ hours, 4 hrs 55 mins on northerly path)** stage of the trail will come as something of an unpleasant surprise for those who were hoping for a gentle few days at the start of the walk to ease themselves into the trip. While not as tough as the final two stages on this walk – nor indeed even as tough as the next one – this hike to the conjoined villages of Lynmouth and Lynton is still fairly taxing and makes for a surprisingly long day. Furthermore, with no cafés or pubs on the way (save for The Blue Ball Inn at Countisbury, just a short distance from Lynmouth, and assuming the refreshment kiosk at Culbone is not going to be resurrected), you'll need to be self-sufficient or this long day is going to feel even longer!

Thankfully there are enough distractions on this stage to help you ignore the quiet screaming coming from your calf muscles including Culbone Church (see box opposite). There are also the rare whitebeams of Culbone Wood, dotted here and there with the remains of several humble leper huts; while a short deviation off the trail will take you to Foreland Point – Devon's most northerly extremity.

Furthermore, you can also take pride in the fact that during the day you march across the border into Devon (which isn't marked on the trail, though occurs at Coscombe Linhay, near the signposted turn-off to Glenthorne Nature Trail). As such, you will have already achieved the feat of completing Somerset's entire contribution to the SWCP – and you're still only on the second day!

The route

The trail out of Porlock Weir begins between the houses behind Millers at the Anchor, climbing up behind the village and onto the thatched and rather decorative **Worthy Toll** – has a toll gate ever been so ornate? Keeping **Toll Cottage** on your left, pass through the more northerly of the two arches then follow the path as it twists its way, under, over and through the overgrown terraces of **Ashley Combe**.

❑ Ashley Combe

Just past Worthy Toll the trail passes through a couple of tunnels which were once an integral part of the gorgeous gardens of Ashley Combe house. The home of Ada Byron (the only legitimate daughter of the poet, Lord Byron), later Countess Lovelace, the house was originally built in 1799 but improved significantly by Lord King, the first Lord Lovelace and Ada's husband who, influenced by the fairy-tale castles of Italy, decided in 1835 to lavish a huge sum in adapting Ashley Combe to please his wife. The tunnels from the road led to the house's tradesman's entrance and were built so that Ada and the other inhabitants didn't have their views of the ornate terraced gardens interrupted by the comings and goings of commoners. Towers, turrets, archways and other follies decorated the terraces, which were walled on three sides but opened out onto the sea, while spiral staircases led between the different levels. A team of Swiss engineers was even brought in to lay a network of carriageways throughout the grounds.

The house fell into disrepair soon after the Countess's death in 1852 and though it found a use as a home for orphans during WWII, it soon became uninhabitable and in 1974 it was pulled down for safety reasons. Plans are afoot to restore the gardens (visit 🖳 www.thephilosophersgarden.com for details) but for the moment, while its true glory has long since faded, it's still fascinating to pick out some of the original features of the gardens – the twisting paths, and the stone benches set into the garden walls – as you walk along the trail from Worthy Toll.

❏ **Culbone Church**
The small church at Culbone is one of the hidden gems of the South-West Coast Path. England's smallest complete parish church, it measures 35ft (10.66m) and seats a congregation of around 30, thus meriting a place in the *Guinness Book of Records*.

However, Culbone church is not just tiny – its origins are also extremely old. It is one of the few buildings that also features in the Domesday Book. At Culbone Stables a Bronze Age stone marker – one of many which were believed to have lined the way between Lynmouth and Porlock – was discovered in 1940. Celtic missionaries from Wales and Ireland travelled to the West Country along this path from about the late 6th century onwards, leading to a revival of the Christian faith in England. One of these missionaries was the patron saint of Culbone, **St Beuno**. Though his link with the church is unclear, it is believed that Culbone became a place of reverence in his day; and the wheeled cross on the Bronze Age standing stone marker acted as a signpost, pointing the faithful to Culbone as an important place of pilgrimage.

The Saxons are believed to have been the first to build a church here, made of wood, which in time was replaced by a stone edifice by the Normans. The oldest part of the church today is probably the sandstone window on the northern side of the chancel (the space around the altar), which is thought to be at least a thousand years old, though many other features are only slightly younger: the font, for example, is believed to be around 800 years old, as is the arch that separates the chancel from the nave (where the congregation sits). The tiny window on the north side of the nave is known as a leper squint – where lepers, who were banned from entering the church, could still watch the services.

One of the most noticeable features of the church is the number of gravestones dedicated to people with the surname 'Red'. Nicholas Red was churchwarden in 1856 (he is responsible for the Ten Commandments on one of the walls of the church) and it is his descendants who populate much of the graveyard. It is believed that the name provided the inspiration for the Ridds in the novel *Lorna Doone*. While you're in the graveyard, look at the church steeple: it was erected in around 1810, though locals swear that it is actually the missing top part of the truncated steeple of St Dubricius (see p86) in Porlock.

The church is still in use, though there is no tarmac leading to it; instead, worshippers have to either take the precarious 4WD track down to the church, or do as you have just done – and walk there!

A lazy meander along a gently undulating path past the **twisted oak trees** of Yearnor Woods soon brings you out onto a better track that winds its way down to **Culbone Church** (see box above) – an essential stop on the SWCP.

The path divides after Culbone Church (Map 7). The main (southern) trail from here heads up the hill, out of the trees, into farmland and from there onto a road – though we use the term loosely, for cars are something of a rarity around here and easily outnumbered by livestock to left and right.

It's difficult to lose your way – just keep heading west past Silcombe and Broomstreet farms, the track eventually dwindling to a footpath. Soon after, it takes a sharp right down **Wheatham Combe** and back into the woods on the lower northern slopes of **Sugarloaf Hill**, where it is reunited with the alternative (northern) route (see overleaf).

Alternative route between Culbone Church and Sugarloaf Hill

This alternative (northern) path is at times rugged and should be trodden carefully but the woodlands it passes through make for a wonderful alternative to the fields above. The areas that you walk through have interesting histories, too.

Splendidly isolated **Culbone Wood** has throughout the ages being home to many deemed too dangerous to remain in mainstream society – from the 'mentally insane' in the 13th century to lepers in the 16th. Meanwhile, **Embelle Wood** and its stony pathways are known to have been used by smugglers carrying their ill-gotten gains away from Embelle Wood Beach. Presumably chosen for its remoteness – despite the presence of a limekiln – the beach is thought to be the most remote in Somerset. Indeed, so remote is it that David Burgess, a self-styled 21st-century Robinson Crusoe, managed to move here and remain almost undetected since 1985! Burgess became the focus of the national press briefly in 2011 after the park authorities finally told him to leave. Following protests, Mr Burgess is now waiting to hear if he can stay.

A note of caution: be wary of landslides. Although generally well signed, landslips are a common occurrence on this section and the diversions made necessary because of them can be sudden, especially around **Broomstreet Combe**. Between there and the reunion with the official path the trail is also particularly steep.

The path continues parallel to the coast now under the woodland canopy, climbing the slopes occasionally to avoid the occasional landslip, then passing through deciduous woodland and coniferous plantations before, having crossed the **Somerset–Devon border**, the path deviates off the large track to visit the 19th-century **stone cross** that marks the Sister's Fountain. The name comes from one of the nieces of the original owner of nearby Glenthorne House who liked to play at this spot. In local legend, the well or spring was created by Joseph of Arimathea by striking his staff on the ground, thus providing much-needed refreshment on his journey to Glastonbury.

Passing through the wild boar gateposts (the entrance to 19th-century Woodland Lodge as well as to Glenthorne House), the route follows the driveway down the hill before taking a narrow trail off to the left, the path now brightly embroidered to left and right with vivid rhododendron and gorse. The way is more exposed now too, a pleasant change after so long in the shade of trees, though patches of woodland still punctuate the trail, particularly when passing the several combes on the way: Wingate, Pudleep Gurt, Swannel and Chubhill. Eventually, with limbs wearying and feet aching, tarmac is reached before Coddow Combe, at which point those with enough fortitude can follow the road down to Foreland Point (see below) and the lighthouse that marks the northernmost tip of Devon, while the rest take the path off left up the slope, the reward for one's efforts being a clear view of Lynmouth.

The path to Foreland Point

For those wishing to see Devon's most northerly point, a short walk down the road on your right will take you to the **lighthouse** at Foreland Point, built in 1900. From here, you can either return on the same path or, if you would like to stick as close to the coast as possible and not retrace your steps, there is also

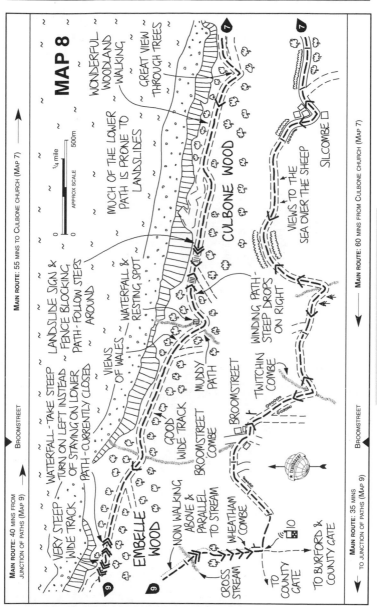

MAP 8

MAIN ROUTE: 55 MINS TO CULBONE CHURCH (MAP 7)

MAIN ROUTE: 40 MINS FROM JUNCTION OF PATHS (MAP 9)

BROOMSTREET

WONDERFUL WOODLAND WALKING

GREAT VIEW THROUGH TREES

MUCH OF THE LOWER PATH IS PRONE TO LANDSLIDES

LANDSLIDE SIGN & FENCE BLOCKING PATH - FOLLOW STEPS AROUND

WATERFALL & RESTING SPOT

VIEWS OF WALES

VERY STEEP WIDE TRACK

WATERFALL - TAKE STEEP TURN ON LEFT INSTEAD OF STAYING ON LOWER PATH - CURRENTLY CLOSED

GOOD WIDE TRACK

MUDDY PATH

CULBONE WOOD

WINDING PATH - STEEP DROPS ON RIGHT

VIEWS TO THE SEA OVER THE SHEEP

SILCOMBE

BROOMSTREET

BROOMSTREET COMBE

EMBELLE WOOD

NOW WALKING ABOVE & PARALLEL TO STREAM

WHEATHAM COMBE

TWITCHIN COMBE

CROSS STREAM

TO COUNTY GATE

TO BURFORD & COUNTY GATE

MAIN ROUTE: 35 MINS TO JUNCTION OF PATHS (MAP 9)

BROOMSTREET

MAIN ROUTE: 60 MINS FROM CULBONE CHURCH (MAP 7)

APPROX SCALE

0   ¼ mile

0   500m

ROUTE GUIDE AND MAPS

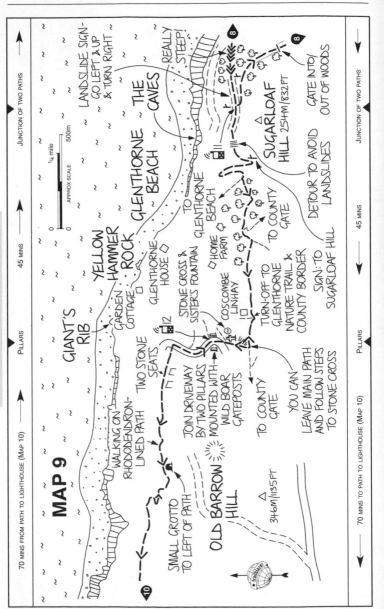

MAP 9

70 MINS FROM PATH TO LIGHTHOUSE (MAP 10) →

PILLARS

45 MINS

JUNCTION OF TWO PATHS

WALKING ON RHODODENDRON-LINED PATH

GIANT'S RIB

YELLOW HAMMER ROCK

GLENTHORNE BEACH

THE CAVES

REALLY STEEP!

LANDSLIDE SIGN-GO LEFT & UP & TURN RIGHT

TWO STONE SEATS

GARDEN COTTAGE

GLENTHORNE HOUSE

STONE CROSS & SISTER'S FOUNTAIN

TO GLENTHORNE BEACH

SUGARLOAF HILL 254M/832FT

GATE INTO/OUT OF WOODS

SMALL GROTTO TO LEFT OF PATH

JOIN DRIVEWAY BY TWO PILLARS MOUNTED WITH WILD BOAR GATEPOSTS

HOME FARM

COSCOMBE LINHAY

TURN-OFF TO GLENTHORNE NATURE TRAIL & COUNTY BORDER

TO COUNTY GATE

DETOUR TO AVOID LANDSLIDES

OLD BARROW HILL 346M/1135FT

TO COUNTY GATE

YOU CAN LEAVE MAIN PATH AND FOLLOW STEPS TO STONE CROSS

SIGN:-TO SUGARLOAF HILL

APPROX SCALE
¼ mile
500m

8
8
10

70 MINS TO PATH TO LIGHTHOUSE (MAP 10) →

PILLARS

45 MINS

JUNCTION OF TWO PATHS

Trailblazer

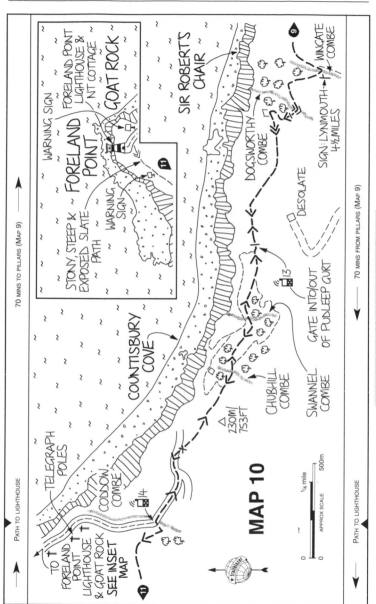

GOAT ROCK

Foreland Point
Lighthouse &
NT Cottage

WARNING SIGN

FORELAND POINT

STONY, STEEP &
EXPOSED SLATE
PATH

WARNING SIGN

SIR ROBERT'S CHAIR

DOGSWORTHY COMBE

DESOLATE

SIGN: LYNMOUTH
4½ MILES

WINCATE
COMBE

GATE INTO/OUT
OF PUDLEEP GURT

COUNTISBURY COVE

CHUBHILL COMBE

SWANNEL COMBE

△ 230M
753FT

TELEGRAPH
POLES

CODDON COMBE

TO ↑
FORELAND POINT
LIGHTHOUSE &
GOAT ROCK
SEE INSET MAP

MAP 10

¼ mile

APPROX SCALE

500m

0

0

70 MINS TO PILLARS (MAP 9)

70 MINS FROM PILLARS (MAP 9)

PATH TO LIGHTHOUSE

PATH TO LIGHTHOUSE

ROUTE GUIDE AND MAPS

a path that continues around The Foreland and rejoins the official coastal path. Note that much of it is exposed and it does involve walking on scree. It is a beautiful if challenging walk (especially if you are carrying a pack) but there is a need for caution.

The fairly uninteresting church of St John the Baptist at **Countisbury** marks the start of the drop down to the harbour, though at this late stage you would be forgiven for calling in first at *The Blue Ball Inn* (Map 11; ☎ 01598-741263, 🖥 www.exmoorsandpiper.com; 11D/3F; ☛; 🐾; £39-42pp, sgl occ £58), formerly the Exmoor Sandpiper, though it has now reverted to the original name it was given in the late 18th century. Each room boasts a bath (though, curiously, not all have a shower!) and they can provide internet access for anyone with a laptop. The food (daily noon-9pm) is quite 'bistro-esque', including a delicious barbecued Exmoor pork belly rib served with chips, and salad (£9.95). Quantock's No 300 seasonal **bus** service stops outside the pub; see pp49-51.

Returning to the trail, the stagger down to Lynmouth seems long and it's a rare person who isn't exhausted by the time they've walked through a patch of woodland to emerge at the back of Lynmouth Manor House. If you, too, feel exhausted, spare a thought for the brave lifeboatmen (see below) of Lynmouth who in 1899 *carried* their craft overland all the way to Porlock Weir to rescue a nearby ship in distress – a journey that took some 10 hours in total!

LYNMOUTH [Map p103]

'*My walk to Ilfracombe led me through Lynmouth, the finest spot, except Cintra and the Arrabida, which I have ever seen.*'
Robert Southey
Lynmouth and its neighbour up the hill, Lynton, combine to form the biggest settlement in the whole of Exmoor National Park. Nicknamed 'Little Switzerland' by the Victorians (who popularised these twin towns as a tourist resort in the 19th century) due to the beauty, tranquillity and steep gradients of its surrounding countryside, the two villages act as a hub for a plethora of paths, with the Two Moors Way, Samaritans Way and Tarka Trail (see box p34) all joining the Coast Path in passing through or terminating here. As such, facilities in these two settlements are fairly comprehensive, with plenty of accommodation and restaurants; and while the majority of these facilities are up the slope in Lynton, there's plenty of businesses catering for the exhausted walker in Lynmouth too.

Two events dominate Lynmouth's history. The first is the famous **Overland Launch** of 1899, when Lynmouth's heroic

lifeboat crew, wishing to rescue a boat in the Bristol Channel but unable to set sail from Lynmouth due to a force-eight gale, opted instead to drag their lifeboat *The Louisa* over Countisbury Hill and down to Porlock Weir; a film (🖥 www.flat-broke films.co.uk/html/louisa.html) may be made based on this.

The second event occurred on Friday 15 August 1952 when, following almost a fortnight of torrential downpours, a cloudburst unleashed 9" of rain on Exmoor that sent a wall of water cascading towards the unsuspecting village, dispersing boulders from the surrounding countryside onto the streets. Thirty-four people lost their lives that day and sixty buildings were destroyed entirely. **Lynmouth Flood Memorial Hall**, down near the harbour, exists as a lasting reminder of the tragedy.

The **Rhenish Tower**, located at the end of the pier and one of only two buildings to have been reconstructed since the flood, was built in 1832 by wealthy local landowner, General Rawdon. The General returned from his grand tour of Europe in

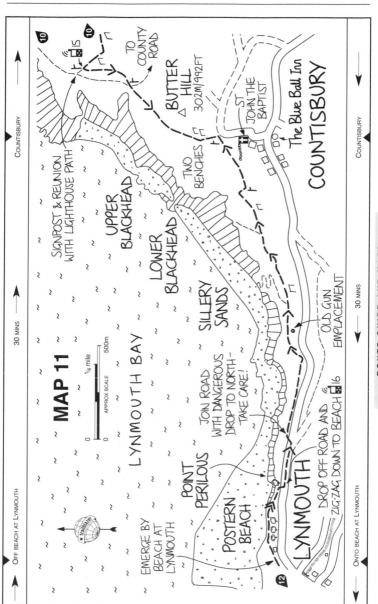

MAP 11

LYNMOUTH BAY

SIGNPOST & REUNION WITH LIGHTHOUSE PATH

UPPER BLACKHEAD

LOWER BLACKHEAD

SILLERY SANDS

JOIN ROAD WITH DANGEROUS DROP TO NORTH– TAKE CARE!

POINT PERILOUS

POSTERN BEACH

EMERGE BY BEACH AT LYNMOUTH

DROP OFF ROAD AND ZIG-ZAG DOWN TO BEACH

LYNMOUTH

OLD GUN EMPLACEMENT

TWO BENCHES

ST JOHN THE BAPTIST

BUTTER HILL 302M/992FT

TO COUNTY ROAD

The Blue Ball Inn

COUNTISBURY

OFF BEACH AT LYNMOUTH — 30 MINS — COUNTISBURY

COUNTISBURY — 30 MINS — ONTO BEACH AT LYNMOUTH

1/4 mile

500m

0

APPROX SCALE

trailblazer

the early 19th century and had the tower built as an imitation of those that he had admired on the Rhine. Once used for pilchard spotting by the local fisherman, the tower has recovered since the flood – much like Lynmouth itself – and has become a sort of symbol of the town.

See p16 for details of festivals and events in Lynmouth and Lynton.

Services

Exmoor National Park Visitor Centre (☎ 01598-752509; late Mar to end Oct daily 10am-5pm; Feb half-term daily 10.30am-3pm, Feb to late Mar Sat & Sun 10.30am-3pm), in the car park next to the road bridge, is full of useful information and literature on the park, though for information on Lynmouth/Lynton you'll need to visit the tourist office in Lynton (see p102), or ask at Lyndale Tearooms (see Where to eat).

Hardings of Exmoor (☎ 01598-753999; mid Feb to Dec daily 9.30am-5pm), at 9 Lynmouth St, has **walking, and some camping, gear**. There is **internet access** at Deeply Dippy (daily 10.30am-4pm; £1.50/first 30 mins, £1 for every half-hour thereafter), on Lynmouth St overlooking the river.

There are two **ATMs**, one in The Fish On The Harbour (see p102) and one in **Lynmouth Stores** (Feb-Dec; daily summer 8.30am-7pm, winter 10am-3.30pm) on Lynmouth St, but both charge a fee of £1.75 and are accessible only during their opening hours. The latter also sells stamps – there being no post office in Lynmouth. For the nearest post office, as well as free cash machines and the better supermarkets, you need to head up the hill to Lynton.

Where to stay

The nearest **camping** option to Lynton is *Sunny Lyn Holiday Park* (☎ 01598-753384, 🖳 www.caravandevon.co.uk; hiker & tent £6, additional person £6; 🐾 £2.50; pay as you go WI-FI) which has a shop (Easter-Oct daily 9am-5pm) and a café (Easter-Oct 8.30-10.15am) that serves breakfasts; shower and laundry facilities are available. The site can be accessed from

either village. From Lynmouth walk down the B3234 (Lynbridge Rd) and it will be on your left by the river.

Lynmouth's **B&Bs** are primarily found beyond the road bridge towards the back of town (ie furthest from the sea). Along Watersmeet Rd you will find several places with many boasting lovely views over both the village and the sea. The most famous is *Shelley's* (☎ 01598-753219, 🖳 www.shelleyshotel.co.uk; 10D/1T; ☞; WI-FI; £37.50-55pp, note: full room rate for single occupancy), a sophisticated place where the Romantic poet chose to honeymoon in the summer of 1812. Although there is a two-night minimum stay policy, they will accept one-night bookings if their diary allows. Others on Watersmeet include: *Bonnicott House* (☎ 01598-753346, 🖳 www.bonnicott.com; 7D/1T; ☞; WI-FI; £30-55pp), a grade-II listed former rectory dating back to 1809 that does evening meals and packed lunches if requested; *Orchard House* (☎ 01598-753247, 🖳 www.lynmouthhotel.co.uk; 2D/1T/2F; ☞; £25-35pp, sgl occ £30-35pp); lovely *Hillside House* (☎ 01598-753836, 🖳 www.hillside-lynmouth.co.uk; 1S/4D/1T; ☞; WI-FI; 🐾; £27-35pp, sgl £35), an 18th-century house though with parts that may date back to the 1400s; *River Lyn View* (☎ 01598-753501, 🖳 www.riverlynview.com; 3D/1T; ☞; WI-FI; 🐾; £27-35pp, sgl occ £35-40); and *East Lyn House Hotel* (☎ 01598-752540, 🖳 www.eastlynhouse.co.uk; 7D/1T; ☞; WI-FI; £30-45pp, sgl occ £40-45) a fairly lavishly decorated and well-maintained hotel which also does early evening meals and offers a pick-up and drop-off service to walkers (though you'll be charged to cover costs).

On the other side of the East Lyn River there are a few more options, of which *Ye Olde Sea Captain's House* (☎ 01598-753369, 🖳 www.thecaptainshouseinlynmouth.co.uk; 1S/6D or T/2F; ☞; WI-FI; 🐾; £28-45pp, sgl £30-35) is the most interesting, having been built for Captain Jack Crocombe, who led the men who dragged the *The Louisa* (see p98) to Porlock Weir. There are drying facilities and packed lunches (£7.50) can be supplied. If booked in advance and subject to a 25-mile limit and payment of a small fee they are happy to provide a luggage-transfer-service. Other options on this side of the Lyn include *Glenville House* (☎ 01598-752202, 💻 www.glenvillelynmouth.co.uk; 3D/1T; ✎; £30pp, sgl occ £35), at 2 Tors Rd, another Victorian edifice; and, next door, *Lorna Doone House* (☎ 01598-753354, 💻 www .lornadoonehouse.co.uk; 4D/2D or T; ✎; 🐾 £3; WI-FI; dinner, bed & breakfast £54-60pp, sgl occ £64-70), the landlords of which have been working in the hospitality industry for over a quarter of a century.

Back in the heart of Lynmouth – and thus nearer the trail – *The Village Inn* (☎ 01598-752354, 💻 www.villageinnlyn mouth.co.uk; 5D/1T; ✎; WI-FI; 🐾; £30-35pp, £45 sgl occ), on the pedestrianised shopping street, provides B&B above a 'traditional', Free House. The inn has been winner of the Lynton and Lynmouth in Bloom competition several times and, in this author's opinion, is a competitor for the friendliest place. *Riverside Cottage* (☎ 01598-752390, 💻 www.riversidecottage.co .uk; 6D/1T; ✎; WI-FI; well-behaved 🐾 £4; £30-40pp, sgl occ £40-50), is virtually opposite and has two floors of balcony-fronted rooms overlooking the harbour and river.

There are quite a few **hotels** in Lynmouth. On the harbour itself, *Rock House Hotel* (☎ 01598-753508, 💻 www .rock-house.co.uk; 1S/5D/2T; WI-FI; 🐾 £5; £47.50-59.50pp, sgl £45) does not take one-night bookings Fri & Sat nights (Mar-Sep). On the opposite side of the harbour and dating back to the 14th century, *The Rising Sun* (☎ 01598-753223, 💻 www.ris ingsunlynmouth.co.uk; 12D/1T; ✎; cottage with double bed; WI-FI; 🐾 ; £60-85pp, sgl occ £90-110) is an olde-worlde place with modern facilities. R D Blackmore is said to have written some of *Lorna Doone* within its walls. Further back from the sea is *The Bath Hotel* (☎ 01598-752238, 💻 www .bathhotellynmouth.co.uk; 10D/8T/3F; ✎; 🐾 ; £37.50-50pp, sgl occ £45-55; mid Jan to mid Nov), an unpretentious place in a great location; the name comes from the fact that it is built on the site of an old inn that used to have its bathwater delivered by

horse and cart from a well beneath Rhenish Tower (see pp98-9).

Finally, *Tors Hotel* (☎ 01598-753236, 💻 www.torshotellynmouth.co.uk; 27D/7T; ✎; 🐾 £5.50; WI-FI; £55-125pp, sgl occ £75-200) is the huge white pile overlooking Lynmouth from high up on the eastern hill, with its own heated outdoor swimming pool; it's a lovely place but the climb up to it can be soul-destroying after such a long day's walk. However, it can be accessed from the path.

Where to eat and drink

There's a fair selection of places to eat in Lynmouth to cater for all budgets. Back near the B&Bs on Watersmeet Rd are some fine tearooms: *Lyndale Tearooms* (☎ 01598-753553; daily 8am-6pm, winter daily usually 9am-5pm but variable) provides decent breakfasts and lunches at very reasonable prices and a cream tea is £4.95. The staff also have good local knowledge, are happy to act as a kind of tourist information centre and can also tell you about the bus services that run by; while across the water *Ye Olde Sea Captain's House* (see Where to stay; daily 10am-6pm) combines cream teas (available all day; £5) and lunches with wonderful views over the river.

For evening grub, *The Rising Sun* (see Where to stay; daily noon-2.30pm & 6-9pm) is one of the more sophisticated pubs on the trail serving, according to them, 'a blend of quality local produce with a European twist'. The menu changes daily and may include Bigsbury Bay oysters (£1.85 each) and a selection of roast shellfish (an eye-watering £28.50). Less complicated fare is available at *The Village Inn* (see Where to stay; food served Easter to Oct daily noon-9pm, Nov to Easter daily noon-2pm & 6-8.30pm) which does some great, honest food (including lamb shank for £9.95) in a warm atmosphere. In the same vein, *The Bath Hotel* (see Where to stay; daily 10.30am-8.30pm, hours differ in winter) have a similarly 'unfancy' menu with a daytime menu that includes jacket potatoes (from £4) and ham, egg & chips (£6.95), and an evening menu with items such as homemade Tribute beer-battered fish and chips for £8.95.

The Fish on the Harbour (☎ 01598-753600; Feb-Oct Tue-Sun noon-8pm) is unlike any other fish eatery on the trail, a nautically themed restaurant with one of the most imaginative menus anywhere; try their crab burger (from £7.95), or Caribbean cod (fish topped with prawns, in an apricot, mango and coconut sauce, all with cheese on top and served with chips and salad) for £10.95. Not to everybody's taste, maybe, but you've got to admire their creativity!

More piscine platters are available at *Le Bistro* (☎ 01598-753302, 🖳 www.lebistrolynmouth.co.uk; Tue-Sat 6.30-10pm; they may also open noon-3pm in the school summer holidays) opposite Shelley's Hotel. The menu changes regularly but always includes a bounty of fresh local fish amongst other meals, such as a mixed nut roast with mushrooms for £11.95, and dishes suitable for a wheat-, gluten- or dairy-free diet. For less formal fish, *Esplanade Fish Bar* (☎ 01598-753798; May-Oct daily noon-7.30pm, to 8.30 or 9pm in summer; mid Feb to May daily noon-3pm; closed Oct-Feb) is one of the best chippies on the trail.

Transport

[See also pp49-51] To return to Porlock or Minehead on **bus** take Quantock's No 300 (Apr-Oct only); while Filers No 309/310 travels to Barnstaple. Buses stop by the car park near the road bridge at the back of the village.

For a **taxi** try Lyn Valley Taxi (☎ 07907-161666).

While the sight of Lynmouth and its pubs is undoubtedly welcome, for many walkers there's one more effort required before the day is out: the zig-zag trail shadowing the direct path of the **Cliff Railway** (☎ 01598-753486, 🖳 www.cliffrailwaylynton.co.uk; mid Feb to early Nov, daily from 10am to between 4pm and 9pm depending on the season, check website for details; £2.25/3 single/return) to **Lynton**. Take it if you're early enough; after all, nobody can begrudge you this after the effort you've put in today. This railway dates back to the late 19th century; prior to its construction holidaymakers were transported between

© BT

Lynmouth and Lynton by pony. The two carriages are connected by a cable that runs around pullies at each end. When water from the West Lyn River fills the 700-gallon tanks of the upper car – at the same time that water empties out of the tanks of the lower carriage – the heavier carriage starts to descend along the 862ft railway, pulling the bottom carriage up as it does so. Simple, but effective!

LYNTON

Though not as attractive, perhaps, Lynton certainly has more amenities than Lynmouth. The **tourist information centre** (☎ 0845-660 3232 or ☎ 01598-752225, 🖳 www.lynton-lynmouth-tourism.co.uk; Easter to end Oct Mon-Sat 9.30am-5pm, Sun 10am-4pm, Nov to Easter Mon-Sat 10am-4pm, Sun 10am-2pm) is in the Town Hall on Lee Rd and has **internet access** (£1/15 mins), as has the **library** (☎ 01598-752505; Tue 10am-noon & 2-4.30pm, Fri 10am-noon, 2-4pm & 5-7pm, Sat 10am-noon) on Market St. The Crown Inn has wi-fi.

The **post office** (Mon-Fri 9am-5.30pm, Sat 9am-12.30pm) is on Lee Rd, while nearby lies Lynton **pharmacy** (Mon, Tue, Thur & Fri 8.30am-6.30pm, Wed 8.30am-1pm & 4.30-6.30pm, Sat 8.30-11am) and, next door, a Costcutter **supermarket** (daily 7am-9pm). There's a Lloyds **bank** (Mon, Wed & Fri 9.30am-3pm) with free **ATM** just down the road.

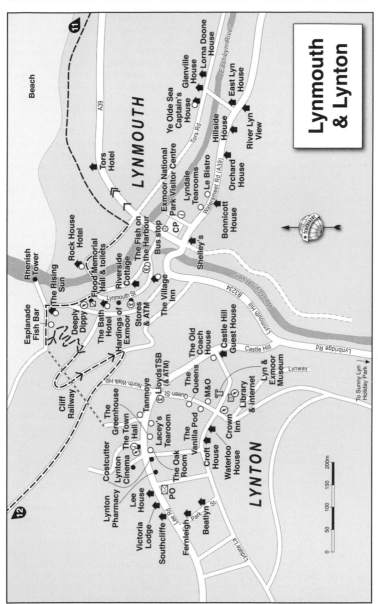

Lynmouth & Lynton

For entertainment, there's a **cinema** (☎ 01598-753397, 🖳 www.lyntoncinema.co .uk) with shows every Friday (£5).

Lyn and Exmoor Museum (🖳 www .visitlynton.co.uk; Easter to Oct Mon-Fri 10am-4pm, Sun 2-4pm; admission £1) has a fairly small collection of farm tools; of more interest, perhaps, is the building in which it is housed, the oldest dwelling in Lynton and perhaps the only museum in Devon which is said to be haunted!

Where to stay

For **camping**, see Lynmouth, p100. To reach the campsite from Lynton, having arrived at the top of North Walk Hill, cross the road to descend Queen St then turn left onto Lynway and follow to the bottom of the hill.

You won't have a problem finding **B&B** accommodation in Lynton, though trying to find one that will take you for just one night is another matter. Luckily, two of the B&Bs that do accept one-night bookings are also two of the more pleasant. Friendly, Georgian *Waterloo House Hotel* (☎ 01598-752575, 🖳 www.waterloohouse hotel.com; 1S/3D/1T; ☛; £42-69.50pp, sgl £35-55), on Lydiate Lane, is the oldest accommodation in Lynton. An evening meal is available (one sitting at 8pm) and the menu includes local ingredients such as Devon Ruby Red beef. Next door, *Croft House* (☎ 01598-752391, 🖳 www.lynton bandb.co.uk; 3D/1D or T/1T/1F; ☛; £38pp; sgl occ £60-76) is another Georgian property, originally built in 1828 for a local sea captain but now welcoming walkers to their individually styled rooms. The house also boasts a lovely little walled garden that's a bit of a sun trap.

On Park St are some more walker-friendly options: *Fernleigh Guest House* (☎ 01598-753575, 🖳 www.fernleigh.net; 2D/1T/2T or F; ☛; 🐾; WI-FI; £30-40pp, sgl occ £41) and, at No 13, *Beatlyn* (☎ 01598-753676; 2D; 🐾; WI-FI; £27.50-35pp).

The main area for accommodation is Lee Rd, where an unbroken line of B&Bs border one side of the road leading up from the tourist office. Few, if any, take one-night bookings in advance.

Southcliffe (☎ 01598-753328, 🖳 www .southcliffe.co.uk; 5D/1T; ☛; WI-FI; £32-39pp, sgl occ £42-49) is typical, a grand Victorian property where every room has a TV and two rooms have a balcony. Elegant *Victoria Lodge* (☎ 01598-753203, 🖳 www .victorialodge.co.uk; 1T or D/7D; ☛; WI-FI; £35-70pp, sgl occ £60-119; minimum of two nights on Fri & Sat) has richly decorated, sumptuous, well-equipped rooms. In a similar style, *Lee House* (☎ 01598-752364, 🖳 www.leehouse-lynton.co.uk; 6D/2T; ☛; WI-FI; £37.50-39pp, minimum booking two nights but flexible so enquire, also for single occupancy rate), at No 27, has been voted one of the best B&Bs in the country by a national newspaper, with lovely individually furnished rooms including one called The Walkers' Rest.

Finally, *Castle Hill Guest House* (☎ 01598-752291, 🖳 www.castlehill.biz; 4D/2D, T or F; ☛; £32.50-47.50pp, sgl occ £45-65; WI-FI in the lounge; mid Feb to Dec) is a large property on Castle Hill, just at the end of the strip of shops before the road starts to descend. A smart-looking place, the owners are very warm and welcoming towards walkers. Their website doesn't allow you to book one-night stays at weekends until a month before you plan to come, though the owners recommend you ring to discuss your requirements and to see if they have any availability.

Where to eat and drink

The choice of food is quite good. Among the different cuisines served in town there's Indian food at *Tanmoye* (☎ 01598-752763; daily 6-10pm), where tandoor chicken is £7.35; and Mediterranean at *The Oak Room* (☎ 01598-753838; café summer daily 10am-5pm, Wed-Mon 6-9pm, winter daily 10am-3pm Thur-Mon 6-9pm) – which is highly recommended and serves dishes such as Spanish-style meatballs (£10.50) and in the evening dinners & tapas.

Some of the many places serving more local fare are *M&O Fish 'n' Chips Takeaway* (☎ 01598-752392; daily summer noon-11.30pm, winter 4-11pm) for fast food; and *Lacey's* (☎ 01598-753520; mid Feb-Oct daily 10am-6pm Nov to mid Feb

11am-4.30pm) for traditional afternoon tea with over 80 teas on offer and cream teas for just £3.95; with *The Old Coach House* (☎ 01598-753360; mid Feb to Oct Mon-Sat 10am-5pm, Sun 9am-6pm) providing worthy competition (cream teas £4.25), with fewer teas but all homemade food (baguettes, jacket potatoes etc), including some products sourced from a friend's garden. In the main season they are expecting to stay open till 8.30pm.

The best place for pub food is *The Queens* (food served noon-3pm & 6-10pm; 🐾), an old pub but one with a modern, 'bistro' feel and some huge portions of grub including 10oz gammon steak (£8.50).

Several places are cafés by day but become restaurants in the evening.

Amongst them *The Greenhouse* (☎ 01598-753358; Easter to Oct daily 10am-9.30pm though they sometimes close in the afternoon, Nov to Easter Mon-Thur, Sat & Sun 11.30am-3pm & 6-10pm), with a largely Italian menu, and, better, *The Vanilla Pod* (☎ 01598-753706; Easter to end Oct café daily 10am-9pm, restaurant 6-9pm; both stay open later if there is demand; in winter evenings only if booked), at 12 Queen St, a lovely place with great food including a delicious duck casserole (£13.95).

Transport
[See also pp49-51] Buses to and from Lynmouth also call in at Lynton.

LYNTON TO COMBE MARTIN   [MAPS 12-17]

This 13¹/₂-mile (21.7km; 6hrs) stage is the longest of the three spent within Exmoor and as your last day in the park it certainly does not disappoint. Including both the weird and mysterious landscape of the Valley of Rocks and the SWCP's highest point, Great Hangman, it is a day of both varied terrain and spectacular scenery: superlatives include Great Hangman itself – which, on its northern side, also happens to be mainland Britain's highest sea cliff, with a vertical face of around 250m (around 800ft) – and one of Britain's biggest waterfalls, Hollow Brook, as well as one of its steepest valleys, Heddon. Then, finally, having conquered all that the path can throw at you, the day ends with a slow descent to the village that, purportedly, has the longest high street in England: Combe Martin. But even without these record breakers this stage would still make for a fascinating day's walking, with ancient abbeys, wild woodland and grazing goats to occupy your attention.

Being the longest stage in Exmoor, and one of the more remote sections of the SWCP, you won't be surprised to find that we recommend you plan your day carefully. There are, after all, only two places where you can get food – one on the path (the tearooms at Lee Abbey), and one a short walk off it (The Hunter's Inn at Heddon) – so you may want to bring your own refreshments; Heddon Valley is a fine and timely place to stop and see if you can spot any of the local wildlife while scoffing your sandwiches, or watching the waves from the shelter of the reconstructed limekiln.

> ❏ **Important note – walking times**
> Unless otherwise specified, **all times in this book refer only to the time spent walking**. You will need to add 20-30% to allow for rests, photography, checking the map, drinking water etc. When planning the day's hike count on 5-7 hours' actual walking.

ROUTE GUIDE AND MAPS

The route

The day begins simply enough by following **North Walk** across the cliff railway and out of town along a path skirting **Hollerday Hill**. There are tremendous views out to sea and along the shoreline. Indeed, so distracting can this prove that it usually comes of something of a surprise when you round a corner and are confronted by the **Valley of Rocks** (see box below) with the appropriately named **Castle Rock** ahead of you, its silhouette like a hilltop fortress overlooking the sea.

There now follows a short but pleasant-enough road walk with **Lee Abbey** on your right. Built in 1850, and an evacuated boys' school during the Second World War, the abbey is now a Christian conference centre. There are some tearooms a little further down the road from the abbey itself. *Lee Abbey Tea Cottage* (summer Tue-Sat 10.30am-5pm) serves a lot of homemade and

---

❏ The Valley of Rocks

'*...covered with huge stones ... the very bones and skeletons of the earth; rock reeling upon rock, stone piled upon stone, a huge terrific mass.*'   **Robert Southey**

The Valley of Rocks is a group of peculiarly weathered rock formations, most with equally unusual names, that was formed by the last Ice Age. Unlike other combes in Exmoor and North Devon, the Valley of Rocks runs parallel with the sea instead of towards it. As a result, this valley is unlike any other in the South-West and, possibly as a result, many myths and legends have grown up around the area.

The names given to many of the rock formations hint at some of these myths. The formations known as **Devil's Cheesewring** and **Ragged Jack**, for example, could refer to a local legend that suggests that the Devil (also known as 'Jack' in local mythology) built a castle here for some of his wives. On returning to the castle one day, the Devil was enraged to discover that they had been indulging in a drunken orgy with a neighbour, an act of betrayal that compelled the Devil, in a fit of temper, to destroy the castle and turn the women into rock – which is the scene that confronts us today.

Since the Devil's residency there have been several other inhabitants in the valley. Evidence of both Iron and Bronze Age settlements have been discovered and amongst the bracken there are the faint remains of stone circles, possibly once used by Druids. Probably the best-known tenant, however, is a fictional one: Mother Melldrum, the soothsayer in RD Blackmore's *Lorna Doone*, who 'kept her winter' here.

Today, the most famous residents are the huge birds of prey that soar and swoop above the valley, along with the Exmoor ponies that graze in the area and the feral goats who clip-clop amongst the rocky outcrops. The current curly-horned inhabitants have occupied the valley since the 1970s, though there are thought to have been goats living here as far back as Neolithic times, making them almost as much a part of the valley as the rocks themselves.

The path through the valley passes between Castle Rock and Ragged Jack. Having joined the road to Lee Abbey, Devil's Cheesewring will be on your left. If, when you're tackling this section, you suddenly become surrounded by crowds of exhausted runners, you will have unwittingly become a part of The Doone Run, an annual long-distance race that takes place each September in the valley.

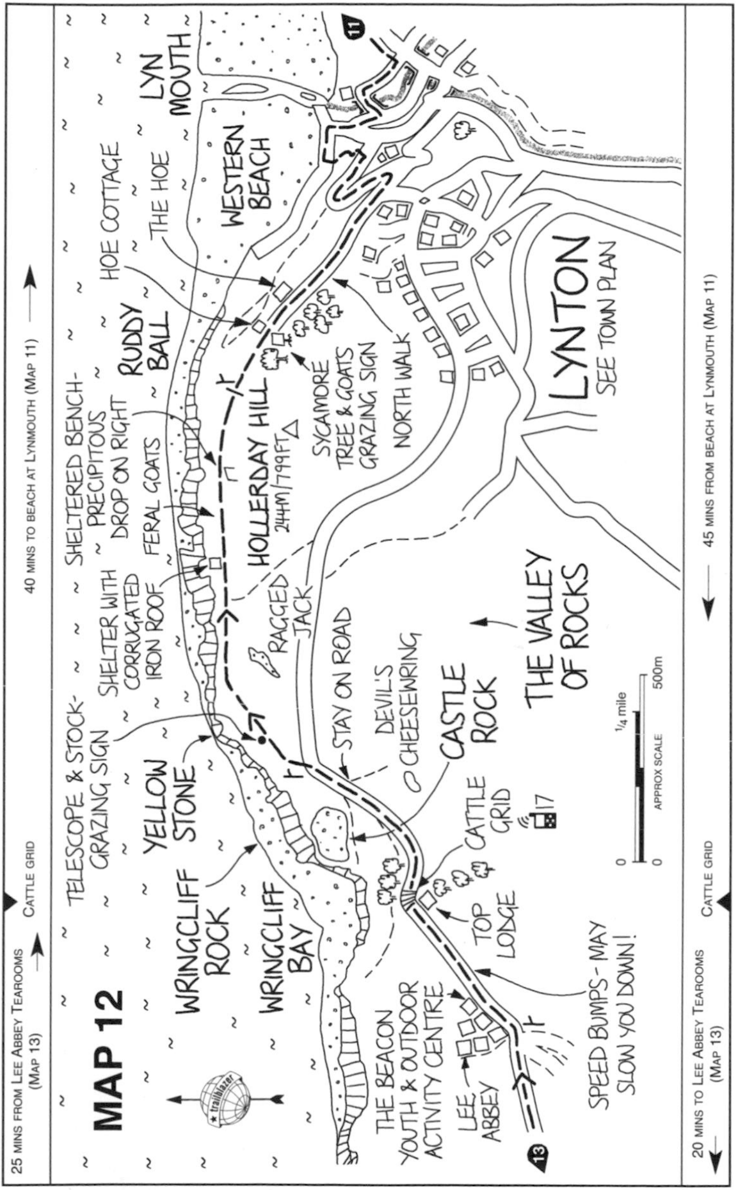

MAP 12

LYN MOUTH

WESTERN BEACH

THE HOE

HOE COTTAGE

RUDDY BALL

SHELTERED BENCH-PRECIPITOUS DROP ON RIGHT

~ FERAL GOATS

SHELTER WITH CORRUGATED IRON ROOF

TELESCOPE & STOCK-GRAZING SIGN

WRINGCLIFF ROCK

WRINGCLIFF BAY

YELLOW STONE

HOLLERDAY HILL 244M/799FT

RAGGED JACK

STAY ON ROAD

DEVIL'S CHEESEWRING

SYCAMORE TREE & GOATS GRAZING SIGN

NORTH WALK

LYNTON SEE TOWN PLAN

CASTLE ROCK

THE VALLEY OF ROCKS

CATTLE GRID

17

TOP LODGE

THE BEACON YOUTH & OUTDOOR ACTIVITY CENTRE

LEE ABBEY

13

SPEED BUMPS - MAY SLOW YOU DOWN!

¼ mile
500m
APPROX SCALE

25 MINS FROM LEE ABBEY TEAROOMS (MAP 13)
CATTLE GRID
40 MINS TO BEACH AT LYNMOUTH (MAP 11)

20 MINS TO LEE ABBEY TEAROOMS (MAP 13)
CATTLE GRID
45 MINS FROM BEACH AT LYNMOUTH (MAP 11)

Fairtrade produce including some delicious cakes and, of course, cream teas (£3.75 for one scone, £4.50 for two).

Shortly after the tearooms you have the option of continuing up the steep and wooded road route, or you can choose the more off-piste **Woody Bay Alternative Route** (see below) around Crock Point.

The Woody Bay alternative route

This route is a delight for those who believe that the Coast Path should stick as close to the shoreline as possible; others, however, will wonder exactly what the point of this short diversion is. There's nothing wrong with it, of course, though on first viewing it doesn't seem to add much to the overall experience, being a simple ramble along field edges bookended by a stroll through woodland. Nor do you even get a good view of the bay after which it is named due to the thick vegetation you pass through (a clear case of not being able to see the Woody for the trees).

Less than 30 minutes after setting off, you are reunited with the main trail.

The two paths do not stay apart for too long and, having reconnected on the road, the SWCP continues through attractive woodland, briefly emerging at a white signpost pointing to such far-flung places as Russia and Iceland. **Hollow Brook Waterfall** presents an impressive distraction, though perhaps not as impressive as you were hoping if it hasn't rained recently: while it is one of the biggest waterfalls in the UK, dropping 200m (656ft) in total, it does so over a total horizontal distance of 400m. That said, there are some 50m drops (off the path) which will have you reaching for your camera.

The path now leaves the woods and takes to the cliffs again, with the views back along the coast little short of extraordinary. **Beacon Roman Fortlet**, excavated in the 1960s and capable of holding around 80 soldiers, still watches the Welsh tribes from the hill above you but the path remains virtually horizontal as far as rocky **Highveer Point**, from where the descent to **Heddon's Mouth** begins.

Despite feeling far from civilisation, it's only a short (10- to 15-minute) jaunt from the path to *The Hunters Inn* (off Map 14; ☎ 01598-763230, 🖥 www.thehuntersinn.net; 7D/2T/1F; ☛; WI-FI; 🐾 £8; B&B £50-70pp, £70-85 sgl occ; dinner, bed and breakfast an additional £25pp), full of charm (some rooms have a four-poster bed) and a good place to stay – if only to delay your exit from Exmoor! The food (daily noon-3pm & 6-9pm) is good too, with baguettes and filling cream teas (3-6pm) served in the afternoon and hearty meals – 8oz venison steak in port sauce (£14.95), for example – served in the evenings; just watch out for the peacocks!

Heddon Valley is actually one of the steepest in England, a fact you'll realise soon enough as the path continues by climbing sharply up a wooded hillside, from where deer can often be seen on the hills opposite while birds of prey circle above. There are good views back down the combe with the roof of the inn emerging through the trees. Continuing on the path, magnificent cliff-top walking leads you onto bare, scrubby **Trentishoe Down**, before a slow descent brings you to the foot of **Great Hangman**. *(continued on p114)*

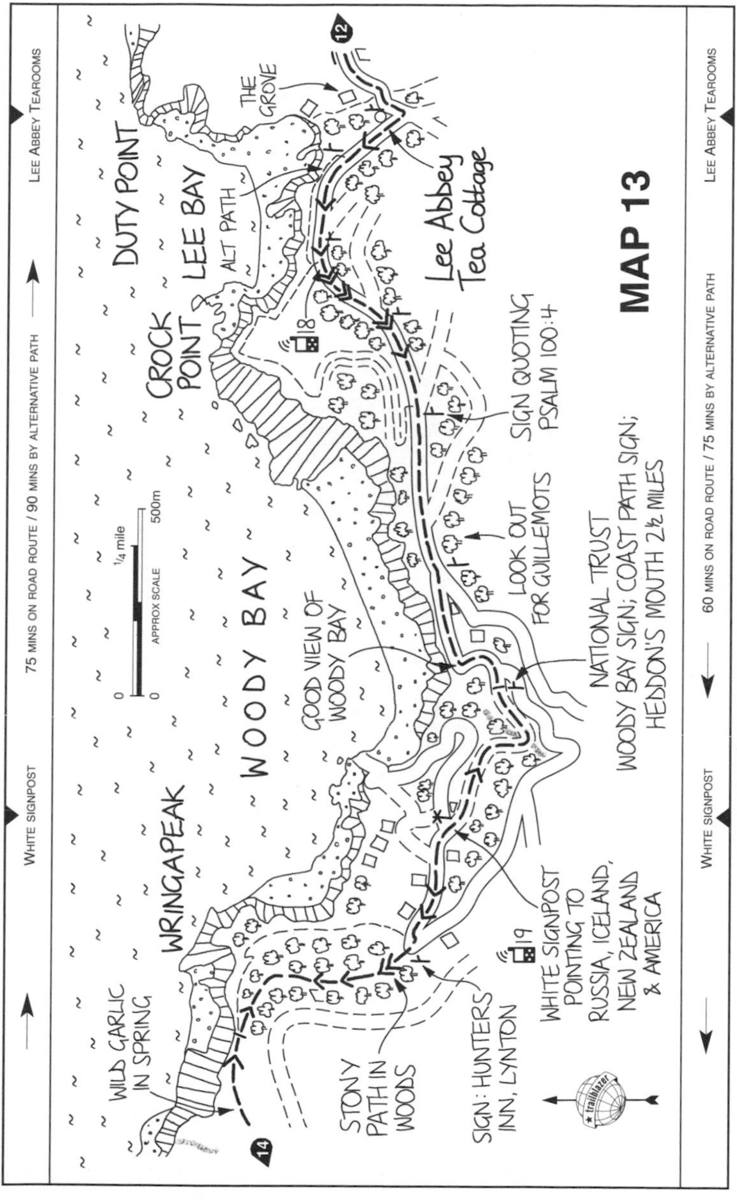
75 MINS ON ROAD ROUTE / 90 MINS BY ALTERNATIVE PATH
WHITE SIGNPOST
LEE ABBEY TEAROOMS
DUTY POINT
LEE BAY
CROCK POINT
ALT PATH
THE GROVE
12
18
Lee Abbey Tea Cottage
MAP 13
SIGN QUOTING PSALM 100:4
LOOK OUT FOR GUILLEMOTS
NATIONAL TRUST WOODY BAY SIGN; COAST PATH SIGN; HEDDON'S MOUTH 2½ MILES
0
0
1/4 mile
500m
APPROX SCALE
WOODY BAY
GOOD VIEW OF WOODY BAY
WRINGAPEAK
WILD GARLIC IN SPRING
14
STONY PATH IN WOODS
SIGN: HUNTERS INN, LYNTON
19
WHITE SIGNPOST POINTING TO RUSSIA, ICELAND, NEW ZEALAND & AMERICA
trailblazer
60 MINS ON ROAD ROUTE / 75 MINS BY ALTERNATIVE PATH
WHITE SIGNPOST
LEE ABBEY TEAROOMS

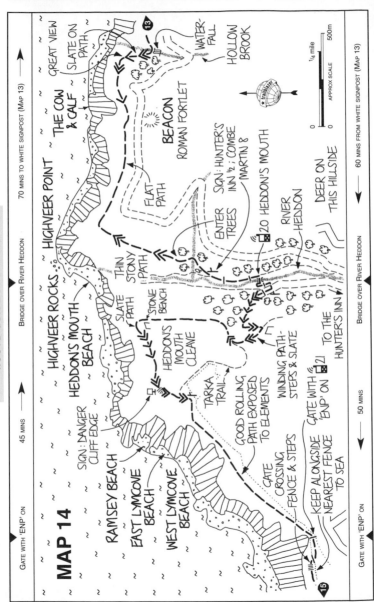

MAP 14

GREAT VIEW
SLATE ON PATH
WATER-FALL
HOLLOW BROOK
THE COW & CALF
HIGHVEER POINT
BEACON ROMAN FORTLET
FLAT PATH
SIGN: HUNTER'S INN ½; COMBE MARTIN 8
20 HEDDON'S MOUTH
ENTER TREES
RIVER HEDDON
DEER ON THIS HILLSIDE
HIGHVEER ROCKS
THIN STONY PATH
HEDDON'S MOUTH BEACH
SLATE PATH
STONE BENCH
HEDDON'S MOUTH CLEAVE
TO THE HUNTER'S INN
SIGN: DANGER CLIFF EDGE
RAMSEY BEACH
EAST LYMCOVE BEACH
WEST LYMCOVE BEACH
TARKA TRAIL
GOOD ROLLING PATH EXPOSED TO ELEMENTS
WINDING PATH - STEPS & SLATE
21
GATE WITH 'ENP' ON
GATE CROSSING FENCE & STEPS
KEEP ALONGSIDE NEAREST FENCE TO SEA

¼ mile
500m
APPROX SCALE

GATE WITH 'ENP' ON — 45 MINS — BRIDGE OVER RIVER HEDDON — 70 MINS TO WHITE SIGNPOST (MAP 13) →

GATE WITH 'ENP' ON — 50 MINS — BRIDGE OVER RIVER HEDDON — 60 MINS FROM WHITE SIGNPOST

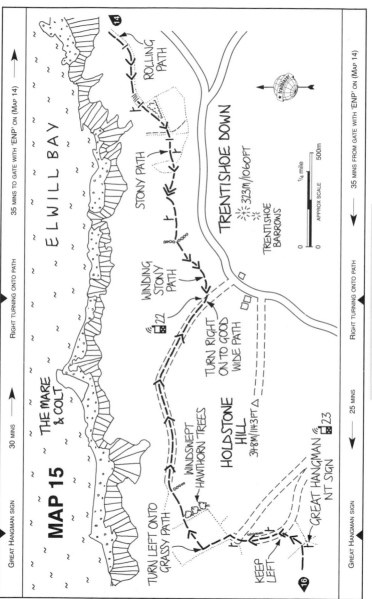

MAP 15

ELWILL BAY

THE MARE & COLT

TRENTISHOE DOWN

313m/1060ft

Trentishoe Barrows

ROLLING PATH

STONY PATH

WINDING STONY PATH

TURN RIGHT ONTO GOOD WIDE PATH

HOLDSTONE HILL
348m/1143ft △

WINDSWEPT HAWTHORN TREES

TURN LEFT ONTO GRASSY PATH

KEEP LEFT

GREAT HANGMAN NT SIGN

APPROX SCALE

¼ mile

0   500m

▲ GREAT HANGMAN SIGN — 30 MINS — ▲ RIGHT TURNING ONTO PATH — 35 MINS TO GATE WITH 'ENP' ON (MAP 14) →

← 35 MINS FROM GATE WITH 'ENP' ON (MAP 14) — ▲ RIGHT TURNING ONTO PATH — 25 MINS — ▲ GREAT HANGMAN SIGN

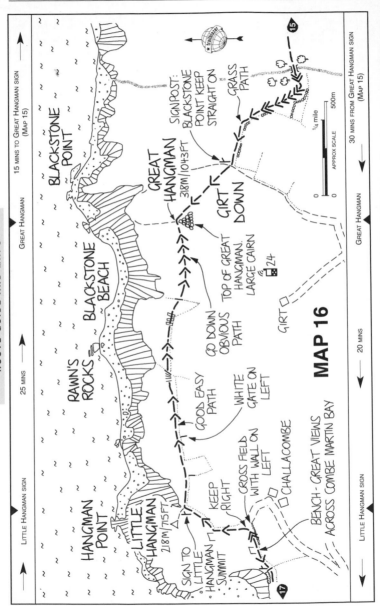

HANGMAN POINT

LITTLE HANGMAN

LITTLE HANGMAN 218M/715FT

RAWN'S ROCKS

BLACKSTONE BEACH

BLACKSTONE POINT

trailblazer

GREAT HANGMAN 318M/1043FT

SIGNPOST: BLACKSTONE POINT KEEP STRAIGHT ON

GRASS PATH

15

GIRT DOWN

TOP OF GREAT HANGMAN. LARGE CAIRN

📷24

GIRT

1/4 mile

500m

APPROX SCALE

0

0

GO DOWN OBVIOUS PATH

WHITE GATE ON LEFT

GOOD EASY PATH

MAP 16

SIGN TO LITTLE HANGMAN SUMMIT

KEEP RIGHT

CROSS FIELD WITH WALL ON LEFT

CHALLACOMBE

BENCH - GREAT VIEWS ACROSS COMBE MARTIN BAY

17

LITTLE HANGMAN SIGN

25 MINS

15 MINS TO GREAT HANGMAN SIGN (MAP 15)

GREAT HANGMAN

30 MINS FROM GREAT HANGMAN SIGN (MAP 15)

GREAT HANGMAN

20 MINS

LITTLE HANGMAN SIGN

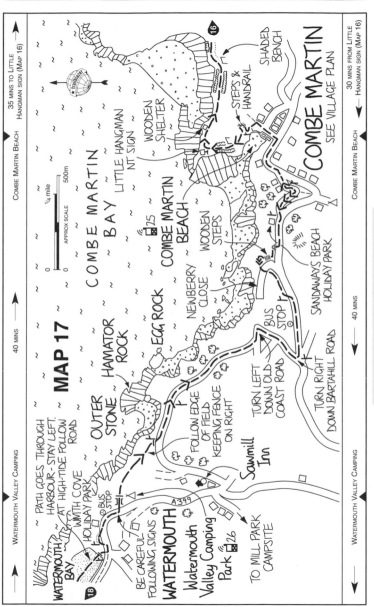

(cont'd from p108) Great Hangman is the highest point on the SWCP and the highest cliff (see p105) in England at 318m or 1043ft (though bear in mind, of course, that you won't be starting your ascent from sea-level but a point approximately 140m above sea level at Sherrycombe – which is a small mercy).

The initial climb will certainly get the heart pounding but you'll also be pleasantly surprised at how brief (hopefully!) the assault is; what's more, the huge **cairn** at the top of Great Hangman is a great spot to survey the land, take photos and enjoy a rest – safe in the knowledge that your day's walking is almost at an end.

The path now has only one way to go and the long, slow walk downwards begins. The path passes by **Little Hangman** (218m/715ft), visitable off to the right of the trail; non-masochists, however, should continue downwards where, shortly afterwards, there are splendid views down to your destination for this stage: **Combe Martin Bay**.

COMBE MARTIN

Combe Martin, anciently Marhuscombe, which lieth low as the name implies, and near the sea, having a cove for boats to land, a place noted for yielding the best hemp in all the County of Devon, and that in great abundance, but in former times famous for mines of tin, and, that which is better merchandise, silver, though Cicero denieth that there is any in Britain.

Tristram Risdon, 1640

Today the hemp fields and mines of tin and silver have all disappeared and if Combe Martin is known for anything now, it is its high street which, so it is said, is the longest in England. (It's a claim that is dubious at best, especially given that much of the street is residential rather than commercial; though it is true that they once featured in the *Guinness Book of Records* for holding the longest street party.)

The town is perhaps not as attractive as some on the route though it's not without some points of interest including the small **Combe Martin Museum** (☎ 01271-889031, 💻 www.combe-martin-museum.co.uk; daily Easter to Oct 10.30am-5pm, Nov to Easter 11am-3.30pm; £2.50), with displays on the industrial, maritime and natural history of the town.

There's also the **Pack o' Cards** pub (see Where to stay), built in 1690 by a local dignitary following a particularly large win whilst gambling, an event that led to his decision to construct the inn with 52 stairs

and 52 windows (52 being the number of cards in a pack), 4 floors (ie the number of suits in a pack), and with 13 doors on every floor and 13 fireplaces throughout (representing the number of cards in a suit)!

See p16 for details of festivals and events here.

Services

There is a **tourist information centre** (☎ 01271-883319; Easter to July daily 10am-2pm, July to Oct daily 10am-5pm, Nov to Easter Fri & Sat 10am-noon) on Cross St, on the left just as you walk into town.

The library has **internet access** (Tue 10am-12.30pm & 2-6.30pm, Wed & Fri 10am-noon & 2-5pm, Sat 10am-noon) though you're better off using the terminals at Devon Fayre Coffee (see p 116; daily 8am-9/10pm) down near the front, where access is just £1 for as long as you want.

The town also boasts a **post office** (Mon-Fri 9am-5pm, Sat 9am-noon) and three **supermarkets** with late opening hours: King St Stores (daily 7am-11pm), Best One Supermarket (Mon-Sat 8am-8pm, Sun 9am-6pm) which offers **cashback** and also has an **ATM**, and a Spar (aka Sue's; daily 7am-8pm) which also has an ATM but doesn't offer cashback. Note that both of these ATMs charge you to take your money out.

There's also a Boots **pharmacy** (Mon-Wed 9am-6pm, Thur & Fri 9am-5.30pm,

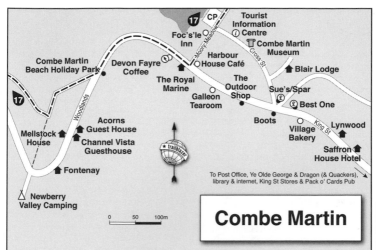

Combe Martin

ROUTE GUIDE AND MAPS

Sat 9am-1pm) and a **walking/camping out-let**, The Outdoor Shop (daily 10am-5pm).

Where to stay

By the standards of this path there's not a great choice of places to stay in Combe Martin, though most are OK and two are positively quirky.

There are two large holiday parks on the outskirts of Combe Martin but the best option for **campers** is *Newberry Valley Camping and Caravanning Park* (☎ 01271-882334, 🖳 www.newberryvalley park.co.uk; Apr-Oct; £12-25 per pitch & two adults; 🐾 £1-2). The facilities are excellent and there's a little shop (daily 8.30am-6.30pm in high season, limited hours in low season) that sells basics only. The site is abundant with wildlife and has won the David Bellamy Conservation & Nature Gold Award six years on the trot! It is located a short distance out of the town on the bend a little way up Newberry Hill.

If you feel that you have a few more miles in you then it is also well worth considering continuing to Watermouth (see p117) where there are some campsites, including a couple that are better value for hikers.

There is a huddle of **B&Bs** on Woodlands, up the hill on the way out of town. The best, perhaps, is *Mellstock House* (☎ 01271-882592, 🖳 www.mell stockhouse.co.uk; 3D/1T/1F; WI-FI; £35pp, sgl occ £40) with a licensed bar and the offer of evening meals. There's also a decent breakfast menu including smoked salmon and eggs, and a drying room too – little wonder that this place is perhaps the most popular with walkers.

Providing close competition is *Fontenay* (☎ 01271-889368, 🖳 www.visit fontenay.co.uk; 1S/1D/1T; the rooms share two bathrooms; 🐾; well-behaved 🐕; WI-FI; £24pp), just before the bend in the road near the top of the hill, a large family house with a nice sideline in selling crafts made from locally sourced driftwood. The bread and other food at breakfast is home cooked and organic where possible and the eggs are from their chickens. Back down the hill, *Acorns Guest House* (☎ 01271-882769, 🖳 www.acorns-guesthouse.co.uk; 5D/1T/1D or F; 🐕 £5; WI-FI; £30-35pp, £40-45 sgl occ) is a huge late-Victorian terrace with friendly owners, while *Channel Vista* (☎ 01271-883514, 🖳 www.channelvista.co. uk; 6D or T; 🐾; WI-FI; 🐕 £4 per visit; £29-

34pp) also has a licensed bar in their pleasant Victorian conservatory and a sweet-natured Patterdale/terrier cross dog. Evening meals and packed lunches are also available here.

There are also some B&Bs in the centre of town. *Blair Lodge* (☎ 01271-882294, 🖳 www.blairlodge.co.uk; 1S/2T/5D/1F; ➼; WI-FI; £33-36pp, sgl £36), at the top of Moory Meadow, just off the main street, is licensed to sell alcohol; evening meals, packed lunches and luggage transfers are also available if arranged in advance. *Lynwood* (☎ 01271-882013, 🖳 wendy drucegofast@mail.gofast.co.uk; 2D/1T; from £30pp), on King St, is a small, good-value place. Much grander, *Saffron House Hotel* (☎ 01271-883521, 🖳 www.saffron househotel.co.uk; 3D/4T or F; ➼; WI-FI; 🐾 £4; £30-37.50pp, £35-40 sgl occ) is a large former farmhouse with its own swimming pool. The hotel lies away from the traffic, up the steps on King St.

Combe Martin also has two pubs in which you may want to spend the night: *The Royal Marine* (☎ 01271-882470, ➼; www.theroyalmarine.co.uk; 3D/2T; £35pp) has two self-contained flats (1D and 1T) in addition to its rooms. Each room has a TV – though there can't be many programmes that could pull you away from the views over the bay towards Hangman. Dogs are welcome in the bar. *Pack o' Cards* (see p114; ☎ 01271-882300, 🖳 www.pack ocards.co.uk; 6D; WI-FI; £37.50-40pp, £42.50-45 sgl occ) still takes guests. Now a listed building, the hotel's rooms are amongst the smartest in town, with some featuring four-poster beds.

Where to eat and drink

Galleon Tearoom (☎ 01271-883732; Mar-Oct daily 10am-5pm) sits close to the front and has a great little terrace which is a delight on a sunny day. Dogs are welcome in this family-run place with breakfasts and cream teas a speciality. Nearby, *Harbour House Café* (Mon-Sat 9am-5pm) offers fair-priced meals with jacket potatoes from £3.40.

Village Bakery (Mon, Tue, Thur & Fri 8am-4pm, Wed & Sat 8am-1pm), on King St, bakes everything on the premises.

Devon Fayre Coffee (Easter-Oct daily 10.30am-6pm depending on demand), on Seaside Hill, is the last café on the way out of town when heading towards Ilfracombe. Serving thirsty customers for 36 years now, they're always happy to see walkers – and with delicious cream teas at £3.95, walkers are usually pretty happy to see them too.

The place with the best reputation in Combe Martin is *Quackers* restaurant (Wed-Fri 6-9pm, Sat noon-3pm & 6-10pm, Sun noon-3pm) at *Ye Olde George and Dragon* (☎ 01271-882282, 🖳 www.george anddragon.uk.com; bar Mon-Wed 4pm-12.30am, Thur 4pm-2am, Fri & Sat noon-2am, Sun noon-midnight), around 2km back from the sea on the main street, a recently refurbished 400-year-old tavern with a restaurant that has daily specials as well as a fixed menu including fillet of sea bass for £12.95. They also do a takeaway service.

Transport

[See also pp49-51] Filer's 300 **bus** service (Ilfracombe to Lynmouth) calls here as does their 301 (Combe Martin to Barnstaple via Ilfracombe). First Group's No 30 also runs to Ilfracombe, via Watermouth & Hele. Buses run along the main street and stop at several places including by the beach.

For a **taxi**, try Andy's (☎ 01271-889200).

COMBE MARTIN TO WOOLACOMBE   [MAPS 17-22]

For this **14¼-mile (23km; 6hrs 35 mins)** stage, and the one after it, the landscape is no longer dominated by the high rolling hills, hanging woodlands, steep-sided canyons and soaring cliffs prevalent in Exmoor. The scenery instead is one of sand and seals, smugglers' coves and surfers, broad beige beaches and bleach-blonde hair. This stage still provides a fairly strenuous workout for your calf muscles, with some stiff climbs, though generally the gradients are kind. That said, the start of the walk is punctuated by some fairly mundane road walking, but this is more than made up for by some great cliff-top walking and some wonderful views of Lundy Island and Ilfracombe – a tourist hot-spot with plenty of amenities. Refreshments are also available at several other spots along the way.

After Ilfracombe the path meanders through the greenery of Torrs Park before following a wonderfully undulating route around Morte Point from where you will be treated to your first views of Woolacombe and her long, gorgeous expanse of sand. Seals, dolphins and basking sharks are frequently spotted from the cliffs around Morte Point (with Rockham Bay being an especially good spot for seals). Whether you'll see one of those exotic British creatures is largely a matter of luck, of course – though one mammal you definitely will see bobbing up and down in Morte Bay as you stroll/stagger into Woolacombe are the local surfers, a largely migratory creature that populates the coastline from Woolacombe to Saunton in huge numbers, particularly in summertime.

The route

There is a need for caution when leaving Combe Martin: both that you take great care whilst walking along the road and that you do not miss the sign that directs you off it. Accompanied by some rather pleasant woodland the path initially takes a rather haphazard route before arriving at **Watermouth Bay**.

WATERMOUTH [MAP 17, p113]

There's not much to Watermouth other than a small, pretty harbour, the old Victorian **Watermouth Castle**, now a theme park (🖳 www.watermouthcastle.com); and, before these, several decent **campsites** of which two stand out.

Watermouth Valley Camping Park (☎ 01271-862282, 🖳 www.watermouthpark .co.uk; Easter-Sep, walkers £5 per pitch plus £5 per additional person, £1 per dog) is a cheap and lovely campsite, perfectly situated on the path and near the pub. (Please note: don't get confused between this campsite and Watermouth Cove Holiday Park next-door.)

Across the road and up the hill from the pub, *Mill Park* (☎ 01271-882647, 🖳 www.millparklimited.co.uk; £6.50-12 for a tent and two people, £15-30 for a 'cocoon', rates depend on season; Mar-Oct) is a smarter affair whose chief recommendation for hikers may be their 'tent cocoons' – two-person wooden huts that make a great alternative to sleeping in a tent, particularly if the weather doesn't look too friendly. However, you need to bring a sleeping bag.

The pub, by the way, is *The Sawmill Inn* (☎ 01271-882259, 🖳 www.thesawmill inn.co.uk; 3D; £30pp, sgl occ £35pp), housed in the original buildings of a watermill. Their food (Jan-Feb Thur-Sat noon-2pm & 6-9pm, Sun noon-2pm; Mar-Dec daily noon-2pm & 6-9pm; school summer holidays 12.30-4pm & 5-9pm) is delicious and the menu may include homemade steak and Tribute ale pie (£8).

A brief dalliance with Watermouth Harbour follows. Tranquil and sleepy it may seem now, but this harbour played an integral part in the allies' Operation Pluto (an acronym for Pipelines Under The Ocean) during WWII. The idea was to lay pipes under the Channel to supply fuel to allied forces, and to test the plan a 51¹/₂-mile (83km) pipe was laid between Watermouth and Swansea across the

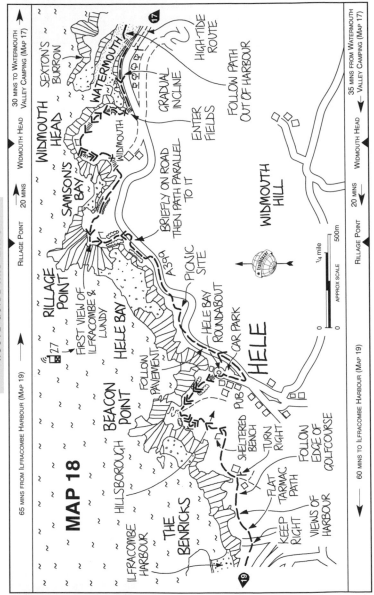

MAP 18

65 MINS FROM ILFRACOMBE HARBOUR (MAP 19)

RILLAGE POINT

WIDMOUTH HEAD 20 MINS

30 MINS TO WATERMOUTH VALLEY CAMPING (MAP 17)

SEXTON'S BURROW

WATERMOUTH

17

HIGH-TIDE ROUTE

GRADUAL INCLINE

FOLLOW PATH OUT OF HARBOUR

ENTER FIELDS

WIDMOUTH HEAD

WIDMOUTH

SAMSON'S BAY

BRIEFLY ON ROAD THEN PATH PARALLEL TO IT

RILLAGE POINT

FIRST VIEW OF ILFRACOMBE & LUNDY

27

HELE BAY

BEACON POINT

A399

PICNIC SITE

WIDMOUTH HILL

FOLLOW PAVEMENT

HILLSBOROUGH

HELE BAY ROUNDABOUT

CAR PARK

HELE

WIDMOUTH HEAD 20 MINS

RILLAGE POINT

35 MINS FROM WATERMOUTH VALLEY CAMPING (MAP 17)

1/4 mile

APPROX SCALE

0

0

500m

trailblazer

THE BENRICKS

ILFRACOMBE HARBOUR

VIEWS OF HARBOUR

KEEP RIGHT

FLAT TARMAC PATH

FOLLOW EDGE OF GOLFCOURSE

TURN RIGHT

SHELTERED BENCH

PUB

19

60 MINS TO ILFRACOMBE HARBOUR (MAP 19)

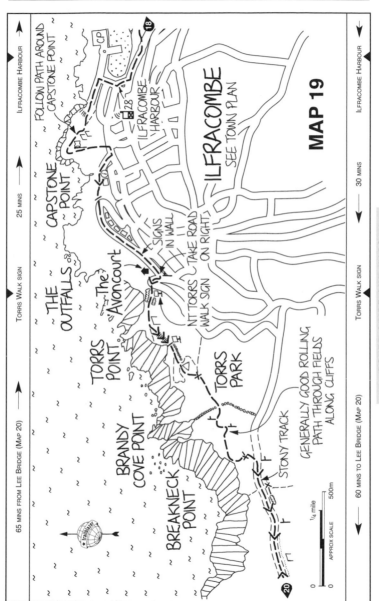

ILFRACOMBE HARBOUR

FOLLOW PATH AROUND CAPSTONE POINT

CP

18

28

CAPSTONE POINT

ILFRACOMBE HARBOUR

ILFRACOMBE
SEE TOWN PLAN

MAP 19

THE OUTFALLS

SIGNS IN WALL

TORRS POINT

The "Avoncourt"

NT TORRS WALK SIGN TAKE ROAD ON RIGHT

TORRS PARK

TORRS WALK SIGN

25 MINS

30 MINS

BRANDY COVE POINT

BREAKNECK POINT

GENERALLY GOOD ROLLING PATH THROUGH FIELDS ALONG CLIFFS

STONY TRACK

20

65 MINS FROM LEE BRIDGE (MAP 20)

60 MINS TO LEE BRIDGE (MAP 20)

¼ mile
500m
0
0
APPROX SCALE

trailblazer

ILFRACOMBE HARBOUR

Bristol Channel. It proved a success and the first pipe was laid under the English Channel to France in 1944 – with further pipes installed for the remainder of the war as the fighting moved closer to Germany.

Some woodland cliff-side walking to **Widmouth Head** follows, from where, sadly, you will get your last good views of Great Hangman. Your eyes will not remain unoccupied for long, however, as from **Rillage Point** another magical spectre arrives on the horizon – that of Lundy Island (see box opposite).

Having passed the edge of **Hele** the path navigates the wooded slopes and fields of **Hillsborough**, from where fabulous views of Ilfracombe and her harbour greet you.

ILFRACOMBE   [Map p122]

'The situation of Ilfracombe is by nature lovely'   **S Baring-Gould** *Devon* (1907)
The first part of Ilfracombe that's visible as you stroll around Beacon Point is the town's harbour.

Whether *MS Oldenburg*, the boat to Lundy (see box opposite), is in dock or not, it's difficult not to be struck by the natural beauty of this little haven. Sheltered between the hills of Capstone and Hillsborough, it's little wonder there's been a harbour here since the 12th century, though, as with just about every resort on the North Devon coastline, the town owes its prosperity largely to the Victorians, whose decision to route the steamships and railways here bought the crowds to Ilfracombe en masse.

Today, the town can be divided into four distinct areas. The **harbour** is the largest in North Devon and, somewhat surprisingly given its rather homely aspect, experiences the world's second highest tidal rise and fall. It is also the place from which to embark on a coastal cruise or sealife safari.

Fore St is the oldest part of Ilfracombe and used to be the town's social and business hub. It is still home to many of the town's better eateries and whilst strolling up or down the steep cobbled street it is easy to envisage the seafaring residents of old staggering out of the George and Dragon, the town's oldest pub, dating from 1360.

The third area is **High St**, the continuation of Fore St (there's a large metal arch separating the two) and a town-centre of sorts. Just after the divide you will find **Walkers Chocolate Emporium** (☎ 01271-867193, 🖳 www.chocolate-emporium.co.uk; Mon-Sat 9.30am-5pm; free admission), a museum dedicated to the humble cocoa bean and all its derivatives; you can also watch chocolate being made.

Also on High St is **Embassy Cinema** (☎ 01271-862323, 🖳 www.merlincinemas.co.uk) as well as most of the banks and other services, although if you have no need for any of these there is little else to justify a visit.

The fourth and final area, the **seafront and The Promenade**, is pretty enough, and the large conical buildings that greet you as you circle Capstone Hill are certainly striking. This is the home of the TIC, a gallery and **Landmark Theatre** (☎ 01271-324242, 🖳 www.northdevontheatres.org.uk), which puts on a wide variety of shows throughout the year. Nearby is the local **museum** (Easter-Oct daily 10am-5pm, Nov-Easter Tue-Fri 10am-1pm; £2.50, £2 concs); it has five rooms, with sections dedicated to sailing, Lundy and the harbour, and makes for a diverting half-hour or so.

St Nicholas Chapel, on Lantern Hill, guards the harbour's entrance. Built in 1321, the chapel's use has changed down the centuries from place of worship to lighthouse to family home; currently it's maintained by Ilfracombe Rotary Club and you can look around (free, although donations are welcome).

See pp15-6 for details of festivals and events held here.

Services

The **tourist information centre** (☎ 01271-863001; Easter to Oct Mon-Thur 9am-5pm, Fri 10am-5pm, Sat & Sun 10.30am-4.30pm, Nov to Easter closed on Sun) shares one of the conical buildings with the theatre.

Internet access can be found at Ilfracombe Library (☎ 01271-862388; Mon 9am-1pm, Tue 9am-5pm, Thur 9am-6pm, Fri 9am-5pm, Sat 9am-1pm; £2.20/30 mins), on Sommers Crescent between the

The Promenade and Fore St, and also at The Genie Café (see Where to eat; £1/30 mins) on the High St.

Also on the High St there is: the **post office** (Mon-Fri 9am-5.30pm, Sat 9am-12.30pm), part of the **general store** McColls (daily 7am-11pm); the **Co-op** (Mon-Sat 7am-9pm, Sun 10am-4pm), which is the best place for food supplies in the centre; the **chemists** Superdrug (Mon-Sat 8.30am-5.30pm, Sun 10am-4pm) and Lloyds (Mon-

❏ **Lundy Island**

Lying 11 miles off the coast of North Devon, where the Bristol Channel meets the Atlantic Ocean, Lundy Island is an extraordinary place in a wonderful location. It is also one that, with careful planning, can be reached by the intrepid pedestrian – and its coastline walked – in just one day.

Measuring 3½ miles long and just a mile wide, the island is renowned for its **wildlife**: approximately 35 species of bird breed on the island annually including puffins ('Lund-ey' means Puffin Island in Norse) and many other seabirds such as razorbills and guillemots. Amongst the landlubbers there are Sika deer and Lundy ponies, while out at sea you may glimpse basking sharks and dolphins.

Standing on the clifftops amongst wildflowers – possibly even next to a famous Lundy cabbage – the walker can stare out across the water and easily imagine why for many centuries Lundy was a favoured hiding place for **pirates**, its remoteness and proximity to both two coastlines and Bristol Channel's bustling shipping lane making it the perfect hideout. **Marisco Castle** is named after a famous family of swashbuckling criminals including William de Marisco, who met a most unfortunate end – in 1242 he was charged with conspiring to kill King Henry III and it is thought that he was the first man to have been hung, drawn and quartered.

Taking less than two hours, *MS Oldenburg* (late Mar to late Oct; 3-5 sailings per week; £34.50/18 adults/children day return, £60/29.50 open return) carries passengers to the car-free island from Ilfracombe and Bideford. Alternatively, in winter a helicopter service (£102 return) runs on Mondays and Fridays from Hartland Point (see p181).

If a single day on Lundy seems inadequate – which it will if you wish to both walk the whole coastline and have time to investigate all its other attractions – there are 23 restored historic buildings on the island in which you can stay, including the castle and a **lighthouse**. The cost varies greatly depending on the size of the property and the season in which you visit, and be aware that some can be rented only on a weekly basis over the school summer holidays. **Camping** (£9-12pp; late Mar to early Oct) is also an option in a field near the island's public house and shop. All accommodation booking must be done in advance as even the campsite is very popular in the summer months. *Marisco Tavern* (bar daily noon-11pm; food served daily noon-2pm & 6-9pm) serves food to suit all budgets.

For more information in regards to sailings, accommodation and the island in general you should contact The Lundy Shore Office (☎ 01271-863636, 💻 www.lundyisland.co.uk) or, for accommodation, The Landmark Trust (☎ 01628-825925, 💻 www.landmarktrust.org.uk).

ROUTE GUIDE AND MAPS

ROUTE GUIDE AND MAPS

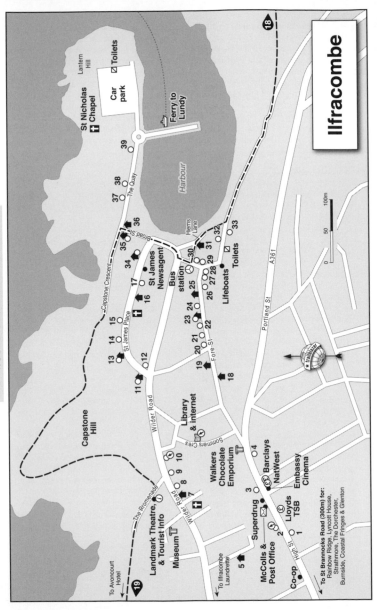

Ilfracombe

Sat 9am-5.30pm) and **banks** with **ATMs** including Barclays, NatWest and Lloyds.

Ilfracombe **Laundrette** (☎ 01271-867719; daily 8am-7.30pm, manned 9.30am-4pm) is at 15 Wilder Rd. Another shop selling general necessities, though nearer the harbour on St James Place, is St James **Newsagents** & Minimarket (daily 8.30am-9pm).

Where to stay

Campers will need to continue onto Woolacombe for the nearest campsite. However, there are, surprisingly, two **hostels** in Ilfracombe: *Ocean Backpackers* (☎ 01271-867835, ☐ www.oceanbackpackers .co.uk; 38 dorm beds/1D/1F; WI-FI; 🐾; £13.50-19pp), at 29 St James Place, is a comfortable place right in the centre of town; it even provides free tea and coffee for its guests. At 12 Fortescue Rd, just off Wilder Rd, *Maplewood House* (☎ 01271-867490, ☐ www.maplewoodhouse.co.uk; 4D/1T/two 8-bed dorms/1F; 🖤; WI-FI; 🐾; £10-19pp exc breakfast) actually describes

itself as a 'backpacking hotel'; breakfast (£5pp) is available if booked in advance, but even so, the prices are remarkable.

There are plenty of **B&Bs** in town. In terms of location, it's hard to beat *Slipway Cottage* (☎ 01271-863035; 4D/1T; 🖤; two rooms share facilities; £28-30pp), right on both the harbour and the trail at 2 Hierns Lane. *Acorn Lodge* (☎ 01271-862505, ☐ www.theacornlodge.co.uk; 2S/6D; WI-FI; £25-29pp, sgl £27) is at 4 St James Place, and *Rocky Cove* (☎ 01271-862281, ☐ www.rocky-cove.co.uk; 2D/2F; 🖤; WI-FI; from £30pp, sgl occ £35) is at No 2. Rocky Cove has its own café (see Where to eat) and both these places have some rooms with views towards Capstone Hill.

The Harbour Lights (☎ 01271-862778, ☐ www.hlhar.co.uk; 2S/4D/1T/ 2F; 🖤; WI-FI; £31-37.50pp, sgl £37.50; end Mar to end Oct), 26 Broad St, is a large, smart place with a licensed restaurant (see Where to eat).

On Fore St there are several Georgian Grade-II listed buildings, two of which we

ROUTE GUIDE AND MAPS

ILFRACOMBE – MAP KEY

Where to stay
5 Maplewood House
7 The Imperial Hotel
11 Rocky Cove B&B
13 Acorn Lodge B&B
16 Ocean Backpackers
18 Wellingtons
19 Crescent House Hotel
23 The Olive Branch
25 Harcourt Hotel
31 Slipway Cottage
34 Capstone Hotel
35 The Harbour Lights
36 The Royal Britannia

Where to eat and drink
1 Grassroots Café
2 The Genie Café
3 Swiss Cottage Café
4 Munchies Kebabs
8 Dolly's Café
9 The Ilfracombe Fryer
10 The Bistro Café
11 Rocky Cove Café
12 Giovanni & Luca
13 Fuschia Tea Gardens
14 6 St James Bistro
15 Curiosity Cottage Tea Rooms

Where to eat and drink *(cont'd)*
17 Double D's Pizza
20 Seventy-One Bistro
21 La Gendarmerie
22 The Terrace
23 The Olive Branch
24 Basil's Restaurant
26 George & Dragon
27 Prince of Wales
28 Take Thyme
29 Ship and Pilot Inn
30 Adele's Café
32 Bus-stop Café
33 S&P Fish 'n' Chips
34 Capstone Hotel
35 Harbour Lights
37 The Smugglers
38 Lynbay Fish 'n' Chips
39 The Quay

can recommend, and one of which has its own restaurant (see Where to eat), namely *The Olive Branch* (☎ 01271-879005, 🖵 www.olivebranchguesthouse.co.uk; 1S/3D/1T; ✒; WI-FI; £35-47.50pp, sgl £45). There's also *Wellington's* (☎ 01271-864178, 🖵 www.wellingtonsrestaurant.co.uk; 2D/1T; ✒; WI-FI; £35pp, sgl occ £40) which now does B&B only.

A little out of town there is a whole stretch of B&Bs. Along St Brannock's Rd are: *Glenton* (☎ 01271-864039; 1S/2D; ✒; £27-28pp), at No 83, where the rooms share facilities; the particularly pleasant *Coastal Fringes* (☎ 01271-865096, 🖵 www.coastalfringes.com; 3D; ✒; £30-35pp, sgl occ £34-39), No 76, with its 1930s/'40s film-themed rooms; *Burnside* (☎ 01271-863097, 🖵 www.burnside-ilfracombe.co.uk; 3D; ✒; WI-FI; £30-35pp, sgl occ £45), No 34, which has a room with a four-poster bed; *The Dorchester* (☎ 01271-865472, 🖵 www.the-dorchester.co.uk; 1S/4D/2F; WI-FI; 🐾 £5; £38-45pp; Mar-Nov), No 59, which is licensed; *Strathmore* (☎ 01271-862248, 🖵 www.the-strathmore.co.uk; 2S/3D/1T/2F; ✒; WI-FI; 🐾 £6.50 per night, half of which goes to a charity, the Dogs Trust; £35-40pp), No 57, which is also licensed; at No 56 *Lyncott House* (☎ 01271-862425, 🖵 www.lyncotthouse.co.uk; 4D/1Tr; ✒; WI-FI; £35-42.50pp, sgl occ £40-45) claims to be Ilfracombe's premier guest house; and *Rainbow Ridge* (☎ 01271-863817, 🖵 www.rainbowridgeguesthouse.co.uk; 2S/4D/1T/1T or F; WI-FI; £22.50-30pp, sgl £25-27.50), at No 53.

In addition to the B&Bs there are plenty of **hotels**. On Wilder Rd, close to the Promenade, is *The Imperial* (☎ 01271-862536, 🖵 www.leisureplex.co.uk; 16S/35D/39T/8F; ✒; WI-FI in public areas; £29-43pp, sgl £36-50), while closer to the harbour, on St James Place, there's *The Capstone Hotel* (☎ 01271-863540, 🖵 www.thecapstonehotel.com; 2S/2D or T/6D/2F; ✒; WI-FI; £27.50-45pp, sgl occ £45), a Victorian place with LCD HD TVs and DVD players in each room; packed lunches are available.

The Royal Britannia (☎ 01271-862939, 🖵 www.royal-britannia.co.uk; 8S/3D/2T/1F; £28-65pp, sgl £28; Jacuzzi in one room; WI-FI in one of the bars; 🐾 £5) is in an even better situation, actually overlooking the boats from its location on Broad St. Back on Fore St there is *Harcourt Hotel* (☎ 01271-862931, 🖵 www.harcourthotel.co.uk; 2S/2D/1D or T/2F; ✒; WI-FI; 🐾 £10 per stay; £33-35pp), and *Crescent House Hotel* (☎ 01271-862096, 🖵 www.thecrescenthousehotel.co.uk; 3S/ 2T/10D/3F; ✒; WI-FI; £38-40pp, sgl £38-40) which started life as a B&B back in 1883 and still contains some lovely Victorian features.

Close to where the path leaves the town, at 6 Torrs Walk Ave, *The Avoncourt* (Map 19; ☎ 01271-862543, 🖵 www.avoncourtilfracombe.co.uk; 2S/6D/1T/1T or F; ✒; 🐾; £32-36pp) is a fairly standard guesthouse which has its own bar and does evening meals (if requested in advance); the owners also provide a pick-up and drop-off service and luggage transfer (£5).

Where to eat and drink
Tearooms and cafés A short stroll along Wilder Rd, will present you with numerous tearooms and cafés, most of which provide breakfasts, lunches and cream teas. Particularly good are *Dolly's Café* (daily 9am-5pm, summer to late) and *The Bistro Café* (☎ 01271-864641; WI-FI; June-Sep daily 9am-9pm, rest of year 9am-4pm but depends on demand).

Also worth a look on St James Place are *Curiosity Cottage* (☎ 01271-863510; Easter-Oct daily 9.30am-4.30pm) which allows dogs in the garden and does cream teas (from £3.90); *Fuschia Tea Gardens* (daily 11am-6.30pm) which is part of Acorn Lodge (see Where to stay) and serves fresh crab; the bistro at *6 St James Bistro* (☎ 01271-866602; Mar-Oct Mon-Sat noon-3pm & 6-9pm, Sun noon-4pm), which serves local produce and does a 10oz rump steak for £11.95; and *Rocky Cove Café* (see Where to stay; July & Aug daily 11am-9pm, rest of year check hours but they are generally open during the day), which is licensed and where the catch of the day is £11.25.

A trip up to High St will lead you to *Grassroots Café* (☎ 01271-867574; Mon-

Sat 9am-3pm, Fri & Sat bistro nights; £12 for a three-course meal, booking preferred) which is well worth a visit, although if arriving later in the day *Swiss Cottage Café* (☎ 01271-864433; June-Oct Mon-Sat 9am-5pm, school summer holidays Sun 9am-5pm, Nov-May Mon-Sat 9am-4pm) may be a better bet.

On the corner of Hiern's Lane and Broad St is *Adele's* (☎ 01271-863268, ⌨ www.adelescafeilfracombe.co.uk; Mar-Dec daily 7.30am-4pm; 🐾); it specialises in gluten-free and vegetarian meals. On Broad St, *Bus Stop Café* (daily 8am-4pm) is good for cheap eats such as cod, chips and peas for £4.25 and hot drinks for less than £1.

Another good budget option is *Genie Café* (daily 9am-4pm; WI-FI) on the High St, which is far smarter inside than it looks from the street and also offers internet access (£1/30 mins).

Take Thyme (☎ 01271-867622; mid Mar-Dec Tue-Sun from 7pm), at 1 Fore St, serves locally sourced fish and beef.

Pubs *The Ship and Pilot Inn* (☎ 01271-863562; food Easter to Oct noon-3pm & 5-8pm) has nine real ales, the majority of which are local, and serves basic pub grub. *The Prince of Wales* (☎ 01271-866391; food served daily noon-9pm; free WI-FI; 🐾)is on Fore St. The menu includes steak & ale pie, chips and gravy for £5.95. Also on Fore St, Ilfracombe's oldest pub, *George & Dragon* (☎ 01271-863851, ⌨ www .georgeanddragonilfracombe.co.uk; bar Mon-Sat 10am-11.30pm, Sun noon-11.30pm; food served daily noon-3pm & 6.30-9pm) has a selection of real ales, a no mobile phones policy and does boozy beef braised in real ale for £7.95.

The Smugglers (☎ 01271-863620; Easter to Nov daily 10am-late, depending on custom), on The Quay, is a quirky place with red leather alcoves, fish tanks set in the wall and seafaring antiquities hanging from the ceiling. Fittingly they do grilled shark for £10.95 or 'simply enormous rainbow trout' for £15.95.

Restaurants For smarter dining there are several places on Fore St.

Seventy-one Bistro (☎ 01271-863632, ⌨ www.seventyone.biz; school summer holidays Mon-Sat 6.30pm to late; Easter to July Tue-Sat 6.30pm to late, rest of year Fri & Sat 6.30pm to late, Thur also if enough bookings) is great and a mouth-watering Devon fillet of beef pan-fried with mixed wild mushrooms and Madeira sauce costs £19.95; while at *La Gendarmerie* (☎ 01271-865984; Easter to Oct Tue-Thur 7-10.30pm, Fri & Sat 7-11.30pm; limited days/hours in the winter) you get two courses for £21 or three for £26.

At *Basil's Restaurant* (☎ 01271-862823; Thur-Tue 6.30-9pm; later by arrangement) a daube of beef with orange and star anise costs £13.95.

Spanish food is available at *The Terrace* (☎ 01271-863482; summer daily from 6pm; winter Wed/Thur-Sat only), a tapas and wine bar. *The Olive Branch* (see Where to stay; daily Easter to end Oct noon-4pm & 6.30-9.30pm) has a varied menu; mains cost £8-12. For Italian you should head to Wilder Rd and *Giovanni & Luca* (☎ 01271-879394; Mar-Oct Tue-Sun noon-2.30pm & 6-10.30pm; winter to 10pm) where pasta dishes cost between £6.45 and £8.50.

Other restaurants include *The Quay* (☎ 01271-868090, ⌨ 11thequay.co.uk; Mar-Oct daily 10am-9pm, Oct-Mar Wed-Sun 10am-9pm), on the road of the same name, where escalopes of pork with buttered parsley potatoes and green salad costs £15.50; *The Harbour Lights* (see Where to stay; end Mar to end Oct daily 6-9pm) where the menu may include roast stuffed shoulder of Exmoor lamb (£14.95), and *The Capstone Hotel* (see Where to stay; daily noon-3pm & 6-10pm) where an Ilfracombe lobster will set you back £27.

Takeaways These include the High St favourite *Munchies Kebabs* (☎ 01271-855666; Sun-Thu 4pm to midnight, Fri & Sat 4pm-3.30am) or *Double D's Pizza* (summer daily 5-10pm, winter Thur-Sun 5.30-9pm) on St James Place, where a 9" Hawaiian is £5.

For fish 'n' chips, and also Japanese king prawns (£6.95), there is *The*

Ilfracombe Fryer (daily noon-10pm) on Wilder Rd; or on The Quay, *Lynbay Traditional Fish 'n' Chips* (daily 11am-9pm) where cod and chips costs £5. If you fancy your fish straight off the trawler *S & P Fish 'n' Chips* (☎ 01271-865923; summer daily 10am-3pm or later depending on demand, winter Thur-Sat 10am-3pm) is on the harbour itself.

Transport

[See also pp49-51] Ilfracombe is well-served by public transport with regular **buses** to most other destinations along the path. To return to Combe Martin take Filers No 300 bus or to go on to Barnstaple take their No 301 or First's No 3; for Woolacombe take Filer's No 302.

For a **taxi** try A Taxis (☎ 01271-865321), or A2B taxis (☎ 01271-867788).

Leaving Ilfracombe the path ventures along the hills and cliffs of **Torrs Park** before passing via *The Blue Mushroom* (Map 20; ☎ 01271-862947, 💻 www.leebay.co.uk/the_blue_mushroom.htm; 1D or T; 🐕 £modest; year-round minimum two-night stay, two nights for two people just £30pp per night, sgl occ £54 per night), a delightful place all by itself with a sun lounge and sea views, before heading down to **Lee Bay**.

LEE

Although the hotel by the trail is shut refreshments are available in the village itself, approximately 3/4 mile up the road. The vale in which the village sits is known locally as 'Fuchsia Valley' due to the abundance of the scarlet flower blossoming in the area's hedgerows at certain times of year.

The Grampus Inn (☎ 01271-862906, 💻 www.thegrampus-inn.co.uk; **food** served daily noon-3pm, Mon-Sat 7-9pm) serves real ales and reasonably priced sandwiches/panini (£4.50-6) as well as a more hearty menu including steak and chips (£13.50) and possibly on the specials board Hungarian beef goulash (£9).

B&B-wise *Grey Cottage* (☎ 01271-864360, 💻 www.greycottage.co.uk; 1D/1D or T/1F; ✦; 🐕; WI-FI; £39pp, sgl occ £49) is within half a mile of the path. Single-night stays are generally not accepted in the school summer holidays but enquiries on the day or just before are welcome. The calendar on their website shows their availability. Packed lunches (£6) and luggage transfer (£13) are both on offer as are evening meals if booked in advance. To get there follow the footpaths that are signed off the coastal path that pass through Whitestone Farm (you may need an OS map for this as it is not unknown for the signs to go AWOL).

Becoming a little more testing, the path now makes its way along Damage Cliffs, a National Trust site. The trail then passes by 19th-century **Bull Point Lighthouse** housed in its own secure compound (the Bull Point Pen?), before following the cliff-tops to **Morte Point**, a place so wild it was once referred to locally as 'the place God made last and the Devil will take first'.

Notice that despite all this natural splendour many of the cliffs and peninsulas have such morbid names: Damage Cliffs, Breakneck Point, 'Morte' (French for 'Death') Point; shipwrecks were common here in the 19th century and many of the geological culprits were named appropriately. Indeed, Morte Point was said to be responsible for five shipwrecks in 1852 alone, while

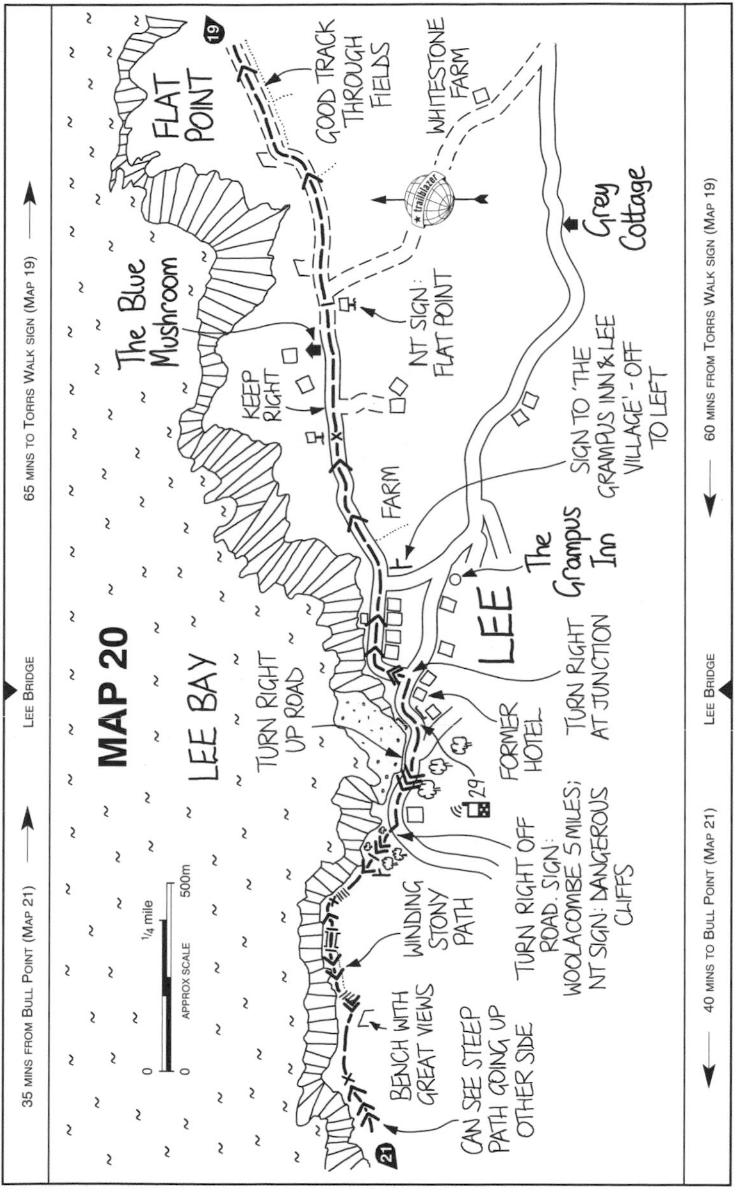

MAP 20
35 MINS FROM BULL POINT (MAP 21)
LEE BRIDGE
65 MINS TO TORRS WALK SIGN (MAP 19)
40 MINS TO BULL POINT (MAP 21)
LEE BRIDGE
60 MINS FROM TORRS WALK SIGN (MAP 19)
APPROX SCALE
0
1/4 mile
0
500m
LEE BAY
FLAT POINT
The Blue Mushroom
GOOD TRACK THROUGH FIELDS
WHITESTONE FARM
trailblazer
Grey Cottage
NT SIGN: FLAT POINT
KEEP RIGHT
FARM
SIGN TO 'THE GRAMPUS INN & LEE VILLAGE' - OFF TO LEFT
The Grampus Inn
LEE
TURN RIGHT AT JUNCTION
FORMER HOTEL
TURN RIGHT UP ROAD
29
TURN RIGHT OFF ROAD. SIGN: WOOLACOMBE 5 MILES; NT SIGN: DANGEROUS CLIFFS
WINDING STONY PATH
BENCH WITH GREAT VIEWS
CAN SEE STEEP PATH GOING UP OTHER SIDE
19
21

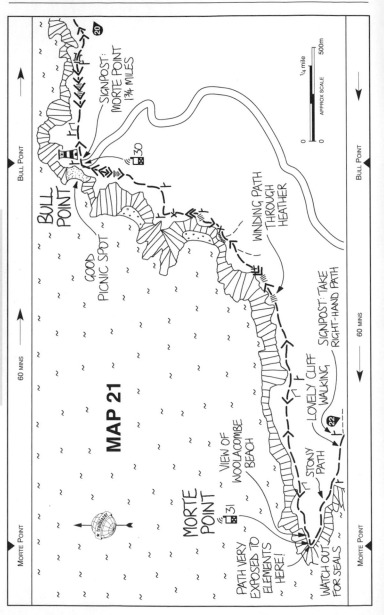

MAP 21

BULL POINT

MORTE POINT

GOOD PICNIC SPOT

SIGNPOST: MORTE POINT 1¾ MILES

WINDING PATH THROUGH HEATHER

SIGNPOST: TAKE RIGHT-HAND PATH

LOVELY CLIFF WALKING

VIEW OF WOOLACOMBE BEACH

STONY PATH

PATH VERY EXPOSED TO ELEMENTS HERE!

WATCH OUT FOR SEALS

60 MINS

1/4 mile

500m

APPROX SCALE

Bull Point

Morte Point

60 MINS

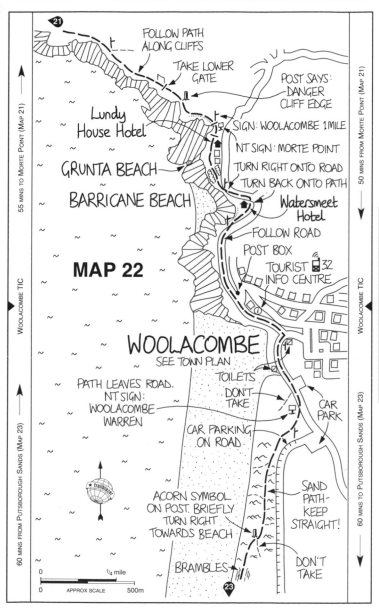

FOLLOW PATH ALONG CLIFFS

TAKE LOWER GATE

POST SAYS: DANGER CLIFF EDGE

Lundy House Hotel

SIGN: WOOLACOMBE 1 MILE

NT SIGN: MORTE POINT

GRUNTA BEACH

TURN RIGHT ONTO ROAD

TURN BACK ONTO PATH

BARRICANE BEACH

Watersmeet Hotel

FOLLOW ROAD

POST BOX

MAP 22

TOURIST INFO CENTRE 32

WOOLACOMBE

SEE TOWN PLAN

TOILETS

PATH LEAVES ROAD. NT SIGN: WOOLACOMBE WARREN

DON'T TAKE

CAR PARK

CAR PARKING ON ROAD

ACORN SYMBOL ON POST. BRIEFLY TURN RIGHT TOWARDS BEACH

SAND PATH - KEEP STRAIGHT!

DON'T TAKE

BRAMBLES

trailblazer

0   1/4 mile
0   APPROX SCALE   500m

55 MINS TO MORTE POINT (MAP 21)

WOOLACOMBE TIC

60 MINS FROM PUTSBOROUGH SANDS (MAP 23)

50 MINS FROM MORTE POINT (MAP 21)

WOOLACOMBE TIC

60 MINS TO PUTSBOROUGH SANDS (MAP 23)

ROUTE GUIDE AND MAPS

Grunta Beach is so named because after one unlucky ship ran aground the cargo of pigs she was carrying ran into the cove – grunting.

As you coax and tease your legs into the final stretch around Morte Point, take time to admire Baggy Point across the bay and stare in awe at the golden sands of Woolacombe's blue-flag beach: surf's up!

WOOLACOMBE

Nestling at the eastern end of Morte Bay, the happy town of Woolacombe has a friendly and pleasant atmosphere. Bustling with surfers in summer, it has all the amenities a coastal-path walker needs – as well as a vast and wonderful **beach** that stretches out to the south for almost two miles (3.2km).

Oddly, the name of the town is said to have nothing to do with the large sheep population that lives hereabouts, but actually comes from Wolmecoma, or 'Wolves Valley', referring to the large wolf population that lived in the woods that existed around here at one time! A small fishing village sprung up centuries later and Woolacombe remained pretty much untouched until a fashion for sea bathing took the country by storm in the Regency period of the early 19th century, leading to the town's conversion into a resort and the construction of some elegant accommodation, some of which still survives.

Services

The helpful and well-stocked **tourist information centre** (☎ 01271-870553, ☐ www .woolacombetourism.co.uk; Easter-Sep Mon-Sat 10am-5pm, Sun Jul-Aug 10am-3pm, Oct to Easter Mon-Sat 10am-1pm) also boasts internet access (£1/15 mins).

For **wi-fi** there's Puffin Café and Jube (see Where to eat). You can take money out at the **cashpoint** at the HSBC on South St (with others that charge for withdrawals at

Jube, Red Barn (see p132) and by the post office – money that you can then spend at the Londis **supermarket** (daily 8.30am-8pm) on West Rd or at Barton **Pharmacy** (Mon-Fri 9am-1pm & 2-6pm, Sat 9am-4pm) opposite. Also on West Rd is the **post office** (Mon-Fri 9am-5.30pm, Sat 9am-12.30pm) at the back of a newsagents. Another **newsagents**, Shirley's (Mon & Tue 6.45am-7pm, Wed-Fri 6.45am-7.30pm, Sat 7am-7.30pm, Sun 7am-6.30pm), near Puffin Café, is well stocked and sells OS maps. Back up on South St near HSBC is a **launderette** (£3 per load).

Where to stay

Campers should head straight for *Woolacombe Sands Holiday Park* (☎ 01271-870569, ☐ www.woolacombe-sands .co.uk; £5-15pp; 🐾 £2.50; WI-FI £3.60/hr; late Mar to Oct) on Beach Rd. Though it's about 15 minutes' walk from the town centre it's a nice place and even has its own bar.

There's no shortage of B&B-style accommodation in Woolacombe, though once again finding places which are suitable for walkers – ie don't mind muddy boots and, most importantly, are willing to accept one-night bookings – is surprisingly difficult. There are, however, two good options on Bay View Rd. The first, *Fairhaven* (☎ 01271-870319, ☐ www.fair havendevon.co.uk; 2D/2D or T; WI-FI; £35-40pp, £45 sgl occ), is a stylish place just a few steps from the path. Rates are at the

---

❏ **Dogs on Woolacombe Beach**

Between April and November dogs are allowed on the beach but only to the south of the stream which lies a couple of hundred metres south of town (ie the main entrance to the beach) – and even then only on a lead. You can release them, however, beyond the large Mill Rock that lies at the back of the beach. There are no restrictions between December and March.

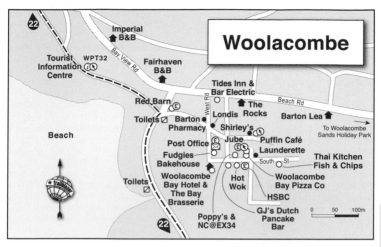

higher end of the spectrum but you are paying for some great views (apart from in the cheaper room) and the fact you don't have to climb the hill out of town.

Just a few metres further up Bay View Rd, *Imperial B&B* (☎ 01271-870594; 1D or T/3F; ☛; WI-FI; small 🐾; £35pp, £50 sgl occ; Apr-Oct) is owned by a local builder (and a relative of one of the owners of Fairhaven). It's a decent place though note that they don't accept one-night bookings in August.

Before you even reach the town there's *Lundy House Hotel* (Map 22; ☎ 01271-870372, 🖳 www.lundyhousehotel.co.uk; 3D/3D or T/2F; ☛; WI-FI; 🐾 £3; £32.50-52.50pp, sgl occ £65-105; Easter to end Oct), with private steps leading directly up from the path. They don't do single-night bookings but for an additional charge will take your luggage to your next accommodation.

You also walk past the large *Watersmeet Hotel* (Map 22; ☎ 01271-870333, 🖳 www.watersmeethotel.co.uk; 1S/13D/9D or T/1T/4F; ☛; WI-FI; £30-87.50pp, sgl occ £40-80), originally built in 1907 as an Edwardian 'Gentleman's residence'.

To find other places in Woolacombe that accept one-night bookings you need to head up Beach Rd. Chic and friendly *The*

Rocks Hotel (☎ 01271-870361, 🖳 www.therockshotel.co.uk; 1S/6D/3T; WI-FI; £39.50-47.50pp, sgl £49-59; add £6 for seaview room) is the first, just 50m up the hill.

About 100m further up, tidy little *Barton Lea* (☎ 01271-870928, 🖳 www.bartonlea.com; 1D/1T/1F; WI-FI; £35-45pp, sgl occ £70) has been providing coastal walkers (amongst others) with accommodation for over 20 years now. The rooms are well furnished.

Woolacombe Bay Hotel (☎ 01271-870388, 🖳 www.woolacombe-bay-hotel .co.uk; Feb-Dec; 33D or T/36F; ☛; WI-FI; £100-125pp, sgl occ £) is by far the grandest place in the town centre; all the rooms are stylish and some are huge. Note that one-night bookings are not accepted for the June half-term and school summer holidays.

Where to eat and drink

Fudgies Bakehouse (☎ 01271-870622; daily 9am-8pm in peak periods, at other times days/hours depend on demand; closed Nov-Feb), on West Rd, is for those who can't wait for Cornwall for their pasty fix. They also serve the locally-made Childhay Manor ice cream with such tempting flavours as Porlock pistachio and Lynmouth lemon meringue.

Puffin Café (☎ 01271-870807; Mon-Thur 9am-3pm, Fri-Sun 9am-5pm; wi-fi free as long as you spend £5), on Barton Rd, is a pleasant laidback café with reasonable prices (full English breakfast £5; cream tea £4). *Poppy's Takeaway* (daily from 10am), on South St, is a worthy rival. Across South St, *GJs Dutch Pancake Bar* (☎ 01271-870992, 🖳 www.gjpancakes.co.uk; Apr-Nov daily 11am-10pm) has a wide variety of pancakes starting from £2.50 for the basic sugar and lemon, rising to £4.50 for the Amsterdammer (cheese, bacon, tomato, mushroom and brie).

There are several other places on South St: *Hot Wok* (Tue-Sat 5.30-11pm, Sun 5.30-10.30pm) is a fairly typical Chinese with dishes from £5. Further up the road are more cheap eats at *Thai Kitchen Fish & Chips* (daily 5.30-9pm) with cod & chips from £7 and curries from £8.

NC@EX34 (☎ 01271-871187, 🖳 www.noelcorston.com; Mar-Nov Sat & Sun noon-3pm & 6-9pm, Wed-Fri 6-9pm), next door to Poppy's, has a delicious menu, much of it locally sourced, including Fowey river mussels (£6.95).

Woolacombe Bay Pizza Company (☎ 01271-871222, 🖳 www.woolacombepizza.co.uk; Apr-Sep daily noon-11pm), opposite HSBC, serves pizzas with standard toppings from £8.50 (free delivery between April and September). Round the corner, *Jube* (wi-fi) is a noisy place with football on the TV and a pounding soundtrack throughout the day. The menu is simple but OK for snacks such as cheesy chips, pizzas (from Woolacombe Bay Pizza Company) and burgers.

On Beach Rd, *The Tides Inn* (☎ 01271-871420, 🖳 www.thetidesinn.co.uk;

food served daily 6-9pm) overlooks the Crazy Golf course from its veranda and has a decent and imaginative menu including venison steak in red wine and redcurrant sauce (£13.75). Below it and part of the same building, *Bar Electric* (Sat & Sun noon-3pm, Wed-Sat 5-9pm) is more of a drinking venue than anything else but also does a mainstream menu of pizzas (from £8.95) and baguettes (from £3.95).

By the main junction in town and with perhaps the best views of the sea, family friendly *Red Barn* (☎ 01271-870264; food served daily 11am-9pm) is one of Woolacombe's livelier places with live music at weekends (Mar-Dec) and a menu including burgers ($1/4$lb cheeseburger £6.95) and breakfasts (Sat & Sun 9.30-11am). The smartest place in town, however, is unsurprisingly *The Bay Brasserie* in Woolacombe Bay Hotel (see Where to stay; Easter to Oct daily noon-11pm, Nov-Dec hours variable), with sandwiches during the day from £7 or for something more substantial you can help yourself to a plate of chilli and lime crab linguine (£14.95).

Transport

[See also pp49-51] As is usual for this path, Woolacombe is once again poorly served by public transport. First Group's No 31 operates to Ilfracombe, as does Filer's No 302, but on Sunday in summer only. First Group also operates the No 303 to Braunton and Barnstaple. There are bus stops on Beach Rd and The Promenade.

The local **taxi** firm is E Zee cabs (☎ 0796-654 8303).

WOOLACOMBE TO BRAUNTON   [MAPS 22-28]

This **$14^3/4$-mile (23.8km; $6^1/2$ hrs inc 10 mins from Velator Bridge to Braunton)** stage is the most diverse in this book. From the cliffs and beaches surrounding Woolacombe and Croyde to the more easygoing terrain through Braunton Burrows – the focal point of the North Devon UNESCO Biosphere Reserve (see box p141) – this is a fulfilling although physically undemanding day's walk.

Magnificent, sweeping views from Baggy Point across the busy sands of Woolacombe and Croyde contrast sharply with the bleaker beauty of Braunton

❏ **Woolacombe to Westward Ho!**
Between Woolacombe and Westward Ho! there are nearly 40 miles of mostly flat and easy walking. For this reason, some choose to cover the miles in just two stages. Whilst doing so means you will get back to the more spectacular parts of the SWCP faster, you also risk exhausting yourself before the final three days to Bude, which are very strenuous indeed. Completing these 40 miles over a longer period of time will allow you to thoroughly explore the towns and villages en route. There is plenty of accommodation en route so a plethora of itineraries is possible (see p29).

This book splits the journey into three sections, but it can be divided into just two stages, or four or more.

Burrows and the lonely Taw Estuary, where the only sounds are the slap of rope against mast or the shrill whistle of an oystercatcher on the wing.

Diverse though the landscape may be on this stage, there can be no doubt that the predominant features are the beaches. There are in fact three vast stretches of golden sand, each separated by a single grassy promontory. The first, Woolacombe, has of course been visible since you rounded Morte Point on the previous stage, and is one of the bigger beaches on the entire path – a vast flat bronze plain that stretches for almost two miles from the town to Baggy Point. Take a stroll around this promontory and you'll then be greeted by the sight of Croyde, Woolacombe's trendier, more glamorous neighbour and rival and a favourite with surfers and families, even though the beach is considerably smaller. While less than an hour's walk from the end of Croyde beach lies the even vaster sands at Saunton.

Indeed, the only disappointment with these beaches is that the SWCP doesn't officially cross any of them, preferring instead to pick its way between the sand dunes at the back of the beach – though only the most pedantic of coastal walkers will choose to stick to the path rather than kick their boots off and stroll along the flats. The exception to this is Saunton Sands, parts of which are used by the army for practice and thus access is limited. But even here the coastal walker is well compensated as the dunes at the back of Saunton form Braunton Burrows Nature Reserve, the largest sand dune system in England and home to rare lizards and snails.

There are numerous places to stop for refreshments along the way including both Croyde and Saunton, though Saunton itself can be bypassed via an alternative path which, if taken, will be the last gradient of any description you'll encounter until Westward Ho!, over two days away. Stick to the main trail, however, and you'll be forced instead to walk along the busy, pavement-

❏ **Important note – walking times**
Unless otherwise specified, **all times in this book refer only to the time spent walking**. You will need to add 20-30% to allow for rests, photography, checking the map, drinking water etc. When planning the day's hike count on 5-7 hours' actual walking.

less Saunton Rd – the worst bit of walking on this path. Continuing on through the Burrows, and along the banks of the Taw – the favoured home of egrets, godwits, herons and oystercatchers – you pass Horsey Island and follow the River Caen, eventually finding yourself on the outskirts of Braunton and the end of this stage.

The route

The day starts simply enough with a walk through the sand dunes of **Woolacombe Warren** and neighbouring **Putsborough Sands**, from where you

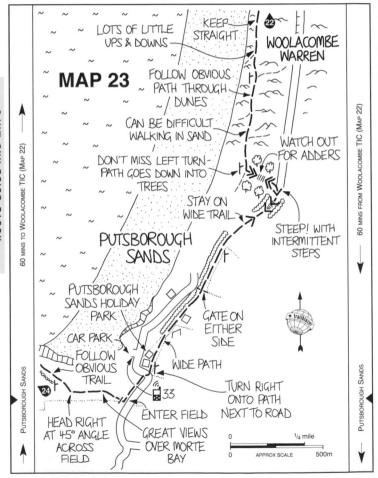

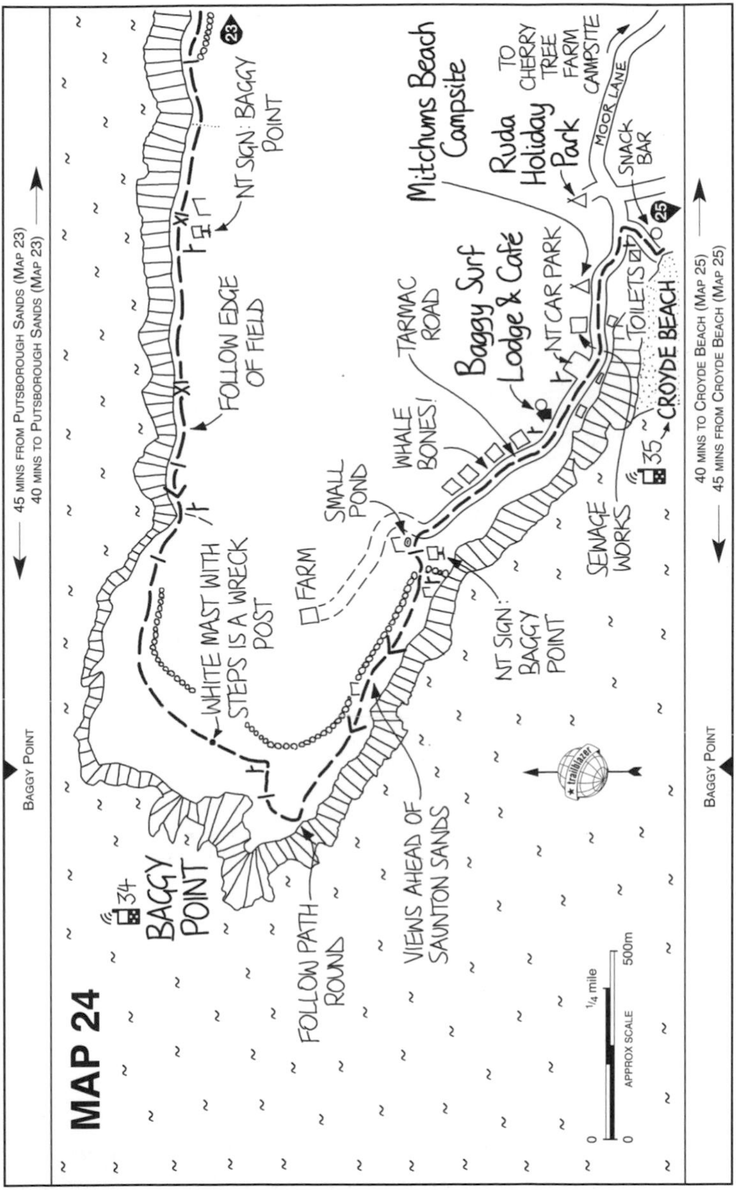

MAP 24

BAGGY POINT

45 MINS FROM PUTSBOROUGH SANDS (MAP 23)
40 MINS TO PUTSBOROUGH SANDS (MAP 23)

23

NT SGN: BAGGY POINT

FOLLOW EDGE OF FIELD

WHITE MAST WITH STEPS IS A WRECK POST

FARM

SMALL POND

WHALE BONES!

TARMAC ROAD

Baggy Surf Lodge & Café

NT CAR PARK

Mitchums Beach Campsite

Ruda Holiday Park

TO CHERRY TREE FARM CAMPSITE

MOOR LANE

SNACK BAR

25

TOILETS

35 → CROYDE BEACH

SEWAGE WORKS

NT SIGN: BAGGY POINT

34 BAGGY POINT

FOLLOW PATH ROUND

VIEWS AHEAD OF SAUNTON SANDS

BAGGY POINT

40 MINS TO CROYDE BEACH (MAP 25)
45 MINS FROM CROYDE BEACH (MAP 25)

¼ mile

APPROX SCALE

0   500m

start the haul to Baggy Point; alternatively, if the tide allows, you can just walk straight along the beach, cutting through the car park at the beach's southern end to rejoin the main trail.

A splendid stroll leads to **Baggy Point**. Owned by the National Trust and a popular spot with climbers, it is also part of an SSSI (see p62) – of scientific interest due to its mixture of Devonian Age (417-354 million years ago) stone. The **white mast** is a 'wreck post' – a spot where, if the sea was too rough to launch a lifeboat but a shipwreck was close enough to the shore, a pulley system would be set up (using a cannon to fire one end of the rope out to the ship) between the point and the ship's mast in order to rescue the stranded sailors. There are tremendous views of Lundy and along the coast to Croyde Bay and Saunton Sands from here.

The clusters of buildings that you can see in the far distance are Westward Ho!, Clovelly and Hartland Point. As you walk around the point admire the views south and imagine the American troops practising for D-day on the sands below you as you stroll into Croyde. General Eisenhower and the Allied

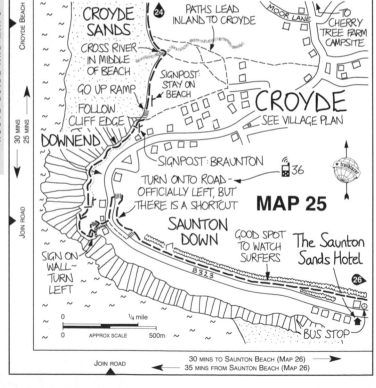

leaders decided that the beaches of Woolacombe, Croyde and Saunton most closely resembled those on France's Normandy coast, and thus they were used for rehearsing for the big day. WWII pillboxes on Croydehoe Farm can still be seen.

CROYDE [Map p138]

Croyde can feel as if its sole purpose is to serve its beach and its world-class surf. However, people were aware of the bay way before surfing took off in Cornwall in the 1960s. The village actually has an ancient heart which you can see if you look amongst the noisy bars of the village centre (which is actually about 15 minutes back from the beach that has earned Croyde its popularity). Indeed, some of the B&Bs and pubs are housed in buildings that are over 300 years old. But if you're not planning on staying in Croyde, you can forego them altogether, for the coast path continues to hug the beach.

The **Village Stores** (Mon-Sat 9am-4pm, Sun 9am-3pm) incorporates a bakery and off-licence, and just a few yards away lies the **post office** (Mon, Tue, Thur & Fri 9am-5pm, Wed & Sat 9am-12.30pm).

If you need money the post office has an **ATM**, as does Billy Budd's (see Where to eat), however both charge £1.85. Debit/credit cards are readily accepted throughout the village but if you're desperate for cash free of charge you will have to go to Braunton.

See p16 for details of the Goldcoast Oceanfest.

Where to stay

Croyde has a number of **campsites**. *Mitchum's* (☎ 0789-189 2897, 🖳 www .croydebay.co.uk; £10-15pp, generally two-night minimum stay; booking recommended especially for the weekend), one of the smaller ones, actually has two locations – one in the village (see village plan) and one by the beach (see Map 24). The opening season changes from year to year (and sometimes only one campsite is open at a time) so check their website for the details.

In contrast *Ruda Holiday Park* (Map 24; ☎ 0844-335 3677, 🖳 www.parkdean touring.com; £14-50 per pitch; mid-Mar to end Oct) is a behemoth and it even has its own Costcutter (mid Mar to end Oct daily 8am-6pm) supermarket and café (daily 10am-6pm, later if resident) – and also a Cascades swimming pool!

Smaller and cheaper than Ruda are *Bay View Farm Campsite* (☎ 01271-890501, 🖳 www.bayviewfarm.co.uk; Easter to end Sep; approx £16) and *Cherry Tree Farm Campsite* (☎ 01271-890495, 🖳 www.cherrytreecroyde.co.uk; £13pp plus a £5-10 bond, see website for details; early June & mid July to early Sep) who, despite advertising a minimum three-night stay policy, will often allow walkers to stay for only one night. To reach the campsite go to the end of Moor Lane then left up Stentaway Lane.

In central Croyde, *The Orchard* (☎ 01271-890364; two-night min on Fri; 🐾; £10 walker & tent; open all year) is the only site in Croyde to allow dogs.

Just as you enter Croyde and slightly before the National Trust car park for Baggy Point, *Baggy Surf Lodge and Café* (see Map 24; ☎ 01271-890078, 🖳 www .baggys.co.uk; 3-bed, 4-bed and 6-bed dorms/4D/1 flat; WI-FI; dorm bed £25-30pp, £50pp in double room) has magnificent views over Croyde beach and offers – surprisingly, given it's such a surfer town – the only **hostel** accommodation. It also has its own **café** (daily 9am-6pm, summer also 6-10pm), which serves a Full Baggy's Breakfast for £4.95.

For **B&Bs** look on Down End which runs into Hobbs Hill – the centre of the village – at its southern end. Close to both the beach and the path you will find *Breakers* (☎ 01271-890101, 🖳 www.croydebreaks .co.uk; 2D or T/1F; WI-FI; from £35pp, sgl occ £45-70; Easter to end Nov), which may not take one-night bookings at the weekend; the small and family-run *Shuna Guesthouse* (☎ 01271-890537, 🖳 www .shunaguesthouse.co.uk; 6D; 🛏; WI-FI; £40-55pp, sgl occ £72-100), and *Oamaru* (☎

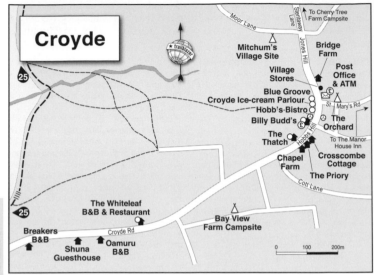

Croyde

To Cherry Tree
Farm Campsite

Moor Lane

Mitchum's
Village Site

Bridge
Farm

Village
Stores

Post
Office
& ATM

Blue Groove
Croyde Ice-cream Parlour

St. Mary's Rd

Hobb's Bistro

The
Orchard

Billy Budd's

The
Thatch

To The Manor
House Inn

Chapel
Farm

Crosscombe
Cottage

The Priory

Cott Lane

The Whiteleaf
B&B & Restaurant

Croyde Rd

Bay View
Farm Campsite

Breakers
B&B

Shuna
Guesthouse

Oamuru
B&B

0   100   200m

01271-890765, 🖳 www.oamarucroyde.co
.uk; 3D/1T; 🛏; WI-FI; £27.50-30pp, sgl occ
£41.25-45).

A little closer to town and with its own
restaurant you will find *The Whiteleaf* (☎
01271-890266, 🖳 www.thewhiteleaf.co
.uk; 3D/1T/1F; 🛏; WI-FI; 🐾 £5; £41-46pp,
sgl occ £62-67). More central still is *The
Thatch* (☎ 01271-890349, 🖳 www.the
thatchcroyde.com; 10D/5T/2F; three rooms
share facilities; 🛏; WI-FI; 🐾; £30-55pp, sgl
occ £40-110) whose rooms are in four different buildings, including some at Billy
Budd's (see Where to eat), Crosscombe
Cottage and The Priory. Almost opposite,
Chapel Farm (☎ 01271-890429, 🖳
www.chapelfarmcroyde .co.uk; 2D/1D or
T/1T/1F; WI-FI; £33-40pp; Mar-Oct) is only
slightly less ancient, having been built in
1709. The owners have been running the
show here for around nine years now but
still retain their enthusiasm.

The most charming place to stay is
right in the noisy centre. The pretty,
thatched *Bridge Farm* (☎ 01271-890422;
1D en suite/1D & 1F share facilities; 🛏;
🐾; £32.50-37.50pp; Easter to end Oct), 8

Jones Hill, is, according to the owner, at
least 400 years old. The place is quirky and
full of character – as you'd expect from a
house this old – and the owners are pleasant
too. It also provides a lovely contrast to the
brash and noisy street outside.

Where to eat and drink
Croyde Ice Cream Parlour, in the centre on
Hobb's Hill, is famed in the village because
of its use of clotted cream as one of its toppings! For a pub meal try *Billy Budd's* (☎
01271-890606; summer Sun-Thur 11am-
11pm, Fri & Sat 11am-midnight, winter
Thur & Sun 5-11pm, Fri & Sat 11am-mid-
night; WI-FI) which has Sky TV and does pizzas (from £7.95) to eat-in or take away and
'subs' such as tuna and onion (£5.95). Pretty
much next door, *The Thatch* (see Where to
stay; daily 8.30am-10pm) is known for its
beef nachos (£10.25). It's a large pub with
surfboards hanging off the walls and daily
surf reports adorning them as well as real
ales such as Proper Job and Tribute.

The Manor House Inn (☎ 01271-
890225, 🖳 www.themanorcroyde.com;
food served noon-10pm), a little out of

town at 39 St Mary's Rd, also serves real ales and you can get seabass, ginger and lime fishcakes for £10.95.

For an à la carte menu made up of local produce there is *The Whiteleaf Restaurant* (see Where to stay; Mon-Sat 7-8.30pm, booking essential); a roast loin fillet of venison costs around £17 (as all the produce is seasonal prices can vary). *Hobb's Bistro* (☎ 01271-890256, ☐ www .hobbsincroyde.co.uk; Mar-Oct daily 7pm-late) is the smartest place in town and has some great dishes including a seafood chowder made with haddock and salmon (£13.95). Just a few yards down the hill, *Blue Groove* (☎ 01271-890111, ☐ www .blue-groove.co.uk; Mar-Dec daily 9am to

late) serves breakfasts, lunches and evening meals, though it's probably best known for its *moules frites* – mussels and fries – for £10.95.

Transport

[See also pp49-51] Stagecoach Devon's 308 runs regularly to Barnstaple, via Saunton, Braunton and Chivenor. If you wish to go north to Woolacombe or Ilfracombe you will need to change in either Braunton or Barnstaple. There are **bus stops** near Billy Budd's in the centre of the village as well as nearer the beach close to Ruda Holiday Park.

For a **taxi** try Croyde Coastal (☎ 07788-703188).

Having navigated **Croyde Sands** a small headland – **Downend** – separates you from Saunton. Round this and the path drops down to the busy B3231 before running around the side of The Saunton Sands Hotel (see p141).

From the car park below the hotel the path heads up the slope on the tarmac, turning off right halfway up (unmarked) to walk around the back of houses before rejoining the B3231 for an unpleasant stretch of pavement-less road walking. Thankfully, there is an alternative.

The alternative route begins after you reach Saunton Sands Hotel, though the price you pay is to climb instead the biggest gradient between Woolacombe and Westward Ho!. This route then passes through a couple of fields before dropping down via elegant Saunton Court to a crossroads, where you rejoin the main trail.

SAUNTON   [MAP 26, p140]

Despite Saunton's far larger beach there are fewer amenities than in Croyde, with scant options for food and accommodation. The beach is renowned for its wildlife, with the possibility of spying oystercatchers, cormorants, and numerous other birds. From the shore you might see porpoise, seals and possibly dolphins in summer. Fisherman have reported foxes and even otters sneaking up behind them in attempts to steal their catch!

The nearest **campsite** is approximately two miles along the road (B3231) although there is an alternative way leading via a series of footpaths to the top of the campsite; this is worth doing as the road is very busy. From the road by Saunton Court, turn left up unmade Hannaburrow Lane to Long

Lane (first turning on the right). Follow this to the road junction, then take a right down Lobthorn Lane, following it down the hill until you can see Lobb Field campsite. *Lobb Fields Caravan and Camping Park* (☎ 01271-812090, ☐ www.lobbfields.com; Mar-Oct; 🐾 £2; rates for walkers on request but expect to pay less than £10pp inc shower/toilet facilities) has internet access, its own snack bar and a laundry room.

There are two **B&Bs**, both a short jaunt inland from the beach and close to where the path leaves the road. *Norboro Guesthouse* (☎ 01271-816210, ☐ www .norboroguesthouse.co.uk; 2D/2T; £30-45pp, sgl occ £45 depending on the time of year) is an Edwardian house that has views across the Burrows. *Saunton Minibreak*

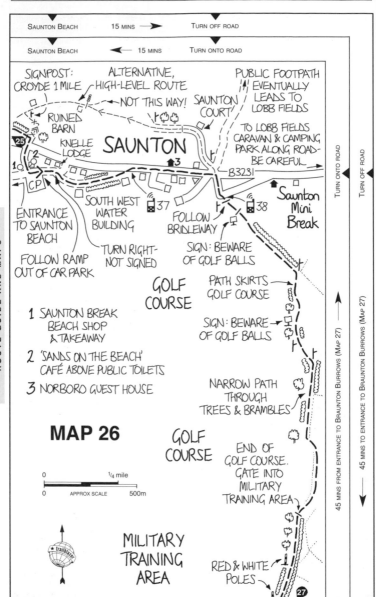

SAUNTON BEACH   15 MINS →   TURN OFF ROAD

SAUNTON BEACH   ← 15 MINS   TURN ONTO ROAD

SIGNPOST: ALTERNATIVE,   PUBLIC FOOTPATH
CROYDE 1 MILE   HIGH-LEVEL ROUTE   EVENTUALLY
    — NOT THIS WAY!   LEADS TO
RUINED   SAUNTON   LOBB FIELDS
BARN   COURT
KNELLE   SAUNTON   TO LOBB FIELDS
LODGE   3   CARAVAN & CAMPING
25   PARK ALONG ROAD -
2   BE CAREFUL
1   B3231
CP

ENTRANCE   SOUTH WEST   37   Saunton
TO SAUNTON   WATER   Mini
BEACH   BUILDING   FOLLOW   38   Break
    BRIDLEWAY
FOLLOW RAMP   TURN RIGHT -   SIGN: BEWARE
OUT OF CAR PARK   NOT SIGNED   OF GOLF BALLS

    GOLF   PATH SKIRTS
    COURSE   GOLF COURSE

1 SAUNTON BREAK   SIGN: BEWARE
  BEACH SHOP   OF GOLF BALLS
  & TAKEAWAY

2 'SANDS ON THE BEACH'
  CAFÉ ABOVE PUBLIC TOILETS

3 NORBORO GUEST HOUSE   NARROW PATH
    THROUGH
    TREES & BRAMBLES

MAP 26   GOLF   END OF
    COURSE   GOLF COURSE.
    GATE INTO
0   1/4 mile   MILITARY
    TRAINING
0   APPROX SCALE   500m   AREA

    MILITARY   RED & WHITE
trailblazer   TRAINING   POLES
    AREA   27

TURN ONTO ROAD   TURN OFF ROAD

45 MINS FROM ENTRANCE TO BRAUNTON BURROWS (MAP 27)

45 MINS TO ENTRANCE TO BRAUNTON BURROWS (MAP 27)

ROUTE GUIDE AND MAPS

B&B (☎ 01271-813672, 💻 www.saunton-minibreak.co.uk; 1T; 🐾; WI-FI; £30pp, £40-45 sgl occ), 1 Warren Cottages, consists of one room (with its own entrance, well-stocked breakfast bar and fridge) in a family home.

The Saunton Sands Hotel (Map 25; ☎ 01271-80212, 💻 www.sauntonsands.com; 90 rooms; 🐕; WI-FI (charge may be made); £101-212pp, web rates £54-109pp, sgl occ £81-153.50) is owned by the local Brend chain. This whitewashed colossus is something of a landmark; indeed, you will see this hotel from as far away as Westward Ho!. The rooms are comfortable without being remarkable – but, given the views along the three-mile beach from most of them, who cares! Note that in the summer school holidays it's week-long stays only,

and at Easter guests are required to stay for a minimum of three nights. Food is served daily (7.30-10am, 12.30-2pm, 6.45-9.30pm).

For **food** there are two options by the sand. *The Saunton Break* is a takeaway (9am-5pm, depending on weather and season) which sells pasties and sandwiches, whilst the recently rebranded *Sands on the Beach* (☎ 01271-891288; Mar-Oct daily 9.30am-9.30pm, hours variable at other times) is owned by the hotel and has a sizeable balcony with magnificent views. A large bowl of mussels costs £12.25, whilst burgers are £10.95. Both establishments will accept payment by card.

If wishing to get a **bus** (see pp49-51), Stagecoach Devon's No 308 runs regularly to Barnstaple, Braunton and Croyde.

The path then heads off along the edge of a **golf course** and through a **military training area** to **Braunton Burrows** (see box below).

Leaving the Burrows you take a sharp left-turn before **Crow Point**, a spit of land popular with fishermen, before taking a path atop an embankment that was built in 1857 to keep marsh, estuary and river apart. During WWII the marshes were turned into a dummy airfield in the hope of distracting the enemy's attention away from the nearby Chivenor Airbase.

On the other side of the estuary you can see the villages of Appledore and Instow, possibly still a day's walk away. Wrecked boats and small fishing craft

---

❏ Braunton Burrows and The North Devon UNESCO Biosphere Reserve

Braunton Burrows is the centre of The North Devon UNESCO Biosphere Reserve (💻 www.northdevonbiosphere.org.uk), an area of 3300 sq km that, according to the United Nations, encompasses a 'world-class environment' rich in wildlife and containing a mix of extraordinary landscapes. As well as the Burrows, the Biosphere Reserve includes **Braunton Marsh and Great Field**, the **Taw and Torridge Estuary**, **Fremington Quay** and **Northam Burrows Country Park**. No wonder, therefore, that there are 63 SSSIs (see p62) within the area's boundaries.

The Burrows themselves are home to a wide variety of flora and fauna, as well as the largest sand dune system in Britain. There are nearly 500 recorded species of **flowering plants** on the site, including such rarities as the sand toadflax, which is unique to the Burrows, the water germander and the round-headed club-rush. There are also 33 species of **butterfly**, over half of Great Britain's regularly recorded species. For enthusiasts, resident is the small blue butterfly (*Cupido minimus*), although you are far more likely to spot a dark green fritillary (*Argynnis aglaja*) or marbled white (*Melanargia galathea*).

Guided tours of the Burrows run regularly throughout the summer. Details can be found on the website.

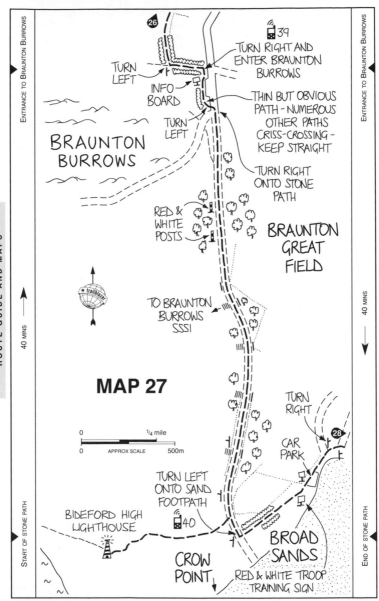

26

📱39

TURN RIGHT AND
ENTER BRAUNTON
BURROWS

TURN
LEFT

INFO
BOARD

THIN BUT OBVIOUS
PATH - NUMEROUS
OTHER PATHS
CRISS-CROSSING -
KEEP STRAIGHT

TURN
LEFT

BRAUNTON
BURROWS

TURN RIGHT
ONTO STONE
PATH

RED &
WHITE
POSTS

BRAUNTON
GREAT
FIELD

TO BRAUNTON
BURROWS
SSSI

MAP 27

0   ¼ mile
0   APPROX SCALE   500m

TURN
RIGHT

28

CAR
PARK

TURN LEFT
ONTO SAND
FOOTPATH

📱40

BIDEFORD HIGH
LIGHTHOUSE

BROAD
SANDS

CROW
POINT

RED & WHITE TROOP
TRAINING SIGN

ENTRANCE TO BRAUNTON BURROWS

40 MINS

START OF STONE PATH

ROUTE GUIDE AND MAPS

ENTRANCE TO BRAUNTON BURROWS

40 MINS

END OF STONE PATH

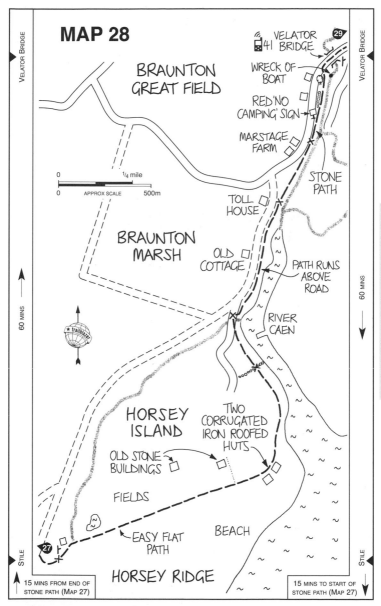

MAP 28

BRAUNTON
GREAT FIELD

VELATOR
📱41 BRIDGE **29**

WRECK OF
BOAT

RED 'NO
CAMPING' SIGN

MARSTAGE
FARM

STONE
PATH

0   ¼ mile

0   APPROX SCALE   500m

TOLL
HOUSE

BRAUNTON
MARSH

OLD
COTTAGE

PATH RUNS
ABOVE
ROAD

★ trailblazer

RIVER
CAEN

HORSEY
ISLAND

TWO
CORRUGATED
IRON ROOFED
HUTS

OLD STONE
BUILDINGS

FIELDS

BEACH

EASY FLAT
PATH

27

HORSEY RIDGE

15 MINS FROM END OF
STONE PATH (MAP 27)

15 MINS TO START OF
STONE PATH (MAP 27)

60 MINS

60 MINS

STILE

STILE

ROUTE GUIDE AND MAPS

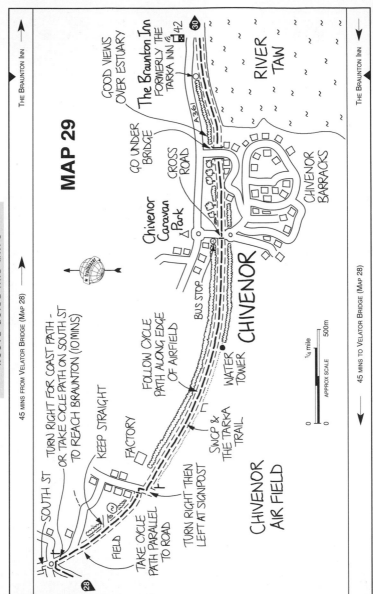

← THE BRAUNTON INN →

45 MINS FROM VELATOR BRIDGE (MAP 28) →

MAP 29

GOOD VIEWS OVER ESTUARY

The Braunton Inn
FORMERLY THE
TARKA INN 🍺 42

30

RIVER TAW

A361

GO UNDER BRIDGE

CROSS ROAD

Chivenor Caravan Park

CHIVENOR BARRACKS

Trailblazer

BUS STOP

FOLLOW CYCLE PATH ALONG EDGE OF AIRFIELD

SOUTH ST

TURN RIGHT FOR COAST PATH – OR TAKE CYCLE PATH ON SOUTH ST TO REACH BRAUNTON (10MINS)

KEEP STRAIGHT

FACTORY

FIELD

TAKE CYCLE PATH PARALLEL TO ROAD

TURN RIGHT THEN LEFT AT SIGNPOST

SWCP & THE TARKA TRAIL

WATER TOWER

CHIVENOR

CHIVENOR AIR FIELD

28

¼ mile
0
0   APPROX SCALE   500m

← 45 MINS TO VELATOR BRIDGE (MAP 28) →

THE BRAUNTON INN →

are dotted about in the sand as you stroll on along the riverside. Between Braunton and the Burrows lie the 350 acres of the **Great Field** – a famous archaeological site and one of only two medieval field systems to survive in England. Some of the 'strip' system which parcelled this land up is still visible.

Eventually you arrive at **Velator Bridge** and, a few hundred metres further on, a roundabout where you have a choice: turn right and continue along the Coast Path, which here, together with the Tarka Trail (see box p34), makes its merry way along a disused rail-track. Or you can turn left, cross the roundabout to South St and head along the disused railway line in the other direction on the marked footpath to Braunton. **Braunton** has several services and is a pleasant-enough village but if you feel up to walking a further 5½ miles there is more to distract you in Barnstaple.

BRAUNTON   [Map p147]

Recorded as Brantona in the Domesday Book, some claim Braunton to be the largest village in England and, as a result, it's more like a small town. Settlement is reputed to have begun in earnest around **St Brannock's Church**, originally founded by the eponymous saint in c550AD as part of his campaign to convert the Celts. His remains are said to be buried there. Braunton's debt to the saint is celebrated with a three-day festival of music, dance and literature around 26 June, St Brannock's Day.

Braunton and District Museum (☎ 01271-816688, 🖳 www.devonmuseums .net/braunton; Mon-Sat 10am-4pm, hours may differ slightly in winter; free) has several interesting displays on the local area spread over two floors. **Braunton Countryside Centre** (☎ 01271-817171, 🖳 www.brauntoncountrysidecentre.org.uk; Apr-Oct Mon-Sat 10am-4pm; free but donation appreciated) has displays about the local nature and also offers 'Braunton Explorers' – personal GPS systems (£5 per day) that guide you via a set of headphones around different areas of interest in the area including the Burrows. Also available are tours of Braunton's industrial past and another entitled 'D-day and the dunes.'

At the time of research the tourist information centre that was in the car park on Caen St had closed; it was unclear when or if it might reopen. There are some leaflets at the museum. For **food** there is a Co-op (Mon-Sat 7am-9pm, Sun 9am-6pm) on

Exeter Rd and if you wish to send any postcards from your trip so far there is a **post office** (Mon-Fri 9am-5.30pm, Sat 9am-12.30pm) on the same road. For a **chemist** there's a Lloyds Pharmacy (Mon-Fri 9am-6pm, Sat 9am-5pm) on Caen St. Nearby, there is an **ATM** outside the Lloyds bank on Caen St. Finally, there's a **launderette** (daily 8am-6pm) on Chaloner's Rd.

Where to stay

Campers should head for Chivenor Caravan Park (see p148), 1¼ miles (2km) further along the trail.

There are several **B&Bs** on quiet South St: *The Brookfield* (☎ 01271-812382, 🖳 www.thebrookfield.co.uk; 1D/3D or T/1F; ☛; WI-FI; £31.50-36.50, sgl occ £50) is a large and luxurious place; comfortable *Stockwell Lodge* (☎ 01271-817128, 🖳 www.stockwell-lodge.co.uk; 1S/1T/3F; ☛; WI-FI; £27-32pp, sgl £44), and cute, thatched *Little Thatch Annexe* (☎ 01271-815328, 🖳 www.littlethatchbraun ton.co.uk; 1D; WI-FI; £30pp, sgl occ £35).

The other options are scattered around town. On Exeter Rd you will find the more contemporary *Green Gates* (☎ 01271-814564, 🖳 www.green-gates.co.uk; 1D/1D suite/1T or F; ☛; WI-FI; £34-36.50pp, sgl occ £45-50), whilst on Saunton Rd there is smart, homely *Lime Tree Nursery* (☎ 01271-816193, 🖳 www.limetreenursery.co .uk; 1S/1F; WI-FI; £24.50-32pp, sgl £45), and the thatched 15th-century *Folly Farm Cottage* (☎ 01271-812148, 🖳 www.folly

farmcottage.com; 1D/1F; WI-FI; £30-33pp, sgl occ £45). At 26 South Park, *Annexe B&B* (☎ 01271-814436, 🖳 www.annexe-accommodation-braunton.co.uk; 1D; WI-FI; £30pp; self service breakfast) offers just one room, though it has its own living room and private entrance; whilst on North St you will find sweet little *North Cottage* (☎ 01271-812703, 🖳 www.northcottagebraun ton.co.uk; 2S share facilities/1D or T/1D; 🐾; WI-FI; £27.50pp).

Finally, right at the northern end of town, near St Brannock's Church, is the 300-year-old cottage *The Laurels B&B* (☎ 01271-812872; 1S/1D/1T, all share facilities; 🖤; 🐾; £30pp) that has been running for over 40 years and is the oldest B&B in the village.

The George Hotel (☎ 01271-812029, 🖳 www.thegeorgehotel-braunton.co.uk; 1S/2D/4T; 🖤 (some rooms share facilities); WI-FI; 🐾; £35-50pp) is a large establishment in the heart of Braunton and it has a thriving bar, restaurant and Thai takeaway (see Where to stay).

Where to eat and drink

Several pubs here serve good food. At *The Agricultural Inn* (☎ 01271-817980, 🖳 www.theaggi.co.uk; food served Easter-Oct Mon-Sat noon-3pm & 5-9pm, light snacks 3-5pm, Sun from 12.30pm, Nov-Easter noon-2.30pm & 5-9pm; 🐾; WI-FI),'The Aggie' as it is known locally, fresh local produce is used and you can get a 10oz rump steak for £13.75. *The Mariners Arms* (☎ 01271-813160; food served end May-Sep Mon-Sat noon-2pm & 6.30-9pm, Sun noon-2.30pm & 6.30-9pm, Oct-May no food at lunch Mon-Thur; well-behaved 🐾) has a big beer garden & Sky TV. All the food is home-cooked; ham, egg & chips costs £5.50. *The George Hotel* (see Where to stay; food served Mon-Sat 8am-2.30pm & 5.30-10pm, Sun 9am-10pm) serves a mixed menu but their speciality is Thai – a weeping tiger (sliced sirloin in a spicy sauce) costs £12.95. *The White Lion* (☎ 01271-813085, 🖳 www.whitelionbraun

ton.co.uk; daily 5-10pm; WI-FI) is known for its Indian food, which it reckons is the best curry this side of Calcutta!

On the opposite side of Caen St there is *Good Fortune* (☎ 01271-817889; Mon & Wed-Sat 5-11pm, Sun 6-11pm), a fairly standard Chinese takeaway, and a few metres further on the *Wild Thyme Café* (☎ 01271-815191, 🖳 www.wildthymecafe.co .uk; school summer holidays Sun-Fri 9am-4pm, Sat 9am-5pm; Sep to mid July daily 9am-4pm, Jan to mid Feb Thur-Mon 9am-4pm), a popular and award-winning café specialising in homemade pizzas (from £5.95) and 'rustic baguettes' from £4. Further along, *CJ's* (☎ 01271-812007; Feb to mid Dec daily 8.30am-4pm) is a sandwich bar which is good for those who aren't planning on stopping for too long. Toasted paninis cost from £3.10.

For an à la carte menu there is *At One* (☎ 01271-814444, 🖳 www.atonedining .com; summer daily 10am-4pm & 6.30-9.30pm, winter daily 10am-4pm, Tue-Sat 6.30-9pm); their steamed Taw Estuary mussels in a creamed white wine sauce starter costs £5.95. They also serve breakfasts and lunches.

For fish 'n' chips try *South Sixteen* (☎ 01271-816445; Mon-Thur 11.30am-2pm & 5-9pm, Fri & Sat to 9.30pm), a restaurant and takeaway which also serves poached salmon in a white wine and chive sauce (£7.70). The best-known eatery in town, however, is the renowned *Squires Fish 'n' Chips Restaurant* (☎ 01271-815533; Mon-Sat 11.45am-10pm), which raises the frying of our humble national dish to an art form and again provides a takeaway service.

Transport

[See also pp49-51] For **buses**, Stagecoach Devon's No 308 passes through Braunton regularly on its way between Croyde and Barnstaple and its 21A service picks up there whilst travelling between Ilfracombe and Westward Ho!. First's No 3 service stops here on its journey between Ilfracombe, Croyde and Barnstaple.

ROUTE GUIDE AND MAPS

Braunton

Annexe B&B

South Park

Lower Park Road

Green Gates B&B

Wrafton Road

Exeter Road

St Brannock's
The Laurels B&B

East St

Chaloners Rd

The Agricultural Inn

Braunton & District Museum & Tourist Info

The George Hotel

Co-op

Post Office

Little Thatch Annexe

Stockwell Lodge B&B

Lloyds Pharmacy

Braunton Laundry

At South Sixteen
One

Toilets

South St

Library

CJ's

The Mariners Arms

The Brookfield B&B

North Cottage B&B

Caen St

Braunton Countryside Centre

Squires Fish 'n' Chips Restaurant

North St

The White Lion

Good Fortune

Wild Thyme Café

Saunton Rd

Lime Tree Nursery B&B

Folly Farm Cottage B&B

0   100   200m

BRAUNTON TO INSTOW   [MAPS 29-34]

After the delights of the previous stages, this **12½-mile (20km; 5hrs 35 mins inc 10 mins Braunton to Velator Bridge)** leg is distinctly more low key. The path continues with the Tarka Trail out of Braunton, hugging the banks of the Taw as it takes a riparian path into Barnstaple – the biggest town on this trail. It then continues along the tarmac until approximately two miles (45 minutes) before Instow, where it suddenly deviates to follow a dyke around the marshes of East Yelland and Instow Barton. (You could, however, stay on the tarmac Tarka Trail which remains straight, providing an alternative to the SWCP.) Scenically, this day is few people's favourite; but, while the terrain will not supply you with much to talk about, the day's walk does pass through some interesting areas. Bird spotters will find much to enjoy with the views across the estuary where egret, curlew and oystercatchers stalk, as well as on Home Farm Marsh, a habitat for all sorts of wildlife. Railway historians might also find something to titillate their senses during the long plod from Chivenor to Fremington, the path being decorated with various bits of ironmongery from its days as part of the long-defunct North Devon Railway. Gourmands will tuck in to the heavenly cream teas at Fremington Quay; while historians will enjoy the architecture of Barnstaple, which also offers numerous options for refreshment.

Even if none of the above particularly appeals there is always the consolation that this walk, and the next to Westward Ho! are, on the whole, pancake flat. As such, it's possible to count off the miles rapidly and indeed it's not unusual for walkers to notch up a mightily impressive 24 miles and combine the two stages in one long day. So, if disused railways, military airfields and mud-flats aren't your thing, prepare to get your marching boots on, clock up the miles and look forward to the more spectacular sights on the path ahead.

The route
The day begins by following the edge of **Chivenor Airfield**. Currently a base for the Royal Marines, the airfield also has two RAF search-and-rescue helicopters stationed there. Just before coming to a roundabout a right turn will lead you to the barracks, while turning left will lead you onto the A 361, on the other side of which is *Chivenor Caravan Park* (Map 29; ☎ 01271-812217, 💻 www .chivenorcaravanpark.co.uk; £11-13 per pitch; 🐾 £1; Mar to end Sep). The site has a small shop, free showers and will charge mobile phones for a small fee.

Shortly after joining Taw Estuary you come to *The Braunton Inn* (Map 29; ☎ 01271-816547, 💻 www.vintageinn.co.uk/thebrauntoninnbarnstaple; food served daily noon-9pm), formerly called The Tarka Inn, a huge crenelated place that used to be a manor house called Heanton Court. It has wonderful views straight over the estuary from its patio, guest ales are served and much of the menu is reasonably priced – a three-course lunch menu (Mon-Sat), for example, costs £10; Sun lunch costs £7.95-9.95.

The route continues on along Taw River to Barnstaple. If you don't wish to visit the town there is an alternative route over the busy new **Taw Bridge**. But if you've got the time, Barnstaple is worth a look.

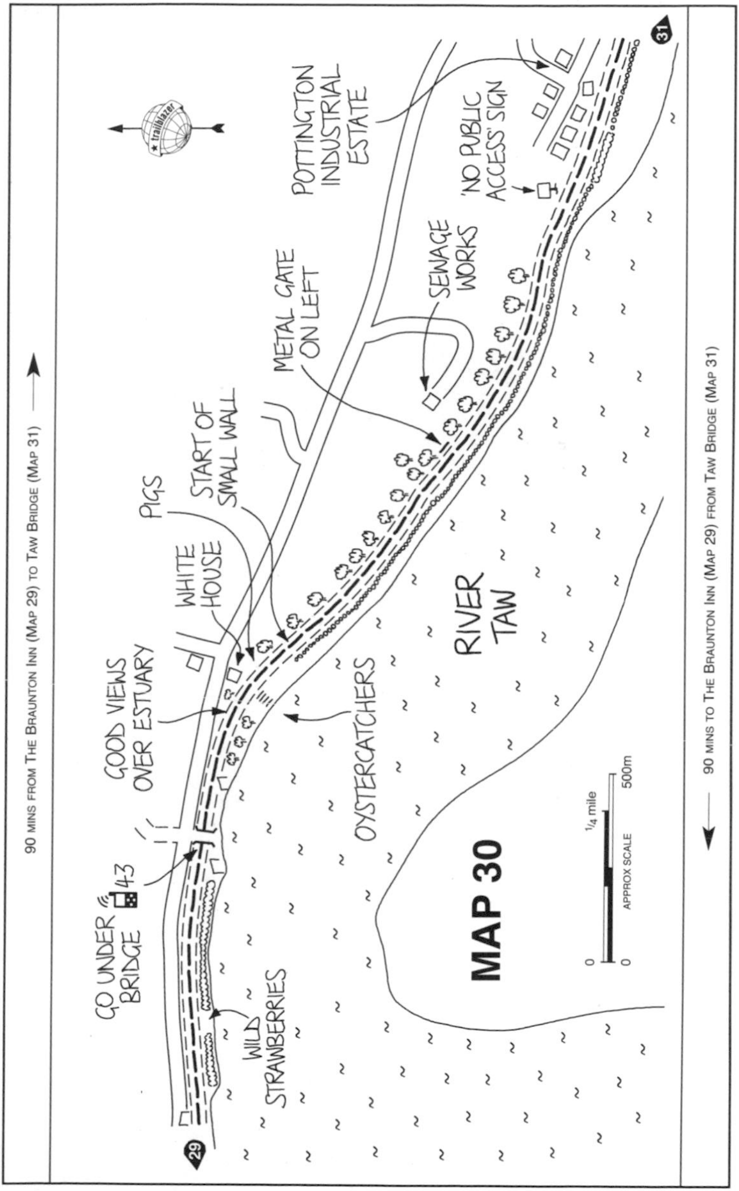

MAP 30

APPROX SCALE

1/4 mile

0 · · · · · 500m

ROUTE GUIDE AND MAPS

29

31

POTTINGTON INDUSTRIAL ESTATE

'NO PUBLIC ACCESS' SIGN

SEWAGE WORKS

METAL GATE ON LEFT

START OF SMALL WALL

PIGS

WHITE HOUSE

GOOD VIEWS OVER ESTUARY

GO UNDER BRIDGE 43

WILD STRAWBERRIES

RIVER TAW

OYSTERCATCHERS

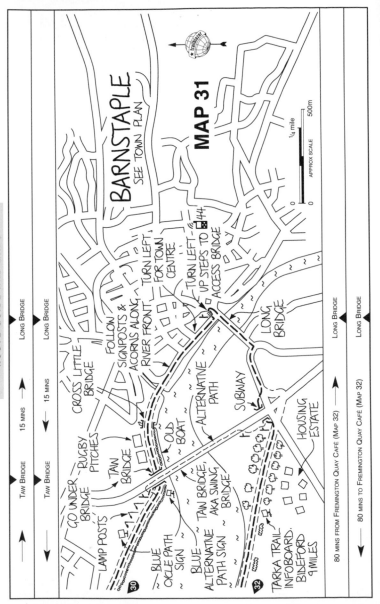

MAP 31

BARNSTAPLE
SEE TOWN PLAN

¼ mile
APPROX SCALE
0   500m

TAW BRIDGE   15 MINS   TAW BRIDGE

LONG BRIDGE   15 MINS   LONG BRIDGE

GO UNDER BRIDGE — RUGBY PITCHES

CROSS LITTLE BRIDGE

FOLLOW SIGNPOSTS & ACORNS ALONG RIVER FRONT

TURN LEFT FOR TOWN CENTRE

TURN LEFT — UP STEPS TO ACCESS BRIDGE

p144

LAMP POSTS

TAW BRIDGE

OLD BOAT

ALTERNATIVE PATH

LONG BRIDGE

SUBWAY

BLUE CYCLE PATH SIGN

TAW BRIDGE AKA SWING BRIDGE

BLUE ALTERNATIVE PATH SIGN

HOUSING ESTATE

TARKA TRAIL INFOBOARD. BIDEFORD 9 MILES

30

32

80 MINS FROM FREMINGTON QUAY CAFÉ (MAP 32)

LONG BRIDGE

80 MINS TO FREMINGTON QUAY CAFÉ (MAP 32)

LONG BRIDGE

BARNSTAPLE [Map p153]

Barnstaple acts as a centre of sorts for North Devon. Historically one of the first four boroughs in England, by the advent of the Norman period the town was already busy and prosperous. Having originally been granted the right to mint coins during the reign of King Athelstan, it had long been a centre of commerce. Indeed, Athelstan also granted the town a charter to hold a market and a fair – both of which remain major cultural and financial contributors to the town today.

Barnstaple Fair is still held each September and the **Pannier Market** (☎ 01271-379084, 🖳 www.barnstaplepannier market.co.uk; Mon-Sat) still operates six days per week for most of the year. (*Pannier*, incidentally, are the wicker baskets that were once used by traders to bring their goods to the market.) Stalls differ daily but are usually a real smörgåsbord, varying from antiques and jewellery to pet supplies and homemade preserves. The market building was constructed in 1855 but plans for the area's development had already begun following the completion of the **Guildhall** in 1827. A remarkably impressive building, the Guildhall includes portraits of – amongst previous councillors – the poet John Gay, who was born in the town. A contemporary of both Samuel Johnson and Alexander Pope, Gay is best known for his satire *The Beggar's Opera*.

On the other side of Butcher's Row from the market and Guildhall are the **parish church**, in existence since 1107, and the Grade-I listed **St Anne's Chapel**. Dating from the early 14th century, the chapel has some splendid features including what some consider to have been a 'charnel house' – a place for storing bones. There are also some wonderfully gruesome gargoyles dotted around the place. Other historical sites which may be of interest include the **Castle Mound**, across the bridge over the Yeo, which was originally the base of a wooden Norman castle; and, if you have the time to be inspecting the doors of almshouses, you'll find bullet holes from the Civil War in one of the doors at **Penrose Almshouses** in Litchdon St.

Barnstaple Heritage Centre (☎ 01271-373003, 🖳 www.barnstapletown council.co.uk; May-Sep Tue-Sat 10am-5pm, Oct-Apr Tue-Fri 10am-4.30pm, Sat 10am-3.30pm; £3.50), on the riverside, runs historical tours of the town and a 'heritage trail', which is free on a Thursday. Should your arrival in town not coincide with any available tour the centre itself aims to take you on a 'Journey through time' with fun displays of the town's past. As well as the Heritage Centre there is **Museum of Barnstaple & North Devon** (☎ 01271-346747, 🖳 www.northdevonmu seum.org; Easter to Oct Mon-Sat 10am-5pm, Oct to Easter to 4pm; free); it has permanent exhibitions including The Tarka Gallery, which deals with the local wildlife, and North Devon at War.

See p16 for details of festivals and events in Barnstaple.

Services

Barnstaple is not short of services and anything you need should be easy to source. In the same building as the museum, the **tourist information centre** (☎ 01271-346747, 🖳 www.staynorthdevon.co.uk; Easter to Oct Mon-Sat 10am-5pm, Oct to Easter to 4pm) is staffed by very helpful and knowledgeable locals and is worth a visit. The **post office** (Mon-Fri 9am-5.30pm, Sat 9am-12.30pm) is on the corner of Boutport and Queen Sts but still only a brief stroll from the river.

The large number of computers in the town **library** (☎ 01271-388593; Mon & Tue 9am-6pm, Wed 10am-5.30pm, Thur & Fri 9.30am-5pm, Sat 9.30am-4pm) on Tuly St, means getting **internet access** (£2.20/30 mins) shouldn't be a problem. There is also a **local studies section** (Mon & Tue 9.30am-5pm, Wed 10am-1pm, Thur & Fri 9.30am-5pm) that is well worth a perusal.

If you're in need of **walking gear** there's a Mountain Warehouse (☎ 01271-372253, 🖳 www.mountainwarehouse.com; Mon-Sat 9am-5.30pm, Sun 10am-4pm) and a Millets (Mon-Sat 9am-5.30pm, Sun 10am-4pm) on the High St, while for **cameras and repairs** there is a Jessops (Mon-

Sat 9am-5.30pm, Sun 10.30am-4.30pm), also on the High St, and the more locally based J & A Cameras (☎ 01271-375037, 💻 www.jandacameras.co.uk; Mon-Sat 9am-5.30pm) on Gammon Walk. Back on the High St there's also a Boots the **Chemist** (Mon-Sat 8.30am-6pm, Sun 10.30am-4pm) and a Superdrug (Mon-Sat 9am-5.30pm, Sun 10am-4pm), **bookshops** such as Waterstones (Mon-Sat 9am-5.30pm, Sun 10.30am-4.30pm) and WH Smith (Mon-Sat 8.30am-5.30pm, Sun 10am-4pm), and a small Co-op **supermarket** (daily 7am-7pm). Out near the railway station there is also a large Tesco.

There are several **ATMs** in the centre including at both HSBC and NatWest.

Where to stay

The accommodation scene in Barnstaple is surprisingly poor. It's not that the accommodation itself is of a low quality, more that there just isn't much of it. This is particularly true when it comes to **B&Bs**, of which there are only a few that we can recommend.

The Old Vicarage (☎ 01271-328504, 💻 www.oldvicaragebarnstaple.co.uk; 1D/1T/1F; ☛; wi-fi; £35-40pp, sgl occ £60), one of the more central options, was once upon a time home to the vicar for the nearby Holy Trinity Church but now finds a purpose by providing accommodation for tired walkers. A five-minute walk from the path, before you enter into town itself, *Crossways* (☎ 01271-379120, 💻 www.barnstaplebedandbreakfastcrossways.com; 2D/2T; wi-fi; from £35pp, sgl occ £45) has good-sized rooms, some of which have been recently refurbished.

The Olive Branch (☎ 01271-370784, 💻 www.olivebranchdevon.co.uk; 1S/1T/1F; £25-35pp) is a pub opposite the post office. It's rather basic but is very close to the action.

Regarding **hotels**, the local Brend chain has three fine representatives in Barnstaple. Right in the centre, there is the elegant Georgian *Royal and Fortescue* (☎ 01271-342289, 💻 www.royalfortescue.co.uk; 4S/44D or T/1F; ☛; wi-fi £6 for 90 mins, £10 24 hrs; 🐾 £5; room only £45-70pp, sgl £30-50). The second, *Park Hotel* (☎ 01271-

372166, 💻 www.brend-hotels.co.uk/the park; 3S/17D/15D or T/4T; ☛; room only £31-41pp, sgl £57-72), is only a five-minute walk away on quieter Taw Vale, overlooking Rock Park and the Taw beyond. Both of these hotels charge £8/11.50 extra for a continental/cooked breakfast.

Surpassing both in terms of style, however, *The Imperial* (☎ 01271-345861, 💻 www.brend-imperial.co.uk; 10S/63D or T/2F; ☛; 🐾 (annexe only); wi-fi; room only £48.50-92.50pp, sgl £87) has rooms whose prices reflect the extra sumptuousness and luxury on offer. A continental/cooked breakfast is £7.50/12.50pp.

Where to eat and drink

There are quite a few options for food in Barnstaple. By far the best, *Boston Tea Party* (☎ 01271-329070, 💻 www.boston teaparty.co.uk/cafe/barnstaple; Mon-Sat 8am-6pm, Sun 9.30am-5pm; wi-fi; 🐾), on Tuly St, is a spacious and modern café that serves a great and varied menu. There is a fine selection of homemade cakes and pastries. A West Country breakfast costs £6.75 whilst a burger will only set you back £7.25. Also available are slightly more alternative dishes such as tagines, and a mackerel and couscous salad.

Close by, on Holland Walk, both *Sheppard's Sandwich Bar* (☎ 01271-375383; Mon-Sat 9am-4pm; 🐾) and *Café Karumba* (☎ 01271-374354; Mon-Sat 9am-5pm, Sun to 4pm) sell sandwiches and coffee to both eat-in and takeaway.

If you're truly determined to get a card stamped or a strawberry-flavoured latte there are also representatives of the national chains including *Costa* (Mon-Sat 7am-6pm, Sun 9am-5pm) and *Caffè Nero* (☎ 01271-379247; Mon-Sat 8am-5.30pm, Sun 9am-5pm), both on the High St. For a quainter experience, try *Old School Coffee House* (☎ 01271-372793; Mon & Wed 9.15am-3pm, Tue & Thur-Sat 9.15am-4pm), 6 Church Lane. It's an interesting place that seems to concentrate more on good service rather than putting syrup in coffee; if Costa is not your thing this probably is. There is a varied menu, all for less than £6: a soup & roll costs a remarkably reasonable £2.75.

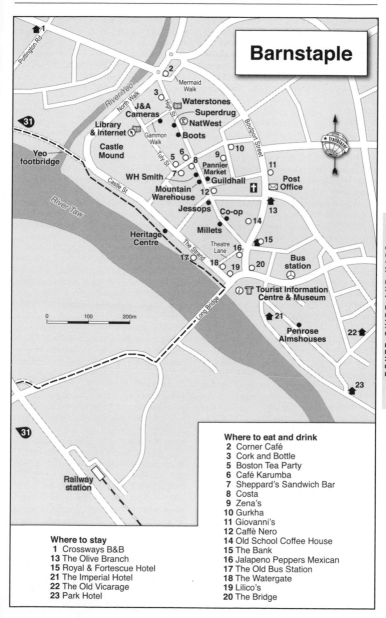

Barnstaple

Mermaid Walk

River Yeo
North Walk
High St.

Waterstones

J&A Cameras
Superdrug

NatWest

Library & Internet
Gammon Walk
Boots

Castle Mound
Turf St.

Yeo footbridge

Castle St.

River Taw

WH Smith

Pannier Market

Guildhall

Mountain Warehouse

Jessops

Co-op

Millets

Heritage Centre

The Strand

Theatre Lane

Bus station

Post Office

Boulport Street

Pottington Rd.

trailblazer

ROUTE GUIDE AND MAPS

Tourist Information Centre & Museum

Penrose Almshouses

Long Bridge

0   100   200m

Railway station

Where to stay
1 Crossways B&B
13 The Olive Branch
15 Royal & Fortescue Hotel
21 The Imperial Hotel
22 The Old Vicarage
23 Park Hotel

Where to eat and drink
2 Corner Café
3 Cork and Bottle
5 Boston Tea Party
6 Café Karumba
7 Sheppard's Sandwich Bar
8 Costa
9 Zena's
10 Gurkha
11 Giovanni's
12 Caffè Nero
14 Old School Coffee House
15 The Bank
16 Jalapeno Peppers Mexican
17 The Old Bus Station
18 The Watergate
19 Lilico's
20 The Bridge

The only place actually on the river between The Braunton Inn (formerly Tarka Inn), outside Chivenor, and the café at Fremington, *The Old Bus Station Café* (☎ 01271-372975, 💻 www.theoldbusstation .co.uk; Tue-Sun 10am-3pm, longer if busy; 🐾) sells Grand Italia coffee, sandwiches/paninis, jacket potatoes and cream teas and also has outdoor seating.

Not far off the path – if you're willing to take a small diversion after Yeo Footbridge – *The Corner Café* (☎ 01271-859555; Tue-Sat 7.30am-4pm; WI-FI; 🐾) is a homely little place that does a special such as vegetable curry or cauliflower cheese everyday for £3.

There are also a few pubs that do food. On the High St *The Cork and Bottle* (☎ 01271-326703; daily 11am-11pm, Fri & Sat to midnight, food served Mon-Sat 11.45am-3pm, Sun noon-3pm; 🐾) does Sunday roasts for £4.95 and a pudding to follow for £1.50. It also serves real ales. *The Bridge* (☎ 01271-343189; food served Mon-Sat noon-3pm & 5.30-10pm, Sun noon-2.30pm & 6-9.30pm, food not served Sun evening in winter) does lunchtime specials for £5.95 as well as a deal where two 8oz steaks and a bottle of wine cost £25.

Wetherspoons has its representative – *The Watergate* (☎ 01271-335410, 💻 www.jdwetherspoon.co.uk; food served 9am-10pm; WI-FI) facing towards the river on The Strand; a beer and burger costs £5.60.

With a great decorative ceiling *The Bank* (☎ 01271-324446; Mon-Fri 11am-3pm & 6-10pm, Sat 10am-5pm & 6-10pm), adjoining The Royal & Fortescue Hotel, started life as a merchant's house some 300 years ago. The menu is imaginative and varied and includes such unusual items as tortilla pancakes filled with seafood in a white-wine cream (£12.95).

For a little spice, *Jalapeno Peppers Mexican Takeaway* (☎ 01271-328877, 💻 www.jalapeno-peppers.co.uk; Sun-Thur from 7pm, Fri & Sat from 6pm) sells burritos

for £7.95, while for something Hispanic, near Long Bridge there's *Lilico's Tapas Lounge & Bar* (☎ 01271-372933, 💻 www.lilicos.co.uk; food served Mon-Thur 11am-2.30pm & 5.30-9.30pm, Fri & Sat 11am-5pm & 5.30-9.30pm) where delicious dusted calamari costs £4.95. At 35 Boutport St, *Giovanni's* (☎ 01271-321274, 💻 www.giovannisdevon.co.uk; Mon-Sat noon-2.30pm & 6-11pm) is, as you may have already guessed, an Italian restaurant with spaghetti bolognaise for £7.25.

There are two good options north of Pannier Market on Market St. *Zena's* (☎ 01271-378844, 💻 www.zenasrestaurant .com; food served Mon-Sat 8.30-11.30am & noon-3pm, school summer holidays Thur-Sat 6-9pm), at 1 Market St, sits by its own courtyard next to the market; its Mediterranean menu is great, it regularly wins awards for being the top restaurant in the region, and it's open for breakfasts too.

A few steps further north, *Gurkha* (☎ 01271-377665, 💻 www.gurkharestaurent .com; Tue-Sat noon-2.30pm & 5.30-11pm) is a Nepalese place that thankfully takes more care with its food than it does with the spelling of the name of its website. Its interesting menu includes such dishes as *lasun chicken* (cooked with garlic, onion, capsicum and spices) for £7.95.

Transport

[See also pp49-51] Barnstaple is the only place on the path to be connected with the national **rail** network. First Great Western runs regular services to Exeter, from where you can connect with other services.

Barnstaple is also very well served by **buses**, with regular services (Filer's No 301, 303 & 309; First's Nos 1, 2, 3 & 303; Stagecoach's Nos 21/21A, 85/85C, 155, 308, 315 & 319) running to Lynton, Ilfracombe, Woolacombe, Croyde, Bideford, Westward Ho!, Clovelly and Hartland. Bude can be accessed by connecting with Jackett's 219 service from Hartland.

From Barnstaple the route follows a long straight path decorated with benches and shelters – mud and sand to one side and fields, in the main, on the other – eventually turning in just before **Penhill Point** and arriving at **Fremington Quay**.

ROUTE GUIDE AND MAPS

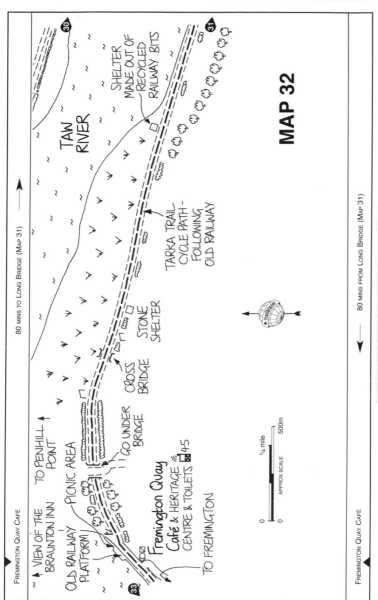

MAP 32

80 MINS TO LONG BRIDGE (MAP 31)

80 MINS FROM LONG BRIDGE (MAP 31)

FREMINGTON QUAY CAFÉ

FREMINGTON QUAY CAFÉ

TAW RIVER

VIEW OF THE BRAUNTON INN

TO PENHILL POINT

OLD RAILWAY PLATFORM

PICNIC AREA

Fremington Quay
Café & HERITAGE
CENTRE & TOILETS

TO FREMINGTON

GO UNDER BRIDGE

CROSS BRIDGE

STONE SHELTER

TARKA TRAIL
CYCLE PATH -
FOLLOWING
OLD RAILWAY

SHELTER
MADE OUT OF
RECYCLED
RAILWAY BITS

30

31

33

¼ mile

500m

APPROX SCALE

trailblazer

FREMINGTON QUAY [MAP 32, p155]

A tranquil spot and a lovely place for a rest, Fremington Quay used to be the busiest port between Bristol and Land's End. The import of coal and the export of, amongst other things, local clay and pottery led to the area thriving throughout the first half of the 20th century. The railway finally closed in 1982; a replica railway station (the old one is on the other side of the trail) houses **Fremington Quay Heritage Centre**.

There are toilets but you have to pay to use them. The centre shares a building and space with *Fremington Quay Café* (☎ 01271-268720, 🖳 www.fremingtonquay.co .uk; daily Apr-Oct 9am-5pm, Nov-Mar 10.30am-4.30pm), a popular place with walkers, cyclists and locals. Serving breakfast until 11am, plus lunches, drinks and snacks, their cream teas (£3.95) are, to put it simply, divine.

Leaving the quay behind, the path crosses the small **bridge** to some disused **lime kilns** on your right. Fields continue to accompany the path on the one side, marshes on the other. **Home Farm Marsh** used to be the site of a dairy farm but since 2002 has been owned by the Gaia Trust, a charity that aims to protect the countryside by promoting sustainable farming and wildlife conservation. Due to the trust's work in returning much of the marsh to its original state as a wetland, wild flowers and birds are once again flourishing – look out for little egret, skylark and bittern. There is a 2km walking route that you can follow around the marsh with information boards helping you to ascertain what wildlife to look out for. (Note: dogs are not allowed on this land). Stray off the path towards the water and you may come across a **granite cross**, erected in memory of Lady Hilda McNeill who drowned there whilst trying to rescue a child in 1904. Be warned that **the waters of the estuary are very fast-running – do not go in**! Note also, that **dogs** are not allowed within the marsh.

The path then runs between **Isley Marsh Nature Reserve** and **East Yelland Marsh**, both of which form part of the estuary's SSSI. Isley Marsh, whilst owned by the RSPB, is mostly consumed by the sea at high-tide so has no breeding birds nesting on it. It is, however, an important habitat for resting birds and between there and the other marshes there is a chance of seeing anything from barn owls to kingfishers. Less spectacular but every bit as fascinating as the kingfisher, East Yelland Marsh is also known to be home to greater horseshoe bats.

The path ambles around Instow Barton Marsh before following the sands of the estuary into Instow. (Note: if walking around windswept marshes doesn't appeal, you can continue along the disused railway track all the way into Instow).

INSTOW   [Map p159]

Instow (🖳 www.instow.net) is a pretty little village, the main highlight of which is its beach and the views it commands across the confluence of the Taw and Torridge rivers. It is a pleasant place to relax in at the end of a day's walk and contrasts splendidly with the hustle and bustle of Barnstaple.

For railway enthusiasts, where the North Devon Yacht Club now stands used to be Instow Railway Station and for those with a nose for trivia, **Instow signal box** (bank holidays and some Sundays, Easter-Oct 2-5pm, Nov-Easter 2-4pm; free, donation appreciated) was the UK's first Grade-II listed signal box.

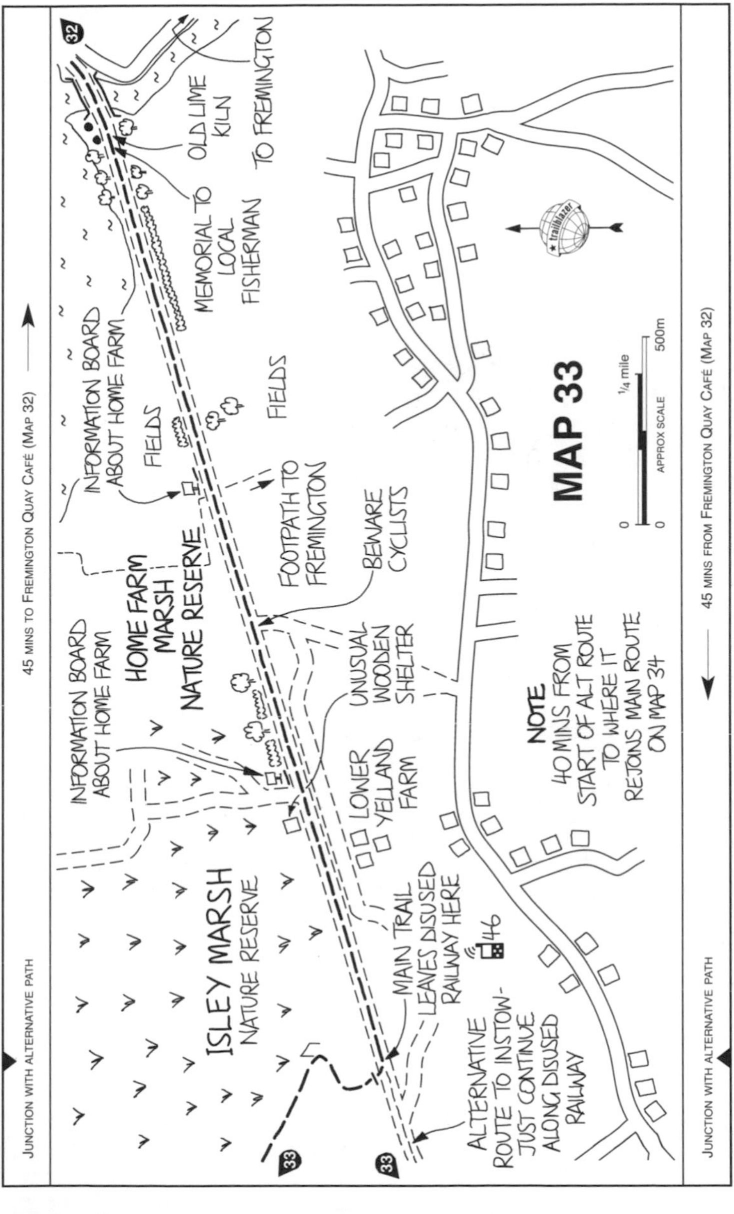
45 MINS TO FREMINGTON QUAY CAFÉ (MAP 32)
JUNCTION WITH ALTERNATIVE PATH
32
OLD LIME KILN
TO FREMINGTON
MEMORIAL TO LOCAL FISHERMAN
INFORMATION BOARD ABOUT HOME FARM
FIELDS
FIELDS
FOOTPATH TO FREMINGTON
HOME FARM MARSH NATURE RESERVE
INFORMATION BOARD ABOUT HOME FARM
BEWARE CYCLISTS
UNUSUAL WOODEN SHELTER
LOWER YELLAND FARM
ISLEY MARSH NATURE RESERVE
MAIN TRAIL LEAVES DISUSED RAILWAY HERE
46
ALTERNATIVE ROUTE TO INSTOW- JUST CONTINUE ALONG DISUSED RAILWAY
33
33
trailblazer
MAP 33
0
1/4 mile
APPROX SCALE
0
500m
NOTE
40 MINS FROM START OF ALT ROUTE TO WHERE IT REJOINS MAIN ROUTE ON MAP 34
45 MINS FROM FREMINGTON QUAY CAFÉ (MAP 32)
JUNCTION WITH ALTERNATIVE PATH

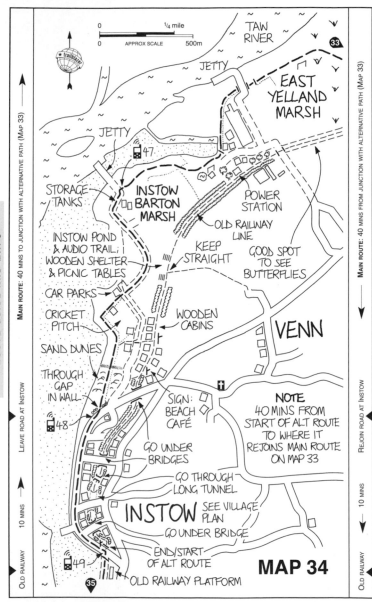

MAIN ROUTE: 40 MINS TO JUNCTION WITH ALTERNATIVE PATH (Map 33)

MAIN ROUTE: 40 MINS FROM JUNCTION WITH ALTERNATIVE PATH (MAP 33)

ROUTE GUIDE AND MAPS

TAW RIVER

33

JETTY

EAST YELLAND MARSH

JETTY

47

STORAGE TANKS

INSTOW BARTON MARSH

POWER STATION

OLD RAILWAY LINE

INSTOW POND & AUDIO TRAIL; WOODEN SHELTER & PICNIC TABLES

KEEP STRAIGHT

GOOD SPOT TO SEE BUTTERFLIES

CAR PARKS

CRICKET PITCH

WOODEN CABINS

VENN

SAND DUNES

THROUGH GAP IN WALL

48

SIGN: BEACH CAFÉ

NOTE
40 MINS FROM START OF ALT ROUTE TO WHERE IT REJOINS MAIN ROUTE ON MAP 33

GO UNDER BRIDGES

GO THROUGH LONG TUNNEL

INSTOW SEE VILLAGE PLAN

GO UNDER BRIDGE

END/START OF ALT ROUTE

49

OLD RAILWAY PLATFORM

35

MAP 34

LEAVE ROAD AT INSTOW

10 MINS

OLD RAILWAY

REJOIN ROAD AT INSTOW

10 MINS

OLD RAILWAY

On the other side of the estuary, through the sails and seagulls, Appledore glistens on a summer's day and if you are willing to bypass Bideford there is a **ferry** (🖳 www .instow.net/ferry.htm) that will take you directly there. Weather permitting, it runs daily throughout the summer months for two hours either side of high tide between 8am and 9pm; the service operates between Instow ferry slip, opposite John's Supermarket, and Appledore Quay. You should always check notices in the villages themselves for the actual operating times. An adult single fare is £1.50, and dogs travel and are charged at the skipper's discretion.

The village feels a little like Porlock Weir in that it has an air of serenity about it, although, also similarly, there are amenities here. For **general supplies** there is John's Supermarket (daily 8am-6 or 7.30pm depending on season), which also includes the **post office** (Mon-Fri 9am-5.30pm, Sat 9am-12.30pm). There is an **ATM** in the shop but it charges £1.85.

For **accommodation** close to the path try *The Wayfarer Inn* (☎ 01271-860342, 🖳 www.thewayfarerinn.co.uk; 5D or T/2F; 🐾; WI-FI; £40pp, £50 sgl occ). It is the first place you come to as you head into town along the beach and is also signed from the Tarka Trail. The rooms are simple but smart and the whole place is very welcoming.

Other possibilities in Instow include *Lovistone* (☎ 01271-860676, 🖳 www.lovi stone.co.uk; 2D; ☛; WI-FI; £32.50pp, sgl occ £45), on the B3233, which has a small communal TV room. There is also the rather austere-looking *Springfield House* (☎ 01271-860895, 🖳 www.springfield-instow.com; 2D private facilities; ☛; 🐾; WI-FI; £42.50pp, sgl occ £65) up the hill on New Rd, which has drying facilities for walkers, a wood-burner, and for a small charge will take baggage on to your next destination. More established, *The Commodore Hotel* (☎ 01271-860347, 🖳 www.commodore-instow.co.uk; 1S/24D or T; ☛; WI-FI; £72-80pp, sgl £82-118.50, sgl occ full rate for rooms with view; dinner, B&B rates also available) is the largest place on the front and is a grand and sophisticated whitewashed affair.

For **food** and refreshments there are several good options. *The Bar* (☎ 01271-860624, 🖳 www.thebarinstow.co.uk; food Mon-Sat noon-2.30pm & 6-8.30pm, Sun noon-8pm, breakfast summer Sat & Sun 9-11.30am; WI-FI; 🐾) serves real ales, locally sourced steaks, and fish specials. In *Instow Arms* (☎ 01271-860608, 🖳 www.instow arms.com; breakfast summer daily 8.30am-noon, lunch noon-2.30pm, light-bites 3-6pm, dinner 6-9.30pm; winter daily 9.30-11.30am, Mon-Sat noon-2.30pm & 6-9.30pm, Sun noon-8pm; WI-FI; 🐾 in the bar) you should make sure you look up and check out the wonderful painting on the ceiling by a local artist. There is a strong focus on locally sourced seafood and Exmouth bay mussels cost £11.95. *The Boathouse* (☎ 01271-861292, 🖳 www.in stow.net/boathouse; food daily noon-2pm, Mon-Sat 6-9.30pm, Sun 7-9pm) is also decorated splendidly, with surfboards hanging off the ceiling and mopeds displayed on the walls. Much of its seafood is served straight off the beach and it has an extensive fish

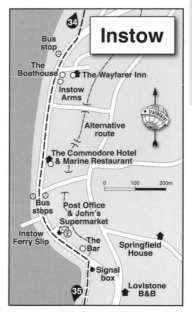

specials menu. Clovelly lobster and crab salad (available in season) costs £29.

The Wayfarer Inn (see p159; daily noon-2.30pm & 6-9pm) serves a full menu as well as bar snacks and daily specials, has a good-sized beer garden, and you can eat your fish dinner whilst the man who caught it sups at the bar. *The Marine Restaurant* at The Commodore Hotel (see p159; restaurant Mon-Sat 7-8.45pm Sun noon-1.15pm & 7-8pm – booking essential in the evening) serves à la carte and adjusts its

menu daily with a strong focus on local and seasonal food. Food is also available in the bar (daily 10am-noon morning coffee, noon-2pm light lunches, 3-5.30pm cream teas, 6.30-8.45pm light meals).

Instow is well-served by public transport. In addition to the **ferry** service (see p159) First's Nos 1 & 2 and Stagecoach's Nos 21 & 315 **buses** run through the town regularly en route between Bideford and Barnstaple (see pp49-51).

INSTOW TO WESTWARD HO!   [MAPS 34-39]

This **11-mile (17.6km; 4hrs 50 mins)** stage is where the coastal path and the Tarka Trail shake hands, embrace and bid a final, fond farewell to each other. Nevertheless, though you finally leave the otter and its old railway line behind at Bideford by crossing the Torridge River, the path still remains flat and easy all the way to Westward Ho!.

From Bideford it follows a slightly incoherent path that twists and turns its way between estuary-edge, road and woodland all the way to Appledore. Leaving this pretty village behind, the route meanders through Northam Burrows Country Park before finally arriving in Westward Ho!, which is not as bad as some will have you believe (though the exclamation mark at the end of

ROUTE GUIDE AND MAPS

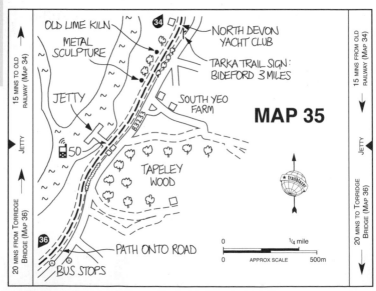

the name does tend to raise expectations that the town struggles to satisfy). There are plenty of options for refreshment on this straightforward stage and you would be well advised to enjoy them as tomorrow the easy walking ends.

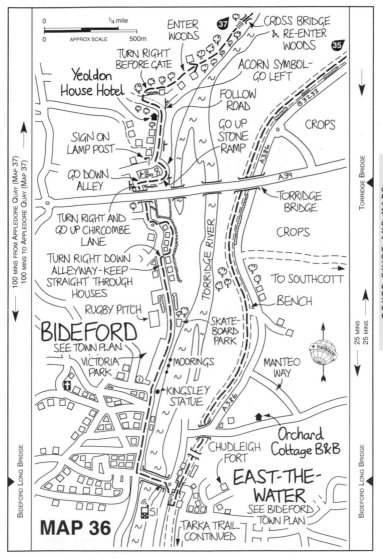

ROUTE GUIDE AND MAPS

So, get a good night's sleep in Westward Ho! and prepare yourself to re-embrace the sharp ups and nigh-on-vertical downs of the jagged North Devon coast!

The route

From Instow continue along the tracks to **East-the-Water** (Stagecoach's No 21/21A **bus** service, see pp49-51, calls here) where you cross the Torridge via the historic Long Bridge to **Bideford**. Looking across the river you can see the route you will follow when leaving the town, as well as the one you've just finished.

BIDEFORD

'All who have travelled through the delicious scenery of North Devon must needs know the little white town of Bideford, which slopes upwards from its broad tide-river paved with yellow sands, towards the pleasant upland in the west.'
Charles Kingsley, *Westward Ho!*

The 'little white town' of Bideford has a long and rich history spanning from Roman times. Pivotal to the town's existence is its position on the Torridge and since the 16th century onwards its primary function has been as a port and place of trade. One of the town's most famous residents, Sir Richard Grenville, set sail from Bideford on several expeditions to the New World. He is also, famously, the subject of Tennyson's poem, *Revenge*, following his death fighting the Spanish during the Battle of Flores in 1591.

There is evidence of The Quay having been here in some form since 1619 and it was refurbished in 2006, a project that included the construction of the **Quay Fountain**, which at high tide shoots 24 jets of water up into the air and out over the river. The 24 jets are supposed to mirror the 24 arches that hold up **Long Bridge**. First constructed from oak in 1280 as a pack-horse bridge, it replaced what was a dangerous ford – the name Bideford is derived from 'By the ford'. Originally the bridge had a chapel at either end. The Quay is also a departure point for ferries to Lundy Island (see box p121).

The current church, **St Mary's**, is actually the third to have been built on the site, having been constructed in 1865 around the original Norman tower. Inside, the font is thought to be from 1080 and is thus the oldest relic in town.

Other sites in Bideford include **Chudleigh Fort** (see Map 36, p161) in East-the-Water, above the path, erected in 1643 during the civil war to defend the town but now an ornamental garden; and the **Pannier Market** – held in Bideford since 1272, when the town was granted charter to hold a market by Henry III, and located on the same site since 1675, though the current building dates 'only' from 1884. Today, as ever, there is as rich a variety of stalls, with trading taking place on Tuesdays and Saturdays year-round. The area is now slightly rundown in parts, though it is also the most interesting of quarters to browse around. Should you have the time **Bideford Heritage Trail** takes you on a tour around the town's most historically significant areas. Information about the tour can be found at the tourist office. If more walking isn't your idea of fun **Burton Art Gallery and Museum** (☎ 01237-471455, 🖥 www .burtonartgallery.co.uk; July-Sep Mon-Fri 10am-5pm, Sat 10am-4pm, Sun 11am-4pm, Oct to June Mon-Sat 10am-4pm, Sun 11am-4pm; free) boasts a number of interesting artefacts and houses a scale replica of Long Bridge, displaying its various forms down the ages. There is also information on many of the town's most famous residents including Edward Capern (1819-94), aka the Postman Poet, a man who could obviously multitask; and the story of the trial of the Bideford witches – who in 1682 became the last women in England to be hanged for witchcraft.

Services

Bideford has a good selection of services. The **tourist information centre** (☎ 01237-

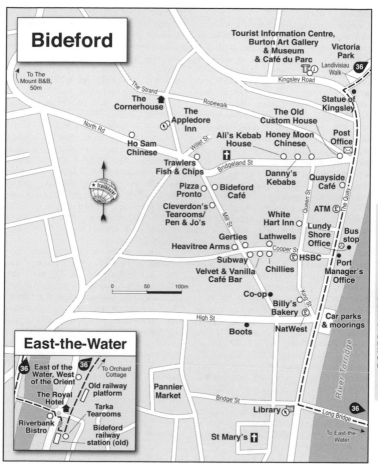

Bideford

To The Mount B&B, 50m

The Strand

The Cornerhouse

Ropewalk

North Rd

The Appledore Inn

Willet St

Ho Sam Chinese

Ali's Kebab House

Bridgeland St

Trawlers Fish & Chips

Pizza Pronto

Bideford Café

Cleverdon's Tearooms/ Pen & Jo's

Mill St

Gerties

Lathwells

Heavitree Arms

Cooper St

Subway

Velvet & Vanilla Café Bar

Chillies

Co-op

Billy's Bakery

Boots

NatWest

High St

Tourist Information Centre, Burton Art Gallery & Museum & Café du Parc

Victoria Park

Landivisiau Walk

Kingsley Road

The Old Custom House

Statue of Kingsley

Honey Moon Chinese

Post Office

Danny's Kebabs

Quayside Café

Queen St

ATM

White Hart Inn

Lundy Shore Office

Bus stop

HSBC

Port Manager's Office

King St

Car parks & moorings

River Torridge

ROUTE GUIDE AND MAPS

trailblazer

0   50   100m

East-the-Water

East of the Water, West of the Orient

To Orchard Cottage

Old railway platform

The Royal Hotel

Tarka Tearooms

Riverbank Bistro

Bideford railway station (old)

Pannier Market

Bridge St

Library

St Mary's

Long Bridge

To East-the-Water

477676; July-Sep Mon-Fri 10am-5pm, Sat 10am-4pm, Sun 11am-4pm, Oct to June Mon-Sat 10am-4pm, Sun 11am-4pm) is in Burton Art Gallery. The **post office** (Mon-Fri 9am-5.30pm, Sat 9am-12.30pm) is nearby on The Quay.

For **internet access** (£2.20/30 mins) try Bideford Library (☎ 01237-476075; Mon & Tue 9.30am-6pm, Thur & Fri 9.30am-6pm, Sat 9.30am-1.30pm) near the

bridge, or The Appledore Inn (see Where to eat).

There are several **ATMs** dotted along the waterfront.

For **food** there is a Co-op (Mon-Sat 7am-7pm, Sun 10am-4pm) on Mill St in the centre as well as a Boots (Mon-Sat, 8.30am-5.30pm) should you need a **chemist**.

Where to stay

Campers looking to pitch their tents in the area should continue walking to Appledore (see p167). Indeed, there is a distinct lack of accommodation in Bideford, which may make the extra 3½ miles to Appledore seem rather appealing to everyone. **B&B** and **hotel**-wise, there are two options in East-the-Water. ***Orchard Cottage*** (Map 36; ☎ 01237-422427, 🖳 www.orchardstudiobideford.co.uk; ●; WI-FI; 33pp, £28.50pp room only, sgl occ rates on request) offers a self-contained unit (1D or T) that comes complete with fridge, microwave, kettle, TV, kitchen area and views across the river to the new bridge, all of which can be rented out on a nightly basis. It's a 15-minute walk from the centre of Bideford though only 10 minutes from the path itself. From the trail, around 200m before you reach Tarka Tearooms at the end of the line, take a right off the path through a gap in the wall; this leads you onto the road to Barnstaple. Head up the slope but rather than following the road left, continue up the hill on what is now Old Barnstaple Rd, then down the other side; Orchard Cottage will be on your left up a private driveway. Also on this side of the river, just before you cross Long Bridge, is ***The Royal Hotel*** (☎ 01237-472005, 🖳 www.royalbideford.co.uk; 5S/25D or T/2F; ●; WI-FI chargeable; 🐕 £5; £37.50-60pp, sgl from £59), arguably the best place in town to stay – though that's not really saying a great deal, and to be honest the service could have been better. Still, the prices are fair and The Kingsley Bedroom is gorgeous, with an ornate, plastered ceiling and original panelling.

The most central **B&B** accommodation sits on The Strand: ***The Cornerhouse*** (☎ 01237-473722, 🖳 www.cornerhouseguesthouse.co.uk; 1S/2D/2T shared facilities; ●; WI-FI; 🐕; £32.50pp, sgl £33) is housed in a pretty 18th-century merchant seaman's house; whilst a little out of town and occupying a very handsome Georgian property on Northdown Rd is ***The Mount*** (☎ 01237-473748, 🖳 www.themountbideford.co.uk; 2S/4D or T; ●; WI-FI; £32.50-40pp, sgl £40).

Where to eat and drink

There are numerous cafés in Bideford, although most involve a short diversion away from The Quay and the path. Having said that, ***Quayside Café*** (Mon-Sat 9am-5pm, Sun 10am-4pm) is where its name suggests and is a pleasant spot for a morning tea or stop for lunch.

Just off the path and attached to the museum and tourist information is ***Café du Parc*** (☎ 01237-429317; Mon-Sat 10am-4pm, to 5pm in summer, Sun 11am-4pm), selling soups and sandwiches amongst other items. Just off the waterfront, ***Billy's Bakery*** (Mon-Sat 8am-4.45pm), at 2 King St, sells lots of yummy takeaway pastry goods and also has a sandwich bar. For late-night grub on a Saturday night head for Mill St and ***Subway*** (Mon-Thu 8.30am-9.30pm, Fri 8.30am-midnight, Sat 8.30am-4am, Sun 10am-4pm).

There are two reasonable pubs overlooking the water. ***The Old Custom House*** (☎ 01237-425267; daily all day; WI-FI; 🐕 allowed in the bar; food served Mon-Fri 10am-3pm & 6-9pm, Sat & Sun 10am-6pm) is a decent place with outside seating that looks towards the harbour and Kingsley statue (see p167). It has a large menu with a full Irish breakfast (including half a pint of Guinness!) for £5.95. Close by on Queen St, ***White Hart Inn*** (☎ 01237-473203, 🖳 www.whitehartbideford.co.uk; daily 11am-11pm, Sun to 10.30pm, food served daily 11am-3pm, Thur 6-8pm; WI-FI; 🐕) serves local real ales and all the meats used for the roast dinners are locally sourced. A Sunday roast costs £6.45.

Closer to the centre of town, up the hill, on Mill St, ***Gerties Café*** (☎ 01237-238011; Mon-Sat 9.30am-5pm, summer school holidays Mon-Sat 9.30am-5pm, Sun to 4pm) sells gluten-free items amongst more 'regular' café food; an all-day breakfast in a roll (£2.50-3). Also on Mill St there's ***Bideford Café*** (Mon-Sat 8.30am-5pm, Sun 9.30am-1pm) and ***Cleverdons Tearooms*** (☎ 01237-472179; Mon-Sat 9am-4pm, Sun 10am-4pm) which does cream-teas and lunches during the day and table service in the evening when it transforms into *Pen & Jo's* (Thur & Fri 4-9pm, Sat 6-9.30pm). A whole dressed crab costs £13.50 whilst a Sunday roast is a very reasonable £6.95. Not far away on Cooper St is *Velvet & Vanilla Café Bar* (☎ 01237-420444, ☐ www.velvetandvanilla .co.uk; Mon-Sat 10am-4pm, Fri & Sat 7pm-midnight), they are licensed so you can drink without eating.

Back on Mill St there is *The Heavitree Arms* (☎ 01237-477187; daily 11am-midnight, food served Sun 12.30-3pm; WI-FI) where a roast dinner costs £5.95; and *The Appledore Inn* (☎ 01237-472496; daily noon-11pm; 🐾; WI-FI), 18 Chingswell St, which serves local real ales including Grenvilles from Jolly Boats and Doom Bar from Cornwall.

A step up in quality, *Lathwells* (☎ 01237-476447, ☐ www.lathwells.com; Easter to Sep Mon-Sat 6.45-8.45pm, Sep to Easter Wed-Sat 6.45-8.45pm) is on Cooper St; 70% of the ingredients here come from within a 25-mile radius of the town. A pan-fried monkfish, wrapped in parma ham and served in a cream and white wine sauce costs £16.95.

Over the bridge in East-the-Water are three more options. *Tarka Tearooms* is housed in a converted old train carriage at the end of the line, where you say goodbye to both the disused railway and the Tarka Trail. It's a lovely little place and does tea on the train for £1.40, and a two-scone cream tea for £4 or £4.50 with strawberries. By the roundabout at the foot of steps leading down from here, *Riverbank Bistro* (☎ 01237-473399, ☐ www.theriverbankbistro .co.uk; Tue-Sat noon-2pm & 6-9pm, Sun noon-2.30pm & 5.30-8pm), is a modern bar and restaurant with a great menu, including such treats as the unusual vegetarian brie, potato, courgette and apple crumble with chips and vegetables (£9.45), or a mixed grill (£17.95) and a great Sunday carvery (£8.50); they also have gluten-free options.

East of the Water, West of the Orient (☎ 01237-425329; Tue-Sat 5-11pm) is a notch above most Chinese restaurants, with an imaginative menu including a starter of Indonesian chicken satay (£4.20), and mains including Peking-style lamb (strips of lamb stir-fried in wine, chilli, beans, hoi sin and soy sauce), all served with vegetables and rice for £9.90.

There are numerous **takeaways**. For Chinese there is *Ho Sam Chinese* (☎ 01237-470084; Sun, Mon, Tue & Thur 5.30-10.30pm, Fri & Sat 5-10.30pm), on North Rd, or *Honey Moon Chinese* (☎ 01237-429633; summer daily noon-2.30pm & 5-11.30pm; winter daily 5-11pm but lunch opening variable), on Bridgeland St, where roast duck with pineapple and young ginger costs £5.50. For something a little spicier, on Cooper St, there's *Chillies* (☎ 01237-422344; daily 5-11pm) where a Persian lamb dish costs £6.95. For kebabs and burgers try *Danny's Kebabs* (☎ 01237-474555; Sun-Thur 4pm-midnight, Fri & Sat 4pm-2am) or *Ali's Kebab House* (☎ 01237-474621; Sun-Wed 4pm-midnight, Thur-Sat 4pm-late), both on Bridgeland St. Other fast-food joints include *Pizza Pronto* (☎ 01237-423000; daily 4pm-midnight) on Mill St, and *Trawlers Fish & Chips* (Mon-Sat noon-10pm, Sun 4-9pm) at No 38, which has a restaurant as well as a takeaway.

Transport

[See also pp49-51] Bideford is well-served by public transport. First's No 1 and 2 **bus** services connect the town with Barnstaple and Westward Ho! via Appledore and Instow, as does Stagecoach's No 21. Stagecoach also run the 319, which travels as far as Clovelly and Hartland where you can connect with Jackett's No 219 to Bude.

For a **taxi** try A1-Cab-it (☎ 01237-666060) or Barry's Taxis (☎ 01237-472724).

ROUTE GUIDE AND MAPS

From Bideford the path takes a slightly convoluted route to Appledore. It initially follows the river. Look out for the *Kathleen and May* – a historic schooner that is often moored in Bideford on one bank or another. Where the road turns away from the water as you leave town you'll find a **statue of**

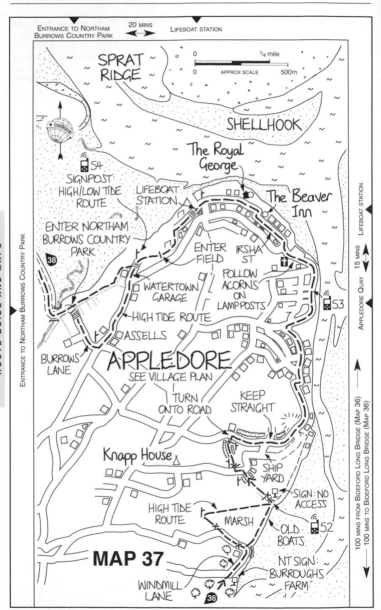

ROUTE GUIDE AND MAPS

ENTRANCE TO NORTHAM BURROWS COUNTRY PARK

Entrance to Northam Burrows Country Park ←→ 20 MINS → Lifeboat station

SPRAT RIDGE

SHELLHOOK

The Royal George

The Beaver Inn

📱54 SIGNPOST: HIGH/LOW TIDE ROUTE

LIFEBOAT STATION

ENTER NORTHAM BURROWS COUNTRY PARK

38

ENTER FIELD

IRSHA ST

FOLLOW ACORNS ON LAMPPOSTS

📱53

WATERTOWN GARAGE

HIGH TIDE ROUTE

ASSELLS

BURROWS LANE

APPLEDORE

SEE VILLAGE PLAN

TURN ONTO ROAD

KEEP STRAIGHT

Knapp House ⌂

SHIP YARD

SIGN: NO ACCESS

HIGH TIDE ROUTE

MARSH

OLD BOATS

📱52

MAP 37

WINDMILL LANE

NT SIGN: BURROUGHS FARM

36

0 — 1/4 mile
0 — 500m
APPROX SCALE

trailblazer

LIFEBOAT STATION

APPLEDORE QUAY ← 15 MINS →

100 MINS FROM BIDEFORD LONG BRIDGE (MAP 36) ←→ 100 MINS TO BIDEFORD LONG BRIDGE (MAP 36)

Charles Kingsley (Kingsley is said to have written much of *Westward Ho!* in Bideford). Beyond this, for 300 yards the tarmac path is known as **Landivisiau Walk** – named after the town's French twin. The park to your left is **Victoria Park**. Hidden amongst the flowerbeds and playing children are a couple of old cannons, thought to have been captured from the Spanish Armada in 1588. There is also a tree in the park planted in 1944 by American Lt Col F Holmes to commemorate the good relations the US army had with the people of Bideford whilst stationed there between 1940 and 1944.

As the ugly but necessary new **Torridge Bridge** looms ever closer the path seems to lose its sense of direction somewhat. The bridge was built in 1987 due to the long-existing problems with the sheer weight of traffic crossing Bideford Long Bridge; indeed, in 1968 some of the bridge had even collapsed. The path then passes by the friendly Victorian *Yeoldon House Hotel* (Map 36; ☎ 01237-474400, 🖥 www.yeoldonhousehotel.co.uk; 7D/3D or T; 🛏; WI-FI; 🐕 £5; £62.50-67.50pp, sgl occ £62.50-85) and meanders between river and farmland, emerging, after a short road-walk, at **Appledore**.

APPLEDORE

Quaint and quirky, Appledore is a lovely little place that, though its location between Bideford and Westward Ho! probably means you won't stay here for the night, really deserves as much of your time as you can give it. At heart it's a typical old West Country fishing village, but one onto which a vivid coat of creativity and craftsmanship has been painted, its centre a jumble of tiny cottages connected by narrow cobbled alleyways in which one finds galleries and workshops, studios and showrooms.

There's also a reasonably interesting museum at the top of town. **Maritime Museum** (☎ 01237-422064, 🖥 www.devonmuseums.net; Mon-Fri May-Sep 11am-12.30pm & 2-4.15pm, Sat & Sun 2-4.15pm, Easter-May & Oct 2-4.15pm; £2) contains exhibitions on Appledore's seafaring history including displays on shipbuilding, fishing and shipwrecks. The house in which it is contained, by the way, was once owned by the father of Jerome K Jerome, author of *Three Men in a Boat*.

See p16 for details of festivals and events in Appledore.

Services

There is some **tourist information** in the **library** (☎ 01237-477442; Tue 10am-1pm, Wed 2-5pm, Thur & Sat 10am-noon) on the front. The library also has **internet access** (£2.20/30 mins). Close by is the **post office** (Mon-Fri 9am-1pm & 2-5pm, Sat 9am-noon) in John's of Appledore, a **general store**.

In the summer months for those who want to return to Instow (or are heading in

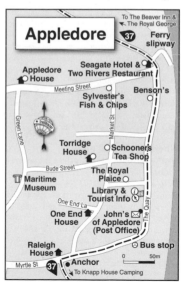

ROUTE GUIDE AND MAPS

the other direction and are happy to miss Bideford) a **ferry** (see p159) runs daily, weather and tide permitting, from The Quay.

Where to stay

There's a good **campsite** at *Knapp House* (Map 37; ☎ 01237-478843; Mar-Oct; £8 per night plus £2pp, 🐾 £2), about a kilometre to the south of Appledore and with its own path leading from the coastal trail.

Regarding **B&Bs**, the grandest is *Appledore House* (☎ 01237-421471, 🖳 www.appledore-house.co.uk; 3D/1T/1F; 🖢; WI-FI; £40-50pp, sgl occ £60-90), a large Victorian pile at the top of Meeting St with stylish, themed rooms (inc bathrobes and slippers), vast views across the rooftops to the estuary and a reputation for great breakfasts.

Other options include: *Raleigh House* (☎ 01237-459202, 🖳 raleighhouseapple dore@gmail.com; 1D; WI-FI; £35pp, sgl occ £40-70), on Myrtle St as you enter the village; the room is on the 2nd floor of an 18th-century house; *One End House* (☎ 01237-473846; 1D/1T; 🖢; WI-FI; 🐾; £35pp, sgl occ £40), on the lane of the same name, one of the charming little 18th-century terraced cottages that make up the centre of the village; and, up the hill at 19 Bude St, *Torridge House* (☎ 01237-477127, 🖳 www.torridgehouseappledore.com; 2D/1T; 🖢; WI-FI; 🐾; £35pp, sgl occ £40), a lovely Georgian place, tastefully furnished and with its own chickens.

Finally, there's 17th-century *Seagate Hotel* (☎ 01237-472589, 🖳 www.seagate hotel.co.uk; 3S/7D/1T/1F; 🖢; £20-40pp, sgl £25-40), at the end of The Quay.

Where to eat and drink

Food-wise, during the day there are several options: *Schooners Tea Shop and Delicatessen* (☎ 01237-474168; daily 10am-4.30pm), on narrow Market St at No 25, sells homemade cakes and does a decent Welsh rarebit (£4.10). On the front, *Benson's Coffee Shop* (☎ 01237-424093, 🖳 www.bensonsonthequay.com; Tue-Fri noon-2pm & 7-9.30pm, Mon & Sat 7-9.30pm), 20 The Quay, describes itself as

an 'adult sanctuary' with no-one under 12 allowed; the menu is a tad more upmarket with Brixham crab sandwich (£6.75), and whole local hake (£16.75). *Appledore House* (see Where to stay) also serve breakfast to non-residents for £6.50 – though do call first.

In the evening, *The Royal Plaice* (☎ 01237-478673; school summer holidays Mon-Sat noon-9pm, Sun 5-9pm; rest of year Mon-Sat noon-2pm & 5-8pm or later if demand) is an unpretentious fish restaurant and takeaway, with a rival takeaway, *Sylvester's Fish & Chips* (☎ 01237-423548; school summer holidays daily noon-9pm, Mar-mid July & Sep-Oct Mon 5-9pm, Tue-Sat noon-2pm & 5-9pm, Nov-mid Mar Tue-Sat noon-2pm & 5-9pm), at the other end of Market St. *Two Rivers Restaurant*, at The Seagate Hotel (see Where to stay; food served Thur, Fri & Sat 6-8.30pm, Sun noon-2pm) has fresh fish, juicy steaks and a nice (if noisy) patio overlooking the estuary. Bar meals (daily noon-2.30pm & 6-8.30pm) are also available.

At the western end of town (see Map 37) on Irsha St are two very popular pubs. *The Royal George* (Map 37; ☎ 01237-474335, 🖳 www.theroyalgeorgeappledore .co.uk; food served daily noon-2pm & 6.30-8pm) boasts an imaginative menu that belies its rather traditional facade, with seabass and ginger fishcakes for £8.95. Before that is *The Beaver* (Map 37; ☎ 01237-474822, 🖳 www.beaverinn.co.uk; restaurant Mon-Sat noon-2.30pm & 6-9pm, Sun noon-8.30pm but Sun lunch to 2.30pm, bar snacks at other times), at No 85, a slightly noisier place with more traditional pub grub including gammon steak for £9.25.

Transport

[See also pp49-51] Appledore is on the Turners Tours **bus** No 16 and 16A circular service that runs to/from Bideford and Westward Ho!. First's No 2 runs to Barnstaple via Fremington, Instow and Bideford. Looking the other way along the coast, Stagecoach's No 21A runs to Ilfracombe via Braunton, Barnstaple, Instow & Bideford.

Leaving Appledore you briefly have a choice between two routes – although as one of them is only accessible at low-tide, nature may well make your decision for you. The two paths soon reunite at the entrance to **Northam Burrows Country Park**. Consisting of 253 hectares of coastal plain and sand dunes the Burrows are an SSSI, due partly to the pebble ridge that separates the Burrows from the sea. The golf course you skirt is The Royal North Devon –

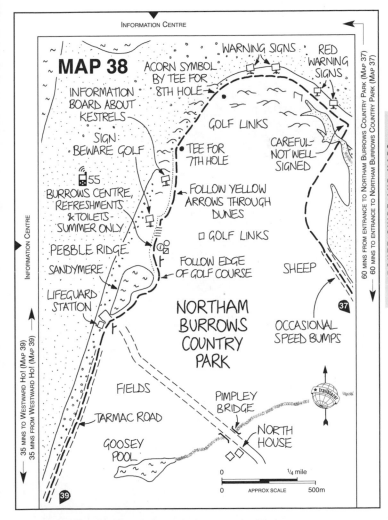

ROUTE GUIDE AND MAPS

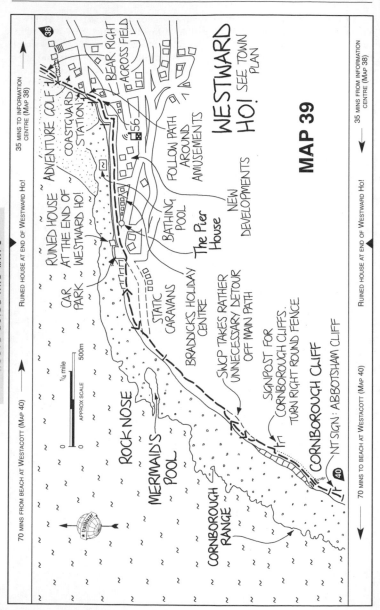

70 MINS FROM BEACH AT WESTACOTT (MAP 40)

RUINED HOUSE AT END OF WESTWARD HO!

35 MINS TO INFORMATION CENTRE (MAP 38)

BEAR RIGHT ACROSS FIELD

ADVENTURE GOLF

COASTGUARD STATION

RUINED HOUSE ~ AT THE END OF ~ WESTWARD HO!

56

FOLLOW PATH AROUND AMUSEMENTS

WESTWARD HO! SEE TOWN PLAN

MAP 39

CAR ~ PARK ~

STATIC CARAVANS

BRADDICKS HOLIDAY CENTRE

Bathing Pool

The Pier House

NEW DEVELOPMENTS

ROCK NOSE

SNCP TAKES RATHER UNNECESSARY DETOUR OFF MAIN PATH

SIGNPOST FOR CORNBOROUGH CLIFFS. TURN RIGHT ROUND FENCE

CORNBOROUGH CLIFF

MERMAID'S POOL

¼ mile

APPROX SCALE

500m

0

0

NT SIGN: ABBOTSHAM CLIFF

40

CORNBOROUGH RANGE

trailblazer

70 MINS TO BEACH AT WESTACOTT (MAP 40)

RUINED HOUSE AT END OF WESTWARD HO!

35 MINS FROM INFORMATION CENTRE (MAP 38)

the oldest links course in England. Be warned: it's not unknown for half-blind amateur golfers to send a wayward shot too close! The main route passes via **The Burrows Centre** (Map 38; ☎ 01237-479708; May-Sep daily 11am-5pm, toilets open 9.30am-5pm), an information centre and small souvenir shop; and from there heads along a long, straight, wide path along the back of the pebble ridge. If you find walking with golfers not to your taste – tide permitting – you can cross the ridge and stroll along the beach all the way to **Westward Ho!**.

WESTWARD HO!

The town of Westward Ho! may come as something of a disappointment to those for whom the name (the only one in England with an exclamation mark and, as far as we know, the only one named after a novel as opposed to the other way round) conjures up images of seafarers, buccaneers and adventure on the high seas.

It's true that this conglomeration of residential care homes and static caravan sites may not be challenging Clovelly or Appledore for any beauty awards in the near future. It also lacks the history of other towns around here, having been built as a holiday resort (the first hotel, The Westward Ho!, was built in 1864, when it was decided that there was money to be made in a tourist development overlooking the Pebbleridge described in the book).

But having said that, those who bother to spend some time in the town often find that they actually grow to really like it. The warmth and openness of the locals is undoubtedly one of the reasons why this is so – and the fact that they all seem so proud of the place is quite infectious after a while. So, while you may not take too many photos as you pass through (though the view over the town's massive beach from the top of town is quite magnificent), don't dismiss Westward Ho! out of hand, despite what other walkers may tell you. The SWCP is all about variety, and whatever else you may think of it, there's nowhere else quite like Westward Ho! on the entire path.

Services

The Co-op **supermarket** (Mon-Fri 7am-11pm, Sat & Sun 7am-10pm) boasts the usual lengthy opening hours, and its rival round the corner, Village Stores (Mon-Sat 7am-9pm, Sun 8am-9pm), has an **ATM** (for which you'll be charged about £1.50). This is the last cash machine on the path before

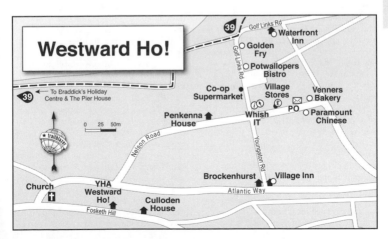

Westward Ho!

Golf Links Rd

39

Waterfront Inn

O Golden Fry

O Potwallopers Bistro

Golf Links Rd

← To Braddick's Holiday Centre & The Pier House

39

Co-op Supermarket

Village Stores

£

Venners O Bakery

PO

Penkenna House

Whish IT

O Paramount Chinese

0 25 50m

★ trailblazer

Nelson Road

Youngaton Rd

Brockenhurst

Village Inn

Church

YHA Westward Ho!

Culloden House

Atlantic Way

Fosketh Hill

Bude, though the hotel at Hartland Quay does cashback. The **post office** (Mon-Fri 9am-5pm, Sat 9am-12.30pm) is just a few metres away.

The information centre at the top of Golf Links Rd is not really for tourists – instead helping locals to find employment and benefits etc – though they do have **internet access** (Mon-Thur 10am-4pm).

Where to stay
For **camping**, *Braddicks Holiday Centre* (Map 39; ☎ 01237-473263; ⌨ www.brad dicksholidaycentre.co.uk; Mar/Apr to Oct; £8-12pp), at the western end of the village, has its reception located at the front of The Pier House Restaurant (see Where to eat).

YHA Westward Ho! (☎ 01237-479766, ⌨ westwardho@yha.org.uk; Apr-Oct; WI-FI; dorm £9.99-17.50pp, £28 per room for two sharing) is at the top of the village on Fosketh Hill and enjoys delightful views over the rooftops and down to the beach. It's a pleasant surprise to find the conservatory and terrace in addition to the more common kitchen and dining-room.

Brockenhurst (☎ 01237-423346, ⌨ www.brockenhurstindevon.co.uk; 2D/1T; WI-FI; £35pp, £45 sgl occ), at 11 Atlantic Way, is conveniently situated opposite the pub. This large house with spotless rooms (with TV) offers walkers a friendly welcome and great breakfasts, with eggs supplied by the chickens in the back garden. The pub, *Village Inn* (☎ 01237-477331, ⌨ www.villageinndevon.co.uk; 3D/1T; ☛) also does B&B and has fine rooms but it is the warmth of the owners that makes this place special.

Recommended by more than one walker, *Penkenna House* (☎ 01237-470990, ⌨ www.penkennahouse.com; 1D with private facilities/1D/1F share facilities; ☛; ☕ but only in outside shed with enclosed garden; WI-FI; £30pp, £35-45 sgl occ), 11 Nelson Rd, is a lovely place. The joy of Penkenna is in the details such as the warmth of the welcome, the super-smart rooms where the owners even supply bathrobes to their guests, the views to the sea and the huge breakfasts.

The views from Penkenna, however,

are surpassed by those of the premier rooms at the Victorian *Culloden House* (☎ 01237-479421, ⌨ www.culloden-house.co.uk; 2D/2T/4F; ☛; WI-FI; ☕; £35-40pp, sgl occ £56-64), Fosketh Hill, which look directly along the main swathe of sand. With its huge rooms the inside of this guest house is a joy too.

On Golf Links Rd, *Waterfront Inn* (☎ 01237-474737, ⌨ www.waterfrontinn.co .uk; 3D/1T/3F; £25-32.50pp, sgl occ £35-40; family rooms for up to five £60-80) is fairly characterless but comfy and good value.

Where to eat and drink
Ask the locals where they would go to eat out and the most popular reply is the *Potwallopers Bistro* (☎ 01237-474494, ⌨ www.potwallopers.co.uk; summer Wed-Sat 11am-2pm & 6.30-9pm, Sun 11am-2.30pm, winter Thur-Sat 6.30-9pm) with a varied menu of hearty dishes including fillet of hake topped with a herb cheese crust and roasted vine tomatoes, served with a sweet balsamic dressing and fresh vegetables (£13.50). However, at the time of research it was for sale so check before going. Next door, *Golden Fry* (☎ 01237-470815; Tue-Thur noon-8.30pm, Fri & Sat noon-9pm, Sun noon-7.30pm) is a good chippy with some seating outside under the awning; they do rock salmon from £3.20.

Right at the top of the hill on Youngaton Rd, *Village Inn* (see Where to stay) serves food daily (noon-2pm & 6.30-9pm) including special offers such as £10 for a fish dish plus dessert.

There's a Chinese restaurant too, *Paramount Chinese* (☎ 01237-477661; summer Tue-Thur & Sun 5-11pm, Fri & Sat 5-11.30pm; in winter they may close earlier), on Nelson Rd, with a takeaway section, and opposite is *Venners Bakery* (☎ 01237-474378; Mon-Sat 8.30am-5pm), serving sarnis and baguettes for take-away only.

Back down at the bottom of Golf Links Rd, *Waterfront Inn* (see Where to stay; food served noon-9pm) has jacket spuds from £5.70 and surf & turf for £13.95.

If all the above are just too far away from the path, *The Pier House* (Map 39; ⌨ www.thepier-house.co.uk; food served daily noon-9pm) at Braddicks Holiday Centre (see Where to stay) is the smartest place in town, with its classic menu (steaks, pies, cod, mussels etc) supplemented by a 'something different' selection that includes more creative cuisine including parmesan and asparagus tart (£9.50).

There are two Hockings **ice-cream vans** on the way into town and right on the trail.

Transport

[See also pp49-51] Westward Ho! is fairly well served by **buses**. First Group's No 1 operates to Barnstaple via Fremington, Instow and Bideford. Stagecoach's No 21 operates a similar route. Turners Tours run the No 16 and 16A circular service between Bideford and Appledore via Westward Ho!.

There are also some National Express **coach** services to Westward Ho! (see p47).

WESTWARD HO! TO CLOVELLY [MAPS 39-43]

This **11-mile (17.7km; 4hrs 35 mins)** section is very much a tale of two terrains. Leaving Westward Ho!, the path assumes a southerly direction along exposed and open cliffs, lacerated, once again, by several deep and fairly testing combes. On reaching Peppercombe, however, the path not only takes a more westerly direction but also changes in nature from clifftop clamber to woodland walk. Aside from a visit to the small huddle of houses that is Buck's Mills, as well as the occasional field, you remain under the forest canopy for pretty much the rest of the stage as the trail leads you towards and then onto Hobby Drive – a wide and gentle tree-shaded track coaxing you to lovely Clovelly.

Note that there is nowhere to get any refreshments on the way and nowhere to stay on the path either (though there are several places a short walk inland). As such, do remember to bring supplies and plan your day properly.

The route

Though the first half of this walk is undoubtedly more testing than the second, it begins in a fairly gentle manner as you escape from Westward Ho! along the path of a disused railway that used to run inland to Bideford. Soon the trail leaves the tarmac to head towards **Abbotsham** and **Green Cliffs**, both owned by the National Trust. Pause at the top of either and you should, weather permitting, make out Saunton Sands and even Baggy Point, which you probably walked around about four days ago! Look south, on the other hand, and the keen-eyed may just be able to make out Clovelly in the cliffs ahead.

There's plenty of walking still to be done. However, the gradients increase as you drop to the beach, briefly, at **Westacott**, and again by the private **Portledge Estate**, before you reach Peppercombe, another National Trust property. **Peppercombe Castle**, labelled on OS maps, is actually an Iron-Age fort though little remains today. Inland along the valley from here, about three-quarters of a mile from the path, is *The Coach and Horses Inn* (off Map 41; ☎ 01237-451214; 1D/1T/1F; 🐾; WI-FI; £30pp, £45 sgl occ; food served summer daily noon-2pm & 6-9pm, winter Sun noon-1.45pm, Tue-Sat noon-2pm & 6-9pm).

The path now meanders along the slopes through **Sloo** and **Worthygate woods** (the border between the two being unmarked) before dropping down to the hamlet of **Buck's Mills**. There's little to detain you here, though there's a

ROUTE GUIDE AND MAPS

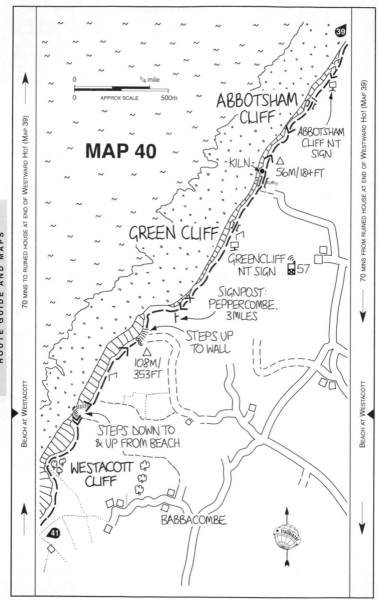

70 MINS TO RUINED HOUSE AT END OF WESTWARD HO! (MAP 39)

70 MINS FROM RUINED HOUSE AT END OF WESTWARD HO! (MAP 39)

ROUTE GUIDE AND MAPS

BEACH AT WESTACOTT

BEACH AT WESTACOTT

0   ¼ mile
0   APPROX SCALE   500m

MAP 40

ABBOTSHAM CLIFF

ABBOTSHAM CLIFF NT SIGN

KILN   △ 56M/184FT

GREEN CLIFF

GREENCLIFF NT SIGN   57

SIGNPOST: PEPPERCOMBE, 3 MILES

STEPS UP TO WALL

△ 108M/353FT

STEPS DOWN TO & UP FROM BEACH

WESTACOTT CLIFF

BABBACOMBE

39

41

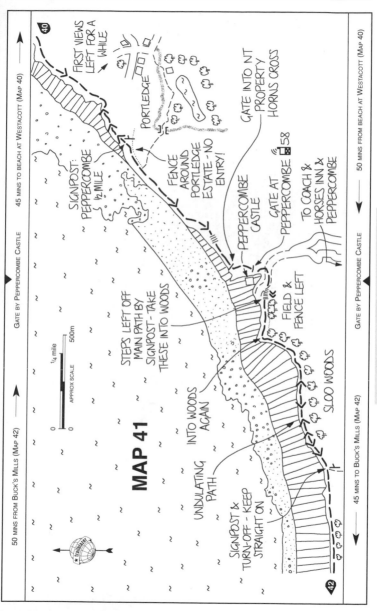

FIRST VIEWS LEFT FOR A WHILE

PORTLEDGE

SIGNPOST: PEPPERCOMBE ½ MILE

FENCE AROUND PORTLEDGE ESTATE - NO ENTRY!

GATE INTO NT PROPERTY HORNS CROSS

PEPPERCOMBE CASTLE

GATE AT PEPPERCOMBE 58

TO COACH & HORSES INN & PEPPERCOMBE

FIELD & FENCE LEFT

STEPS LEFT OFF MAIN PATH BY SIGNPOST- TAKE THESE INTO WOODS

¼ mile

500m

APPROX SCALE

INTO WOODS AGAIN

MAP 41

SLOO WOODS

UNDULATING PATH

SIGNPOST & TURN-OFF - KEEP STRAIGHT ON

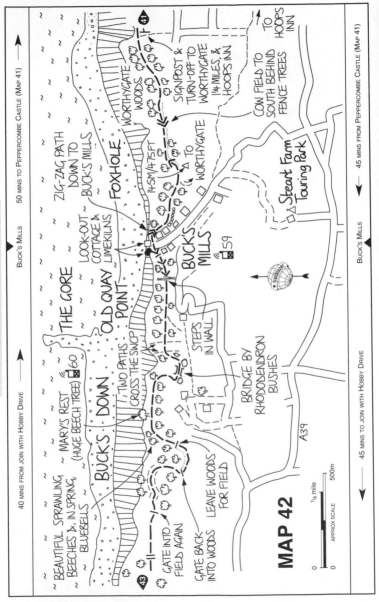

40 MINS from JOIN with HOBBY DRIVE →

50 MINS to PEPPERCOMBE CASTLE (MAP 41) →

BUCK'S MILLS ►

45 MINS from PEPPERCOMBE CASTLE (MAP 41) →

BUCK'S MILLS ►

45 MINS to JOIN with HOBBY DRIVE →

BEAUTIFUL SPRAWLING BEECHES &, IN SPRING, BLUEBELLS

MARY'S REST (HUGE BEECH TREE) 📷 60

THE GORE

ZIG-ZAG PATH DOWN TO BUCK'S MILLS

FOXHOLE

WORTHYGATE WOODS

SIGNPOST & TURN-OFF TO WORTHYGATE
1¼ MILES & HOOPS INN

TO HOOPS INN

COW FIELD TO SOUTH BEHIND FENCE TREES

LOOK-OUT COTTAGE & LIMEKILNS

OLD QUAY POINT

BUCK'S DOWN

1¼SM/475FT

TO WORTHYGATE

Steart Farm Touring Park

TWO PATHS CROSS THE SWCP

BUCK'S MILLS

📷 59

STEPS IN WALL

BRIDGE BY RHODODENDRON BUSHES

A39

LEAVE WOODS FOR FIELD

GATE INTO FIELD AGAIN

GATE BACK INTO WOODS

43

MAP 42

¼ mile

500m

APPROX SCALE

0

0

couple of old **limekilns** down at the bottom of the road by the beach and on the way is **Look-out Cottage**, a tiny studio used from the 1920s to the 1970s by artists Mary Stella Edwards and Judith Ackland, who renamed it The Cabin and whose work now hangs in Burton Art Gallery (see p162) at Bideford. It has barely been touched in the 40 years since the artists left it. Inland, *Steart Farm Touring Park* (Map 42; ☎ 01237-431836; 🖳 www.steartfarmtouringpark .co.uk; early Apr to end Sep; backpacker plus tent £5 plus £1 per extra person; 🐾) lies around 15 minutes from the path. The rate includes free hot showers and there are also laundry facilities. Make sure you've got your own food – the nearest place to eat is about two miles (3km) east along the busy A39: *The Hoops Inn & Country Hotel* (off Map 42; ☎ 01237-451222, 🖳 www.hoops inn.co.uk; 9D/4D or T; 🍺; WI-FI in main bar; 🐾 £5; £32.50-52.50pp, sgl occ £65; food available daily 8.30am-9.30pm; snacks/sandwiches only in the after-noon out of the main season) is a lovely thatched place. The menu includes sir-loin steak with all the trimmings (£18.95).

The woods on the other side of the hamlet are, if anything, even more beau-tiful than those you've just left, with some huge beech trees and gigantic rho-dodendron bushes shading the way. Emerging briefly into meadows above the trees, the path plunges into the shade again to reach **Hobby Drive**, a 19th-century 'bridleway' that provides an easy and picturesque stroll into Clovelly, leisurely snaking its way along the cliffside, with benches placed here and there to the right of the trail to encourage wayfarers to tarry a while and appreciate the views down onto the rooftops of Clovelly. Hard to believe, in such a tran-quil place, that according to legend in a giant cave below the trail lived a cer-tain John Gregg and his family, who made their living robbing, murdering and eating passers-by around 250 years ago. These days, the most dangerous crea-ture you're likely to encounter is the occasional pheasant strutting along the path or scampering through the undergrowth. Just over an hour after joining the Drive you reach its end and arrive at one of the more unique and individual set-tlements on the entire South-West Coast Path...

CLOVELLY [MAP 43, p179]

Clovelly (see box below) is one of the loveliest villages on the entire SWCP. Four-hundred feet of cobbled street rolling down a narrow cleft in the coastline of North Devon, lined on either side by wonderfully preserved cottages which, from certain aspects on the sea, appear to have been stacked on each other's shoulders. It really is the most photogenic of places.

The gradient of the main street – which bears the names Up-a-Long and Down-a-Long – is enough to prevent traffic from

---

The village was built sheer up the face of a steep and lofty cliff. There was no road in it, there was no wheeled vehicle in it, there was not a level yard in it. From the sea-beach to the cliff-top two irregular rows of white houses, placed opposite to one another, and twisting here and there, and there and here, rose, like the sides of a long succession of stages of crooked ladders, and you climbed up the village or you climbed down the village by the staves between, some six feet wide or so, and made of sharp irregular stones. **Charles Dickens**, *Message from The Sea*

driving down it (though there is a road linking the harbour with the top of the village which is used by Land Rovers to shuttle the elderly and the lazy to the harbour). Instead, goods are brought in by sled from the top of the village, while rubbish is taken to the bottom where it is removed by boat. In between are some gorgeous little cottages, each full of character and entirely individual.

Much of the credit for the place's wonderful state of preservation is down to the fact that Clovelly is actually privately owned, the Hamlyn family acquiring the fishing village as part of their purchase of the entire Clovelly Estate in 1738. One of the family, Christine Hamlyn, spent years restoring many of the cottages on the main street; her initials and a date can be seen carved into many of the structures.

For such a small village (the estimated population for the entire ward of Clovelly Bay is only 1616), Clovelly has a surprising number of claims to fame: the village was a boyhood home of Charles Kingsley, who returned here years later to write some of his best work, including *The Water Babies*; Charles Dickens also wrote about it (though he calls it, appropriately enough, 'Steepways'); Rex Whistler painted it, as did JMW Turner; and Wedgewood used cameos of the village on their china service. It is also mentioned in the Domesday Book.

The opening of the huge **visitor centre** above the village – and the subsequent charging of an **entrance fee** (£5.95) to visit the village – are controversies over which coast-path walkers can remain in blissful ignorance, for the entrance into Clovelly along The Hobby bypasses the entrance gates altogether, thus allowing walkers (at least at the time of research) to enter the village without paying.

There are two small museums, both open daily, approximately 9am-5pm: **Kingsley Museum** celebrates the life and work of the author, but perhaps more interesting is the **Fisherman's Cottage**, across the courtyard, where the cob-and-stone dwelling has been preserved in a 1930s' style with a sail loft and even a covered well. At the foot of the village, beyond the

19th-century **Lifeboat Station**, is a waterfall, behind which you'll find a cave where the Arthurian magician Merlin was supposedly born.

Services
The **Visitor Centre** (☎ 01237-431781, 🖳 www.clovelly.co.uk; daily school summer holidays 9am-6:30pm; Easter to mid July & Sep to end Oct 9.30am-5.30pm Nov to Easter 10am-4.15pm) is very much concerned with Clovelly and knowledge on other parts of Devon is slight. In the village itself you'll find a fairly poorly stocked **shop** (daily 9.30am-5 or 6pm).

Where to stay, eat and drink
Regarding **accommodation**, *Red Lion Hotel* (☎ 01237-431237, 🖳 www.clovelly.co.uk; 9D/2D or T/6F; ✒; WI-FI; 🐾 £10; £32.75-35.35pp, sgl occ £50-53) is a bit of a landmark in the town, situated right by the harbour at the bottom of the village, and it's a lovely old place too. Bookending Clovelly at the top end of the village and owned by the same company, *New Inn Hotel* (☎ 01237-431303, 🖳 www.clovelly.co.uk; 1S/6D/1F; ✒; WI-FI; 🐾 £10; £55.75-60.75pp) is perhaps the most elegant place in the village; the smart rooms have a sea view or, in one case, a balcony overlooking the street. New Inn also own *New House* (contact details as above) across the road, with slightly inferior rooms (5T/6D/1F; ✒; WI-FI; 🐾 £10) for £32.75-41pp. Two of the rooms here are en suite but the rest share facilities. Patrons are allowed to use all the facilities available over the road.

There are more options further up the hill in Higher Clovelly, beginning about 1km from the top of the main village; sometimes these B&Bs offer a pick-up/drop-off service from/to the path. If no lift is available, to reach them from the end of Hobby Drive take the path signposted towards Wrinkleberry. Once you reach this tiny hamlet, walk past the school and on your left is another footpath clearly signed through the fields that takes you to the foot of Burscott on the edge of the village. *Dyke Green Farm* (off Map 43; ☎ 01237-431699; £6pp; Easter to Oct) offers **camping** and is

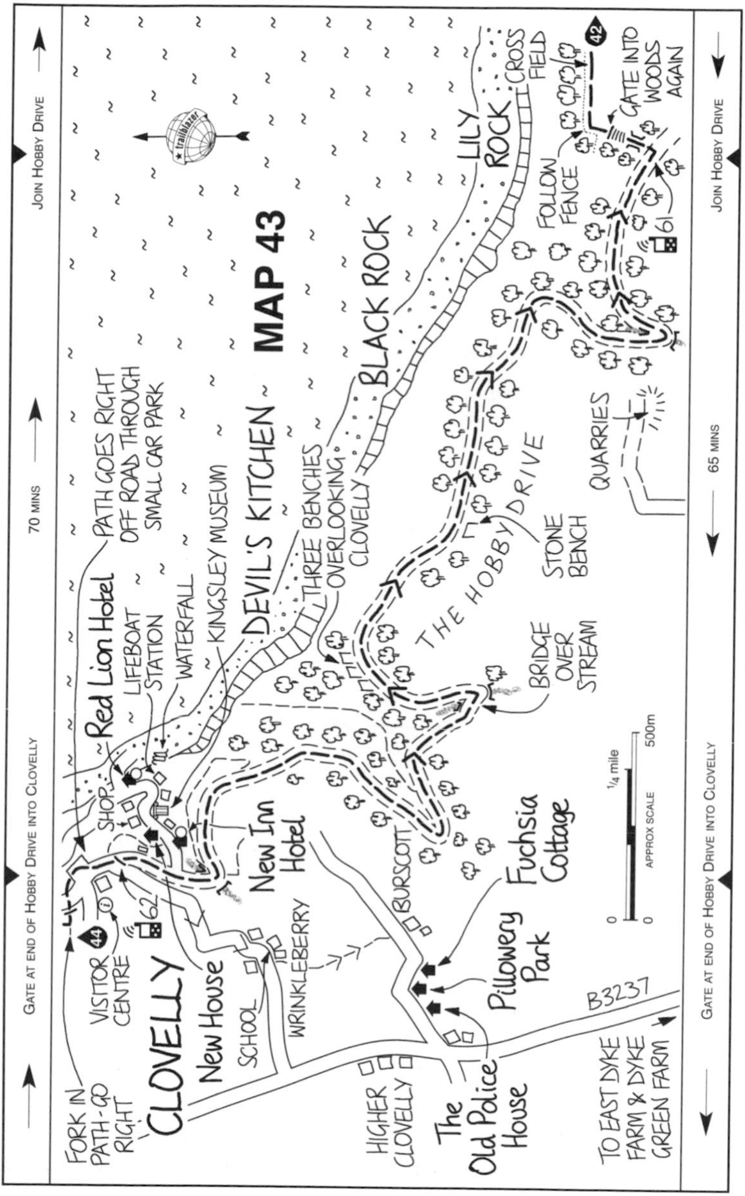

MAP 43

JOIN HOBBY DRIVE →

70 MINS →

GATE AT END OF HOBBY DRIVE INTO CLOVELLY

PATH GOES RIGHT
OFF ROAD THROUGH
SMALL CAR PARK

Red Lion Hotel ~

LIFEBOAT
STATION

WATERFALL

KINGSLEY MUSEUM

~ DEVIL'S KITCHEN ~

BLACK ROCK

LILY
ROCK

42

CROSS
FIELD

GATE INTO
WOODS
AGAIN

FOLLOW
FENCE

61

JOIN HOBBY DRIVE ←

THREE BENCHES
OVERLOOKING
CLOVELLY

THE HOBBY DRIVE

QUARRIES

65 MINS ←

STONE
BENCH

BRIDGE
OVER
STREAM

SHOP

New Inn Hotel

BURSCOTT

Fuchsia
Cottage

Pillowery
Park

B3237

¼ mile

APPROX SCALE

500m

0

0

GATE AT END OF HOBBY DRIVE INTO CLOVELLY

ROUTE GUIDE AND MAPS

FORK IN
PATH - GO
RIGHT

VISITOR 44
CENTRE

62

CLOVELLY

New House

SCHOOL

WRINKLEBERRY

HIGHER
CLOVELLY

The
Old Police
House

TO EAST DYKE
FARM & DYKE
GREEN FARM

JOIN HOBBY DRIVE →

a friendly place. Shower facilities are 20p. The only problem is that it's well over a mile from the path, lying at the very southern end of the village: head to the end of Burscott and turn left. However, the effort in getting there is worth it. Next door, *East Dyke Farmhouse* (☎ 01237-431216, 🖵 www.bedbreakfastclovelly.co.uk; 1D/1T/1F; ◥; WI-FI; £30-35pp, £40-45 sgl occ) is a lovely friendly place, a grand 19th-century building with exposed beams and flagstone floors. You are free to explore Clovelly Dykes, a 200-year-old Iron Age hill fort, lying just beyond their back garden. They also offer lifts and packed lunches for a fee.

There are three smaller places on Burscott. The first you reach from the coast path is tidy, efficient, walker-friendly *Fuchsia Cottage* (☎ 01237-431398, 🖵 www.clovelly-holidays.co.uk; 1S/1D/1D or T; ◥; £30pp); packed lunches are available. Just up the road is *Pillowery Park B&B* (☎ 01237-431668, 🖵 www.clovelly accommodation.com; 1D en suite/2T with private facilities; WI-FI; £30-35pp, sgl occ £40-41); packed lunches are available. Around 10 metres further on is *The Old Police House* (☎ 01237-431256, 🖵

www.clovellybandb.co.uk; 1D private bathroom/1T en suite; ◥; 🐾; £27.50pp, sgl occ £30). If booked in advance the owner can cook an evening meal, prepare a packed lunch and possibly offer a pick-up/luggage transfer service too.

When it comes to **food**, there are three choices in the village – *Cottage Tearooms* are open during the day and boast a lovely outside eating area. The two hotels also serve food: *The Red Lion* (see p178; food served daily noon-2.30pm & 6.30-8.30pm, restaurant 7-8.30pm) unsurprisingly boasts some fine fresh dishes, available both in the bar and its restaurant area. Two/three courses, including such treats as oven-roasted monkfish for mains and sticky toffee pudding are £24.50/29.50. A similar deal is available at the *New Inn* (see p178; food served daily noon-2.30pm & 6.30-8.30pm, noon-2pm to 8pm in winter) though the menu is different. Here you may find roast rack of lamb on a bed of mashed potato.

Transport

[See also pp49-51] Stagecoach's No 319 **bus** connects Clovelly with Barnstaple, Hartland, and Bideford.

CLOVELLY TO HARTLAND QUAY   [MAPS 43-48]

The final two stages of this walk are renowned for being amongst the wildest, most remote and most spectacular on the entire SWCP.

The paucity of amenities and accommodation on the trail also mean that walkers really need to plan their walk on this stretch thoroughly. True, when it comes to **accommodation** there are several B&Bs, a (YHA) hostel and a campsite, but these are sometimes a fair hike away and should definitely be booked in advance. Similarly, for **food** you need to plan well: the first stage is fairly straightforward, with a small tearoom right on the trail and a pub at the end. But the second stage has nothing actually on the path save for an outdoor café just a mile or two before Bude. Otherwise, the only options are a great tearoom and pub at Morwenstow that are both about a third of a mile (500 metres) off the trail; which, on a day that's already 16 miles long, is quite a demanding diversion!

One way round this, of course, is to ask your accommodation to make a packed lunch for you; or, of course, you could make it yourself – though as the poorly stocked shop in Clovelly is the only place selling provisions on these last two stages, the chances are you won't be eating that well.

However, assuming you *have* planned properly, there is much to look forward to on both these stages. The reputation of the second stage for being the toughest and amongst the most awe-inspiring on the entire path is well known but there's plenty to appreciate on this first stage to Hartland Quay too. The first part of this **10¹/₂-mile (16.9km; 5hrs 5mins)** walk is gentle enough, beginning with a stroll through the woods of Gallantry Bower and Snaxland before you indulge in a meadowside meander along the clifftops of Beckland and Brownsham. So far, so familiar. But then one rounds Hartland Point, the path takes an abrupt turn to the south ... and things get a little more dramatic. Wild seas crash against rocks carved by time and tide into alcoves and archways, canyons and caves, tunnels and towers, where grey seals slumber and seagulls soar. It's a land of rock and reef, storm and shipwreck, lonely, baleful shorelines and looming, brooding skies; while, above it all, a 19th-century lighthouse and the enigmatic ruins of a much older tower sit in stoical silence – untouched and untroubled by the chaos below.

The route

Your first task on this stage is to avoid the scary-looking (but presumably benign) steers of the Clovelly Court estate as you skip through fields and forest, passing on your way two curious man-made structures tucked away among the trees. The first, just 10 minutes from Clovelly itself, is **The Cabin**, built in the 19th century by Sir James Hamlyn Williams (a former owner of Clovelly Estate) and now used, bizarrely, as a venue for weddings. The second, reached via a tunnel of rhododendrons, is an ornate wooden pagoda-style structure known as **Angel's Wings**, which was carved by a former butler of the estate.

More woodland wandering ensues as you make your way to **Mouthmill Beach**, once the haunt of smugglers but now the home to a ruined limekiln and, more famously, **Blackchurch Rock** with its two sea-sculpted 'windows'. Climbing out of the valley you now follow an endless series of fields towards Hartland Point, the only features of note being firstly **Windbury Castle**, an Iron Age fort that has largely disappeared due to erosion, though the keen-eyed expert can still make out parts of the southern ramparts amongst the undergrowth; and, just a short walk further on, a **memorial** to a Wellington bomber that crashed at the foot of Beckland Cliff in 1942.

Eventually, around four hours after setting off, you pass the turn-off to *West Titchberry Farm* (Map 46; ☎ 01237-441287; 1D/1T share facilities/1F en suite; ✆; £26.50-30pp, sgl occ £32-35), a typical Devon longhouse and B&B that offers packed lunches and evening meals (if requested in advance) and a pick-up/drop-off facility (subject to a small charge) for walkers. (Its neighbour, by the way, East Titchberry Farm, is a 17th-century National Trust property with its own malthouse that's unfortunately closed to the public.)

Shortly afterwards – though it's been visible a long way beforehand – is the giant white golf-ball-on-a-tee that is the **radar station**. At its foot is *Hartland Point Kiosk* (Apr-Sep daily 10.30am-5 or 6pm, Sep-Apr Mon & Fri 9am-1pm only to meet the Lundy helicopter, see box p121); a rest stop is hard to resist at this stage, though note that they do not have a toilet. From here, it's but a short skip to **Hartland Point**, where the Bristol Channel meets the Atlantic and the SWCP begins to head in a more southerly direction after so long heading west.

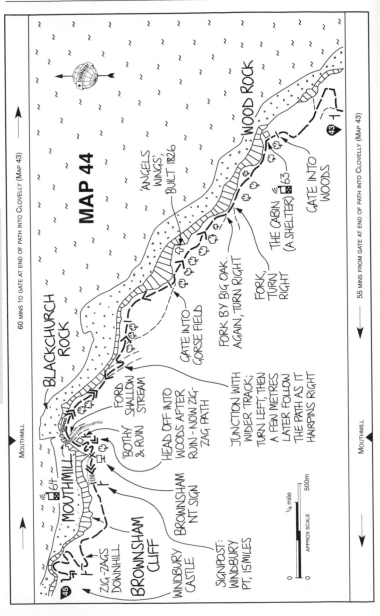

MOUTHMILL

◀ 60 MINS TO GATE AT END OF PATH INTO CLOVELLY (MAP 43) ▶

MAP 44

BLACKCHURCH ROCK

WOOD ROCK

'ANGELS' WINGS', BUILT 1826

GATE INTO GORSE FIELD

FORK BY BIG OAK AGAIN, TURN RIGHT

FORK, TURN RIGHT

THE CABIN (A SHELTER) 🏚63

GATE INTO WOODS

🏚43 1

55 MINS FROM GATE AT END OF PATH INTO CLOVELLY (MAP 43)

FORD SHALLOW STREAM

'BOTHY' & RUIN

HEAD OFF INTO WOODS AFTER RUIN - NOW ZIG-ZAG PATH

JUNCTION WITH WIDER TRACK; TURN LEFT, THEN A FEW METRES LATER FOLLOW THE PATH AS IT HAIRPINS RIGHT

MOUTHMILL 🏚64

BROWNSHAM NT SIGN

WINDBURY CASTLE

BROWNSHAM CLIFF

ZIG-ZAGS DOWNHILL

SIGNPOST: WINDBURY PT, 1½ MILES

45

MOUTHMILL

¼ mile

APPROX SCALE

0   500m

0

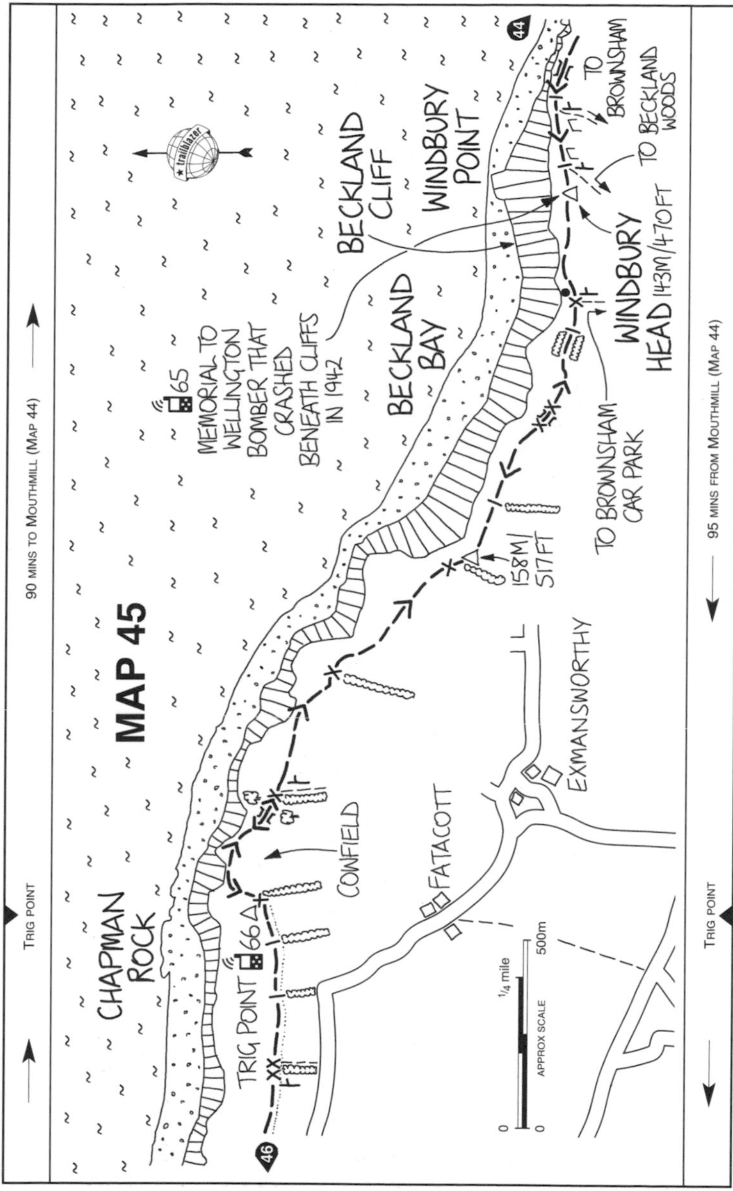
MAP 45
90 MINS TO MOUTHMILL (MAP 44)
95 MINS FROM MOUTHMILL (MAP 44)
TRIG POINT
TRIG POINT
CHAPMAN ROCK
TRIG POINT 66
COWFIELD
FATACOTT
EXMANSWORTHY
158M/517FT
65
MEMORIAL TO WELLINGTON BOMBER THAT CRASHED BENEATH CLIFFS IN 1942
BECKLAND BAY
BECKLAND CLIFF
WINDBURY POINT
WINDBURY HEAD 143M/470FT
TO BROWNSHAM CAR PARK
TO BECKLAND WOODS
TO BROWNSHAM
44
46
APPROX SCALE
1/4 mile
500m
0
0

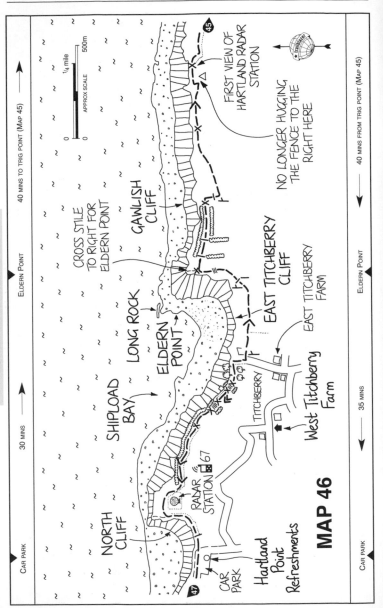

MAP 46

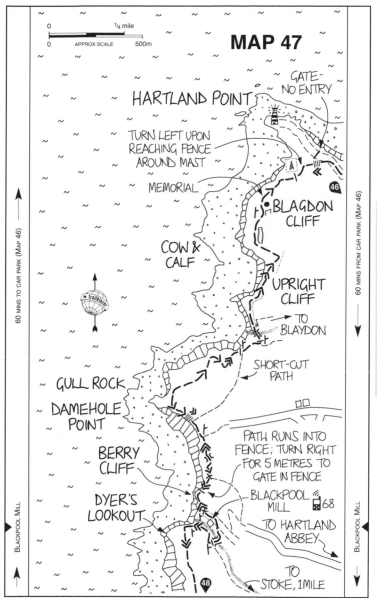

MAP 47

0 ———— ¼ mile
0 ———— APPROX SCALE ———— 500m

GATE-
NO ENTRY

HARTLAND POINT

TURN LEFT UPON
REACHING FENCE
AROUND MAST

MEMORIAL

A

46

BLAGDON
CLIFF

COW &
CALF

UPRIGHT
CLIFF

TO
BLAYDON

SHORT-CUT
PATH

GULL ROCK

DAMEHOLE
POINT

BERRY
CLIFF

PATH RUNS INTO
FENCE; TURN RIGHT
FOR 5 METRES TO
GATE IN FENCE

DYER'S
LOOKOUT

BLACKPOOL
MILL 68

TO HARTLAND
ABBEY

TO
STOKE, 1MILE

48

trailblazer

60 MINS TO CAR PARK (MAP 46)

60 MINS FROM CAR PARK (MAP 46)

BLACKPOOL MILL

BLACKPOOL MILL

ROUTE GUIDE AND MAPS

The point is marked by the **lighthouse**, built in 1874 and said to be visible up to 25 miles away.

Though you're on the homeward stretch, there's still plenty to be done on this leg before you can finally call it a day. Passing a **memorial** to the *Glenart Castle*, a hospital ship that was torpedoed by a German U-boat in 1918 with the loss of 153 men and women out of a total of 186 on board, the path takes you on several steep descents, the second leading towards **Gull Rock**, the third towards the isolated valley of **Blackpool Mill**. Heading up and out of here, the path finally flattens as it crosses **The Warren**, decorated by the ruins of a **tower** – once a folly, so it is believed, but which now makes a nice frame for your photo of the village church in the distance. From here, the way is straightforward to **Hartland Quay**, turning right down the hill by Rocket House.

HARTLAND QUAY, STOKE & HARTLAND
Hartland Quay
There's little to Hartland Quay other than the hotel. This hotel, converted from what were once stables and customs houses, hints at the importance of this spot as a major port in Tudor times. A storm in 1887 destroyed the quay, and these days there's only a small modern slipway. Nevertheless, the past can still be glimpsed in the hotel's very own museum, with photos and mementoes of various shipwrecks that have occurred on this stretch of shoreline over four centuries. (They've plenty of raw material to choose from, for it's said that this coastline has approximately ten shipwrecks per mile!)

As for the accommodation, *Hartland Quay Hotel* (☎ 01237-441218, 🖳 www .hartlandquayhotel.co.uk; 3S/3T/4D/7F; ☞; WI-FI; from £45pp) offers rooms that are the perfect place to nurse sore feet while gazing out over the crashing surf. The hotel's bar, *The Wreckers' Retreat* (food served daily 11am-2.30pm & 6-9pm plus 3-5.30pm in summer) is also decorated with photos and souvenirs of local shipwrecks. The bar serves local ales (including many from St Austell brewery) and does a nice line in healthy portions of resuscitating food.

Stoke
If you can't get a room at Hartland Quay hotel, you'll have to head half a mile inland to this tiny settlement, centred around the 14th-century **Church of St Nectan**, known and famed for its soaring tower, said to be

the highest in Devon and for centuries a vital landmark to sailors at sea. Nearby is an excellent **campsite** and a small B&B. The former is *Stoke Barton Farm* (☎ 01237-441238, 🖳 www.westcoun try-camping.co.uk; £5.50-6.50pp; end Mar to end Oct), a great place with hot showers and owners who are helpful and can arrange a packed lunch for you – they plan to have a small camp shop with the main essentials and may even be able to sell you a tin of dog food if you're desperate. Booking is recommended and is essential for peak periods. They even have their own short-cut from the path (see map opposite).

As for the **B&B**, *One Coastguard Cottages* (☎ 01237-441011, 🖳 www.coast guardcottagestoke.com; 2D; ☞; WI-FI; £30pp, sgl occ £35) is a friendly and welcoming B&B that, thanks to its fine reputation and relative proximity to the path, is more than used to seeing walkers. A good service they provide too, with comfortable rooms, as well as evening meals and packed lunches subject to prior arrangement. They can also provide (for a fee) luggage transfer and lifts to/from the path or other villages.

Hartland
Though around 2½ miles (3.75km) from the path, coastal walkers may find themselves in Hartland as it's the nearest village to this section of the path with shops and facilities, as well as a few places providing B&B, some of which offer packed lunches and a pick-up/drop-off service if arranged in advance.

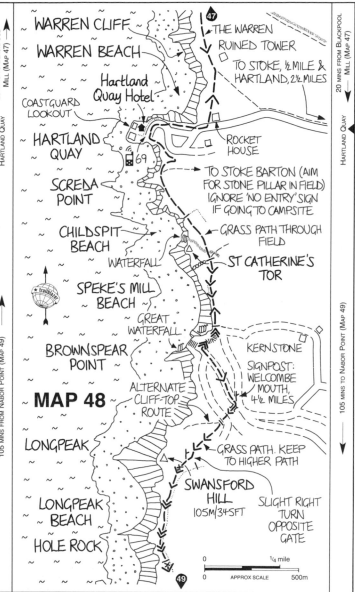

WARREN CLIFF

WARREN BEACH

THE WARREN

RUINED TOWER

TO STOKE, ½ MILE &
HARTLAND, 2½ MILES

Hartland
Quay Hotel

COASTGUARD
LOOKOUT

ROCKET
HOUSE

HARTLAND
QUAY

69

TO STOKE BARTON (AIM
FOR STONE PILLAR IN FIELD)
IGNORE 'NO ENTRY' SIGN
IF GOING TO CAMPSITE

SCREDA
POINT

GRASS PATH THROUGH
FIELD

CHILDSPIT
BEACH

ST CATHERINE'S
TOR

WATERFALL

SPEKE'S MILL
BEACH

trailblaze

GREAT
WATERFALL

KERNSTONE

BROWNSPEAR
POINT

SIGNPOST:
WELCOMBE
MOUTH,
4½ MILES

ALTERNATE
CLIFF-TOP
ROUTE

MAP 48

LONGPEAK

GRASS PATH. KEEP
TO HIGHER PATH

SWANSFORD
HILL
105M/345FT

SLIGHT RIGHT
TURN
OPPOSITE
GATE

LONGPEAK
BEACH

HOLE ROCK

0   ¼ mile

0   APPROX SCALE   500m

47

49

25 MINS TO BLACKPOOL MILL (MAP 47)

HARTLAND QUAY

105 MINS FROM NABOR POINT (MAP 49)

20 MINS FROM BLACKPOOL MILL (MAP 47)

HARTLAND QUAY

105 MINS TO NABOR POINT (MAP 49)

The **post office** (Mon-Fri 9am-5.30pm & Sat 9am-12.30pm) is in the well-stocked general **shop** Christmas Stores (Mon-Sat 8am-9pm, Sun 8am-1pm & 4.30-7.30pm). You can withdraw cash from the post office if it is open and you have a suitable account (see p26); if not there is an **ATM** that charges £1.85. Nearby, *The Pop-in* (☎ 01237-441488, ⌨ www.thepopinstore .com; daily 8am-7.30pm) sells hot pasties and sandwiches, has a **coffee machine** and offers **cashback** (subject to a minimum spend).

Two Harton Manor (☎ 01237-441670, ⌨ www.twohartonmanor.co.uk; 1S/1T/1D; ♥; WI-FI; 🐾; £30-36pp, sgl £30), next to The Hart Inn (see column opposite), is actually the west wing of a 400-year-old manor house. The double room is en suite but the others share facilities. In addition to B&B they offer woodblock-printing lessons. Alternatively, try *7 Goaman Park* (☎ 01237-440005, ⌨ richard.yeates@tiscali .co.uk; 1D; ♥; £25pp, £35 sgl occ) who only provide B&B for coastal-path walkers. As they are two miles from the path they will pick-up/drop-off for free but a charge is made for luggage transfer.

The Granary at Leigh Farm (☎ 01237-441918; caroline_heard@tiscali.co .uk; 1D self-contained; WI-FI; £30pp, £40 sgl occ) is about a mile inland from the coast to the south-west of Hartland village.

The Anchor Inn (☎ 01237-441414; ⌨ www.theanchorinnhartland.co.uk; 6D/3T/ 3F; ♥; WI-FI; 🐾; £30pp, £40 sgl occ) sits in the centre of the village and is one of two popular pubs here. It is a traditional boozer with real ale (they are in the CAMRA guide), pool and darts and the occasional live music or karaoke evening. They offer a free pick-up and drop-off service as well as packed lunches (from £2).

The Anchor also one of the better places for **food** (served summer Mon & Wed-Sat noon-2pm & 6-9pm, Sun noon-3pm & 6-9pm; winter Thur-Sat noon-2pm & 6-9pm, other days subject to demand), with good grub made from local produce and a Sunday carvery.

However, there is another pub in the village whose food reputation is even higher: *The Hart Inn* (☎ 01237-441474, ⌨ www.thehartinn.com; food served Tue-Thur noon-2pm & 6-9pm, Fri & Sat noon-2pm & 5-9.30pm, Sun noon-2.30pm) is the heart of the village, an old place with roots going back to the 14th century. The menu varies, depending on the ingredients available, but may feature a delicious 'matador stew' of beef cooked with root vegetables, chorizo, pancetta in puy lentils, and red wine (£12.75); sandwiches are available at lunch time.

Much more humble but no less delicious, there's a good chippy, *The Square Chip* (Mon-Thur 5.30-9pm, Fri noon-2pm & 5.30-10pm; Sat 5.30-11pm) nearby too.

Hartland is the only place on the peninsula connected by a **bus service**. Stagecoach's 319 runs via Bideford and Clovelly to Barnstaple, connecting with Jackett's 219 service between Hartland & Bude.

Other accommodation around Hartland

For those who think they'll find this last stretch a tad too demanding there are several B&Bs in the area. Many of these offer evening meals, packed lunches and most will, for a fee (or even free), offer lifts from and to the path. Note that though they may say that they are only a short distance from the trail, there is often no path between the two so walking to them may take much longer than you'd anticipated.

Further information on the peninsula and other accommodation options can be found at ⌨ www.hartlandpeninsula.co.uk.

The Old Farmhouse Hescott (☎ 01237-441709, ⌨ www.oldhescottfarm house.co.uk; 2D/1T; ♥; 🐾; £25-30pp, sgl occ £35-40) lies 1½ miles from the path and around two miles west of Clovelly but offers a free pick-up & drop off service as well as evening meals (£12.50 for two courses with a vegetarian option) and packed lunches (£3-6).

Situated just two miles from Higher Clovelly and a similar distance from Hartland – though offering a pick-up and drop-off service from anywhere between Barnstaple and Bude for a donation to the charity she supports in the Gambia – *Southdown B&B* (☎ 01237-431504, 🖳 maryfmcoll@hotmail.com; 1D/1F; ➴; 🐾; WI-FI; £30pp, sgl occ £40) provides packed lunches (£3.50) and evening meals but these must be by arrangement (£12.50 for three courses).

Highdown Cottage (☎ 01237-441131, 🖳 www.highdowncottage.co.uk; 1D/1F; WI-FI; 🐾; £25pp) is a B&B with self-contained accommodation lying about three quarters of a mile from the path and just under two miles as the crow flies north-east of Hartland village with good home cooking and wonderful views. They offer a free pick-up and drop-off service, do evening meals (£12 for two courses) and packed lunches (£5).

Two miles north of Hartland, *Gawlish Farm* (☎ 01237-441320; 4F; ➴; WI-FI; from £29-30pp, sgl occ from £35) is less than a mile off the path. It provides a pick-up and drop-off service and packed lunches (£5-6) as well as evening meals (£12/14 for two/three courses) or they can drop you off at The Hart Inn in Hartland.

Finally, approximately eight miles from Hartland and seven miles from Clovelly, in the tiny hamlet of **Bradworthy**, *Lake House* (☎ 01409-241962, 🖳 www.lakevilla.co.uk; 1D/1T and four self-catering cottages; ➴; 🐾; WI-FI; £31-38pp, sgl occ £44-48; rates for the cottages on request) offers a pick-up and drop-off service (which is useful, as they are nowhere near the path), so you can leave your luggage behind while hiking if staying for more than one night; contact them for details. Packed lunches are available and for an evening meal there is a nearby pub.

HARTLAND QUAY TO BUDE   [MAPS 48-55]

By the time you reach this stage you should be well on your way to becoming acclimatised to your new, itinerant way of life; your feet hardened, your back strong, and your legs like two solid tubes of reinforced steel emanating from the bottom of your shorts.

You are now, in short, a walker.

Which is just as well, for this stage is said to be the most taxing in the entire book; indeed, by common consent it's actually the hardest on the entire South-West Coast Path! It's a **15½-mile (24.9km; 8hrs 30 mins)** slog across soaring summit and plunging combe that includes, by our reckoning, ten *major* ascents and descents as you scramble across valley after valley, with no refreshments along the way until right near the end (though it's possible to divert off the path to Morwenstow where there both a wonderful tea room and a marvellous pub).

Thankfully, the rewards are manifold: the views along the way, especially the panorama at Higher Sharpnose Point, the vista south from Steeple Point and the aspect from Yeolmouth Cliff back to Devil's Hole, are little short of magnificent. If surveying the scenery is difficult due to inclement conditions you can find shelter in the huts of writers Robert Hawker, near Morwenstow, and Ronald Duncan, above the border with Cornwall. While if the weather is good, it seems churlish not to pay a visit to the endless stretch of sand before Bude, the perfect place to cool one's corns and paddle in the sea. All this, and we haven't even mentioned the waterfalls (with a particularly fine example at Speke's Mill Mouth), Iron Age forts, Roman sites, radio stations ... and the sheer joy of being on one of the remotest and most beautiful stretches of coastline this country can offer. Plus of course, nothing can beat the feeling that, at the end of this day, you will have completed the walk described in this book –

which is no small achievement. While for those who are walking the entire trail – and thus for whom this book was little more than an *hors d'oeuvre* – you too can celebrate the fact that you've finished your time in North Devon, and you won't be seeing this county again for another 300 miles!

The route

Despite the fearsome reputation of this stage, the beginning of the walk is rather gentle as you leave Hartland Point to head towards the triangular promontory of **St Catherine's Tor**. The path ignores the scramble up the Tor (which is believed to have had a Roman villa on its summit), preferring instead to follow Wargery Water upstream, a waterway that ends its journey in impressive fashion by plummeting over the cliffs to the north of the Tor. Those who miss this waterfall (which, after all, is not actually on the path) needn't be too concerned, for the next valley, **Speke's Mill Mouth**, has, if anything, an even more spectacular version, and one that is easily visible just a few metres from the path.

Climbing out of the combe – the first of many calf-popping ascents – up Swansford Hill and past the turn-off to YHA Elmscott (see below), the path is rather uneventful to **Nabor Point**, even joining a road at one point, and only gets exciting again at **Embury Beacon**, where the path runs alongside the defensive earthwork of an Iron Age fort. Yet another vertiginous descent follows, this time at **Welcombe Mouth**, where the path crosses the stream on stepping stones. It's a beautiful spot surpassed in its noteworthiness for walkers only, perhaps, by the next laceration in the surface of the land: **Marsland Valley**. Another steep combe, it is here on its northern slopes that you'll find the **hut of Ronald Duncan**. Author, poet, playwright and pacifist, Duncan is perhaps best known for writing the libretto of Benjamin's Britten's opera *The Rape of Lucretia*; but also for this lovely hut that he constructed so he could have views over the sea while writing. You can often pick up free copies of his work in the hut.

ELMSCOTT

If you're not too exhausted, walking along the path 1½ miles or so to Elmscott is a good idea. It's an easy, short walk from the path and will reduce the distance you need to walk on the next stage. Furthermore, the accommodation is rather pleasant. *YHA Elmscott* (☎ 01237-441367, or ☎ 0845-371 9736, john.goa@virgin.net; 32 beds: 1T/three 4-bed dorms/three 6-bed dorms; £16-18/18-20 members/non-members) is one such, originally built as a school in Victorian times and now a cosy hostel with a small shop (Easter to Oct) and good kitchen facilities (which is just as well as meals aren't provided and there's nowhere to eat around here). The farm on which it is set is also a **B&B**: *Elmscott Farm* (☎ 01237-441276, 🖳 www.elmscott.org.uk; 2D/1T; 🛏; £30pp) lies about 400m from the path.

Struggle down the steps to the floor of the valley and you cross the **border into Cornwall**, the exact boundary marked by a bridge and a signpost welcoming you to 'Kernow' (as they call it round here). But while the county might have changed, the path remains as challenging as ever as you traverse yet more stamina-sapping undulations at **Litter Mouth** and **Yeol Mouth** and around **St Morwenna's Well** – so easy to write, so exhausting to complete.

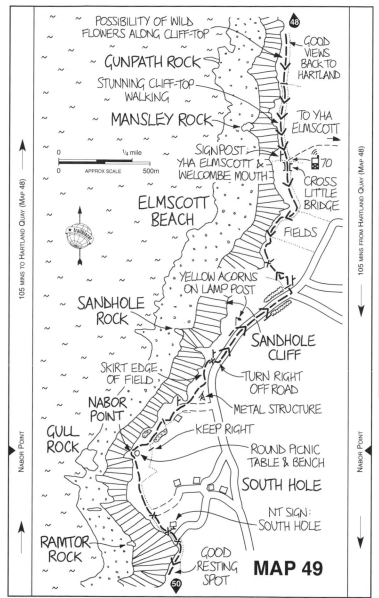

POSSIBILITY OF WILD FLOWERS ALONG CLIFF-TOP

GOOD VIEWS BACK TO HARTLAND

GUNPATH ROCK

STUNNING CLIFF-TOP WALKING

MANSLEY ROCK

TO YHA ELMSCOTT

SIGNPOST: YHA ELMSCOTT & WELCOMBE MOUTH

📵 70

CROSS LITTLE BRIDGE

0   ¼ mile

0   APPROX SCALE   500m

ELMSCOTT BEACH

FIELDS

★ trailblaze

YELLOW ACORNS ON LAMP POST

SANDHOLE ROCK

SANDHOLE CLIFF

SKIRT EDGE OF FIELD

TURN RIGHT OFF ROAD

NABOR POINT

METAL STRUCTURE

KEEP RIGHT

GULL ROCK

ROUND PICNIC TABLE & BENCH

SOUTH HOLE

NT SIGN: SOUTH HOLE

RAMTOR ROCK

GOOD RESTING SPOT

MAP 49

105 MINS TO HARTLAND QUAY (MAP 48)

105 MINS FROM HARTLAND QUAY (MAP 48)

NABOR POINT

NABOR POINT

ROUTE GUIDE AND MAPS

ROUTE GUIDE AND MAPS

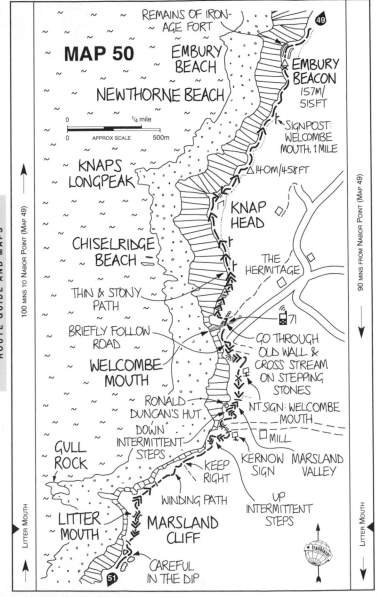

MAP 50

REMAINS OF IRON-AGE FORT

EMBURY BEACH

NEWTHORNE BEACH

49

EMBURY BEACON 157M/ 515FT

SIGNPOST: WELCOMBE MOUTH, 1 MILE

△ 140M/458FT

¼ mile

0   APPROX SCALE   500m

KNAPS LONGPEAK

KNAP HEAD

CHISELRIDGE BEACH

THE HERMITAGE

THIN & STONY PATH

BRIEFLY FOLLOW ROAD

71

WELCOMBE MOUTH

GO THROUGH OLD WALL & CROSS STREAM ON STEPPING STONES

RONALD DUNCAN'S HUT

NT SIGN: WELCOMBE MOUTH

DOWN INTERMITTENT STEPS

MILL

GULL ROCK

KEEP RIGHT

KERNOW SIGN   MARSLAND VALLEY

WINDING PATH

UP INTERMITTENT STEPS

LITTER MOUTH   MARSLAND CLIFF

CAREFUL IN THE DIP

51

100 MINS TO NABOR POINT (MAP 49)

90 MINS FROM NABOR POINT (MAP 49)

LITTER MOUTH

LITTER MOUTH

trailblazer

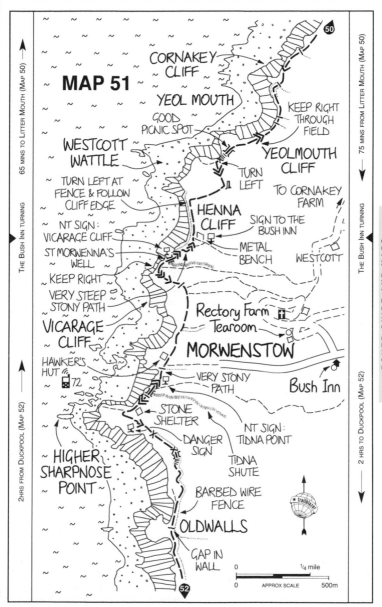

MAP 51

CORNAKEY CLIFF

YEOL MOUTH

KEEP RIGHT THROUGH FIELD

GOOD PICNIC SPOT

WESTCOTT WATTLE

YEOLMOUTH CLIFF

TURN LEFT AT FENCE & FOLLOW CLIFF EDGE

TURN LEFT

TO CORNAKEY FARM

NT SIGN: VICARAGE CLIFF

HENNA CLIFF

SIGN TO THE BUSH INN

ST MORWENNA'S WELL

METAL BENCH

WESTCOTT

KEEP RIGHT

VERY STEEP STONY PATH

VICARAGE CLIFF

Rectory Farm Tearoom

MORWENSTOW

HAWKER'S HUT 72

VERY STONY PATH

Bush Inn

STONE SHELTER

NT SIGN: TIDNA POINT

DANGER SIGN

TIDNA SHUTE

HIGHER SHARPNOSE POINT

BARBED WIRE FENCE

OLDWALLS

GAP IN WALL

65 MINS TO LITTER MOUTH (MAP 50)
THE BUSH INN TURNING
2HRS FROM DUCKPOOL (MAP 52)
75 MINS FROM LITTER MOUTH (MAP 50)
THE BUSH INN TURNING
2 HRS TO DUCKPOOL (MAP 52)

50

52

ROUTE GUIDE AND MAPS

★ Trailblazer

0   1/4 mile
0   APPROX SCALE   500m

Thankfully, soon after the latter, it's possible to get off the rollercoaster for a while by taking the short diversion to the hamlet of **Morwenstow**.

MORWENSTOW   [MAP 51, p193]

There's little more to this ancient settlement than a church, a tearoom and a pub. All three, however, are full of character. The church is dedicated to St Morwenna and St John the Baptist, and while the earliest part of the current church is Norman, there is believed to have been a church on this site since Anglo-Saxon times. The Rev Hawker, of Hawker's Hut fame (see box p196), was one of the vicars here.

Opposite sits the award-winning *Rectory Farm Tearoom* (☎ 01288-331251, 🖳 www.rectory-tearooms.co.uk; week before Easter to end Oct daily 11am-5pm, possibly later in peak season; winter hours variable, check their website), part of a charming 13th-century farm that's been serving cream-topped scones to hungry walkers for over 50 years now. To the south, the 13th-century *Bush Inn* (☎ 01288-331242, 🖳 www.bushinn-morwen stow.co.uk; 1D/2D or T; ☞; WI-FI; 🐕 £6.50;

£42.50pp, sgl occ £47.50) provides B&B and serves food (daily 11am-9pm Fri & Sat 9.30pm). The menu changes regularly but may include beer-battered pollock with chips for £10.50 and a delicious 10oz char-grilled sirloin steak with field mushroom, garlic & herb butter & chips for £17.50. They also do packed lunches (£6.50). Ask the owners to point out some of the ancient features of the inn, including the lepers' squint, through which the diseased of the parish were fed scraps, and a monastic cross carved into a flagstone in the floor.

Cornakey Farm (off Map 51; ☎ 01288-331260, 🖳 www.cornakey-farm .co.uk; 1D/1F; ☞; WI-FI; £32pp; Easter to Oct) is set in gorgeous lush farmland around half a mile north of Morwenstow and only 400m from the path; indeed, the path actu-ally crosses the farm's land. Evening meals are available at the Bush Inn but they will provide a packed lunch (about £2.50).

Those who forego the delights of Morwenstow will instead continue along **Vicarage Cliff**, in time coming to the cliff-face path to **Hawker's Hut** (see box p196), built by a local vicar from the timbers of shipwrecked craft.

Still the relentless gradients of the path continue as you clamber in and out of the valleys of **Tidna Shute** and **Stanbury**, the latter, in this author's reckon-ing, the steepest of all today's climbs. Your reward at the top is an enormous **radio station** from where, at its southern end, the first views of Bude can be glimpsed. Another steep valley, **Duckpool**, follows, where in July at dusk you can see the rare spectacle of glow worms. Along this coast, over 150 ships have been wrecked between Morwenstow and Bude. No wonder Alfred, Lord Tennyson, described this stretch thus:

> *But after tempest, when the long wave broke*
> *All down the thundering shores of Bude and Bos.*
> **Alfred, Lord Tennyson**, *The Birth of King Arthur*

Duckpool is also the last serious challenge on this stage. The gradients finally relent now and the path, though still long and undulating, is more merciful than it has been previously on this stage. Cafés start to appear on the route too, including *Sandymouth Café* (Map 53; ☎ 01288-354286; 🖳 www.sandy mouth.com; Easter to Oct daily 9am-6pm; weekends only in winter) and the lovely eatery, *Margaret's Rustic Tea Room* (which has actually been here since

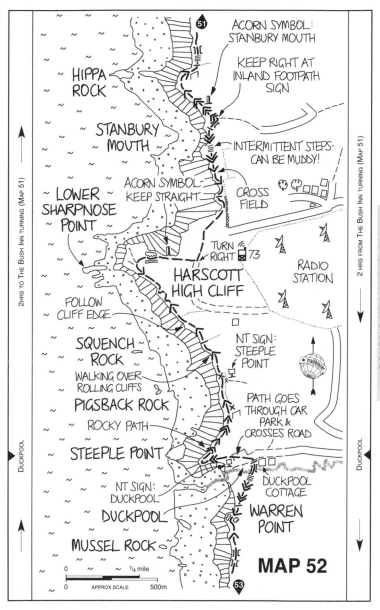

ACORN SYMBOL:
STANBURY MOUTH

KEEP RIGHT AT
INLAND FOOTPATH
SIGN

HIPPA
ROCK

STANBURY
MOUTH

INTERMITTENT STEPS-
CAN BE MUDDY!

ACORN SYMBOL-
KEEP STRAIGHT

CROSS
FIELD

LOWER
SHARPNOSE
POINT

TURN
RIGHT 73

HARSCOTT
HIGH CLIFF

RADIO
STATION

FOLLOW
CLIFF EDGE

SQUENCH
ROCK

NT SIGN:
STEEPLE
POINT

WALKING OVER
ROLLING CLIFFS

PIGSBACK ROCK

PATH GOES
THROUGH CAR
PARK &
CROSSES ROAD

ROCKY PATH

STEEPLE POINT

DUCKPOOL
COTTAGE

NT SIGN:
DUCKPOOL

WARREN
POINT

DUCKPOOL

MUSSEL ROCK

0   ¼ mile

MAP 52

0
APPROX SCALE   500m

2HRS TO THE BUSH INN TURNING (MAP 51)

DUCKPOOL

2 HRS FROM THE BUSH INN TURNING (MAP 51)

DUCKPOOL

ROUTE GUIDE AND MAPS

❑ **Hawker and his hut**

Writer, maverick and saviour of shipwrecked sailors, Robert Stephen Hawker was born in 1803 and became vicar of the St Morwenna and St John the Baptist Church at Morwenstow in 1834. Prior to his arrival the church had had no serving clergy for well over a century and, lacking any guiding moral influence, the coastline in this region had instead become a base for smugglers and wreckers (who used to lure passing ships onto the rocks, regardless of the safety of those onboard, so they could then loot the wreck of its cargo).

Hawker, horrified at the behaviour of many of his parishioners, went out of his way to both ameliorate their behaviour and educate them in the errors of their ways. The hut that he built out of driftwood into the cliff-face, and which still carries his name, was originally designed as a lookout, so Hawker could warn any ships of the dangers of navigation. He also used the hut as his study, from where he could compose such works as '*Footprints of Former Men in Far Cornwall*', which included an account of the wrecking of the *Caledonia* in 1842, and where he also received friends such as Charles Kingsley and Alfred, Lord Tennyson.

Contemporary sources describe Hawker as a bit of an eccentric, given to wearing colourful clothes, dressing up as a mermaid, and excommunicating his cat for mousing on a Sunday. But he was also extremely compassionate and introduced the practice of giving the bodies of shipwrecked sailors a Christian burial (where previously they had been allowed to bob in the ocean for days). The **figurehead of** *Caledonia* marks the spot in Morwenstow Church where the crew are buried. Nearby is a granite cross into which the words 'Unknown Yet Well Known' are carved, a tribute to the thirty or so bodies of seafarers that he buried nearby. He is most remembered, however, as the man who introduced the Harvest Festival into the Christian calendar, having invited his congregation to a service in October 1841 to give thanks to God for his bounty; and as the composer of '*The Song of the Western Men*', which has become something of a 'national' anthem for Cornwall.

Hawker died in 1875, the mourners at his funeral wearing purple rather than the traditional black. He was survived by his wife, who was forty years his junior – plus, of course, by his small driftwood hut, today the smallest building in the entire portfolio of the National Trust.

the '40s when Margaret's mum ran the place), with outside seating by the stream at **Northcott Mouth**, and wonderful cream teas served from an old green caravan. But by now even this idyllic place may not be enough to halt your determined march to Bude ... which you should reach, weary, exhausted and happy, about 2-2¹/₂ hours after leaving Duckpool.

BUDE   [MAP 55, p201]

Bude is a small, compact seaside town with plenty of charm and character that sprawls out from its famous beach, Summerleaze.

Summer, bank holidays and during the jazz festival (see p16) are when this normally sleepy little town springs into life and it can become quite hectic. However, arrive at any other time and you shouldn't have

any trouble booking accommodation and making your way around town.

If you have an inclination to explore, the **castle** with its **heritage centre** (☎ 01288-357300, 🖳 www.bude-stratton.gov .uk; Mon-Fri & Sun Easter to Oct 11am-5pm, Nov to Easter 11am-4pm; £3.50), which, should you have developed an

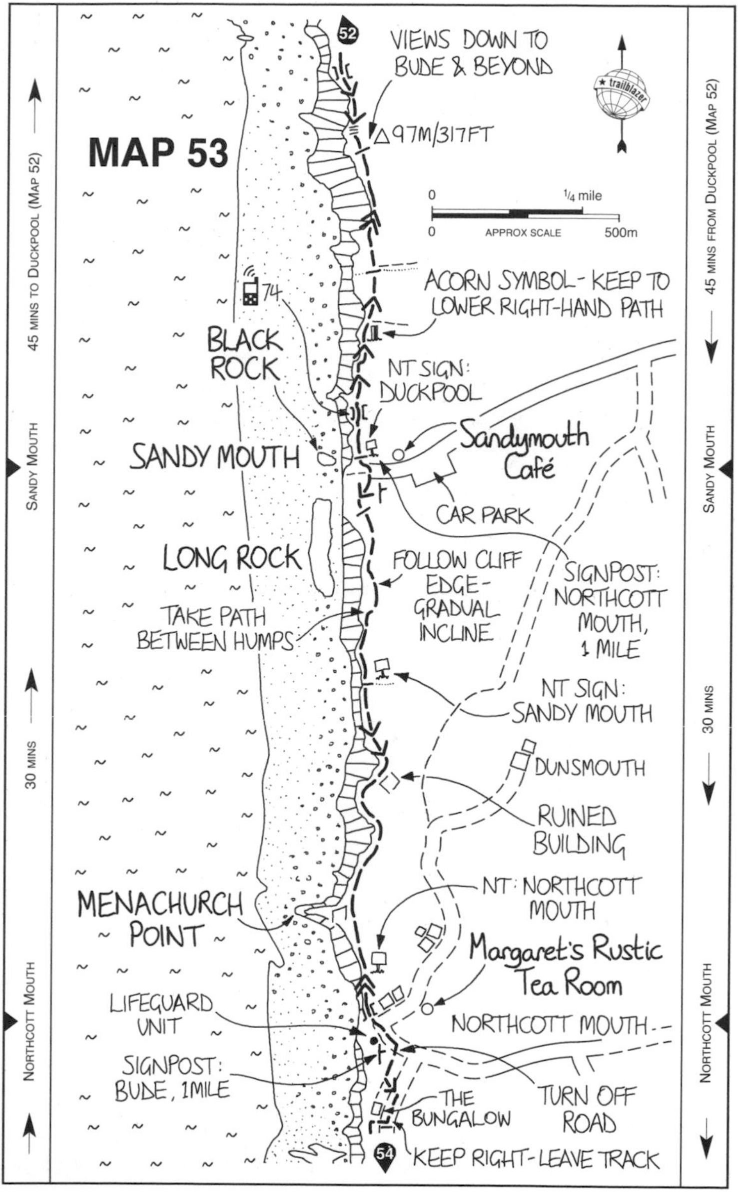

MAP 53

VIEWS DOWN TO BUDE & BEYOND

△97M/317FT

ACORN SYMBOL - KEEP TO LOWER RIGHT-HAND PATH

BLACK ROCK

NT SIGN: DUCKPOOL

SANDY MOUTH

Sandymouth Café

CAR PARK

LONG ROCK

FOLLOW CLIFF EDGE - GRADUAL INCLINE

SIGNPOST: NORTHCOTT MOUTH, 1 MILE

TAKE PATH BETWEEN HUMPS

NT SIGN: SANDY MOUTH

DUNSMOUTH

RUINED BUILDING

NT: NORTHCOTT MOUTH

MENACHURCH POINT

Margaret's Rustic Tea Room

NORTHCOTT MOUTH

LIFEGUARD UNIT

SIGNPOST: BUDE, 1MILE

THE BUNGALOW

TURN OFF ROAD

KEEP RIGHT - LEAVE TRACK

45 MINS TO DUCKPOOL (MAP 52)

45 MINS FROM DUCKPOOL (MAP 52)

SANDY MOUTH

SANDY MOUTH

30 MINS

30 MINS

NORTHCOTT MOUTH

NORTHCOTT MOUTH

ROUTE GUIDE AND MAPS

0   1/4 mile
0   APPROX SCALE   500m

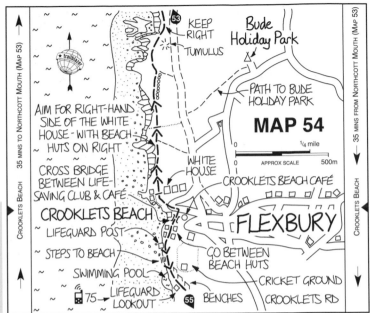

❏ Bude Canal

Bude Canal was dug to transport mainly sand inland from the seashore so that it could be spread on the fields to improve the soil which was rather poor in parts of north Cornwall. The Canal was the brainchild of one John Endyvean, the intention being to link up with the River Tamar at Calstock, thus providing a waterway between the Bristol Channel and the English Channel, 90 miles of canal to span just 28 miles as the crow flies.

The full scheme was never realised although by 1823 some 35 miles of canal were in operation. Once the railways were built the use of the canal began to decline and by the Second World War it became ineffective as a waterway. Today only a short stretch remains between Bude and Helebridge.

A project to restore the canal with the aid of a £45m grant from the Heritage Lottery Fund was completed in 2009. Whilst the lock-gates giving access to the open sea suffered damage in the early part of 2008 during some huge storms, the canal itself is currently in good working order. At the Helebridge end, **Weir Nature Centre** at Whalesborough Farm opened in 2011. It is a 40-minute walk along a flat tarmac path by the side of the canal.

You can also hire rowing boats and pedalos to take out on the canal from **Bude Rowing Boats** (☎ 0796-868 8782; Good Fri to end Sep daily 10am to late).

interest in shipwrecks or any other nautical matters whilst walking the cliffs, may be of interest. It also includes displays on the Bude Canal and the geology of the Cornish coast. Should budgetary constraints be a concern **Willoughby Gallery**, where the museum holds its exhibitions, is free. **Bude Canal** (see box opposite) runs along next to the centre. Also nearby is the **Bude Light**, a Millennium project built to commemorate the life of Sir Goldsworthy Gurney, a Cornish scientist and inventor.

Bude is known for its **Jazz Festival** (see p16) which usually takes place at the end of August (but won't in 2012) so be aware of the increased demand for accommodation during this period and remember to book in advance.

Services

Bude Tourist Information and Canal Centre (☎ 01288-354240, 🖳 www.visit bude.info; Mon-Sat 10am-5pm, to 6pm in the school summer holidays, Sun 10am-4pm) has a comprehensive listing of accommodation in the area and the enthusiastic staff are willing to help. **Internet access** (60p/15 mins) is available as well as wi-fi for customers.

Bude **Library** (☎ 0300-123 4111; Mon, Tue & Fri 9am-5pm, Thur 9am-6.30pm, Sat 10am-4pm; wi-fi) also provides access to the internet (£1.80/30 mins) as well as having a good Cornish reference section. Internet access (£1/20 mins) is also available at Coffee Pot Café (see Where to eat).

Bude's main **post office** (Mon-Fri 9am-5.30pm, Sat 9am-12.30pm) is at the top of Belle Vue, the main shopping street. There's also a **sub-post office** (same hours) which is part of a newsagents (daily 7am-5.30pm) on the other side of The Crescent from the tourist office.

For **food** shopping there is a Sainsbury's (Mon-Sat 8am-8pm, Sun 10am-4pm), a Co-op (Mon-Sat 8am-10pm, Sun 10am-4pm) and a Local Plus (Mon-Sat 7am-10pm, Sun 8am-10pm). For a **chemist** there is a Boots (Mon-Sat 9am-5pm), while for **walking gear** there is a Mountain Warehouse (Mon-Sat 9am-5.30pm, Sun 10am-4.30pm), and there's a

good **bookshop**, Spencer Thorn Bookshop (☎ 01288-352518; Mon-Sat 9am-5pm, Sun 10am-4pm in summer).

There are several **banks** including a NatWest (Mon-Fri 9am-4.30pm) and a Lloyds (Mon-Fri 9am-5pm, Wed 10am-5pm), both of which have **cash machines**; you will also find ATMs at all the town's supermarkets and convenience stores.

Finally, if you should need a **launderette** (Mon-Thur 8.30am-5pm, Fri 8.30am-8pm, Sat 9am-5pm, Sun 10am-5pm) there's one tucked away off Lansdown Rd.

Where to stay

Campsites and hostels For **campers**, before you even enter Bude – and with a path leading to it from near Crooklets Beach – **Bude Holiday Park** (Map 54; ☎ 01288-355955, 🖳 www.budeholidaypark .co.uk; £6.70-8.70pp for walker and tent; 🐾 £2; Apr-Nov) is reasonably priced and has a good selection of amenities including a laundry, shop and café. Arrive during peak times, however, and be prepared for a lot of screaming, excitable children in this family-orientated park.

The ten-minute stroll out of town to **Upper Lynstone Caravan & Camping Park** (☎ 01288-352017, 🖳 www.upperlynstone .co.uk; Apr to end Sep; 🐾; camping £7-9 for walker & little tent, £13.50-19 for two people and a tent) is well worth the effort. The location is perfect for those continuing on the trail as it backs on to the cliffs and the coastal path to Upton and Widemouth Bay. There is also a well-stocked shop, free showers and a laundry. One idea that may be worth considering if travelling in a group and wishing to remain in Bude for a few days (though not in the peak season) is hiring one of their caravans – three nights in a caravan costs £45 per night for the van, and as you can fit up to six people in each one this could be a cheap alternative to a B&B.

Previously a holistic healing centre, **NorthShore Bude Backpackers** (☎ 01288-354256, 🖳 www.northshorebude.com; 🛏; four 4-bed dorms; two 6-bed dorms, 3D/ 1T/1F; £16-18 for a dorm bed, £18.50-22.50pp, £30 sgl occ, only in low season)

ROUTE GUIDE AND MAPS

has some en suite rooms and everything a walker needs: internet access (£2/hour), a drying room and a laundry (£4 per wash, if available). It also benefits from a big and clean living area and kitchen (meals are not provided) and Sky TV. Booking is recommended all year but especially for the high season as it can get very busy.

B&Bs and guesthouses B&B-style accommodation is scattered about the town.

Near the campsite and a little out of town along Vicarage Rd is *The Elms* (☎ 01288-353429; 3D/1F; ☛; Mar-Oct; £28pp, sgl occ £40).

Both more central and pretty much on the SWCP are *Riverview* (☎ 01288-359399, 🖳 www.riverviewbude.co.uk; 1D/1T; ☛; WI-FI; 🐾; £26-32pp, sgl occ £31-37), which is run by a local artist (but unfortunately was for sale at the time of research although it may continue as a B&B under new ownership); and *Breakwater House* (☎ 01288-353137, 🖳 www.breakwater house.co.uk; 2D, 1D or T; ☛; WI-FI; £39-44pp, sgl occ £49-54) which is at the luxury end of the scale. Whilst they take only two-night bookings they will consider one-night stays should you call requiring accommodation that night.

On or around Burn View you will find *Links Side Guest House* (☎ 01288-352410, 🖳 www.linkssidebude.co.uk; 1S/3D/1T/ 1F; ☛; £25-35pp, sgl £27-40), which even has laptops to borrow for those who want to take advantage of the wi-fi; *Palms Guest House* (☎ 01288-353962, 🖳 www.palms-bude.co.uk; 2S/1D/1T/1F; ☛; WI-FI; Apr-Oct; £26-38pp, sgl £35-38), which serves a varied breakfast, including smoked haddock; *Sea Jade Guest House* (☎ 01288-353404, 🖳 www.seajadeguest house.co.uk; 4S/4D or T; WI-FI; £30-35pp) on Burn View; *Sunrise* (☎ 01288-353214, 🖳 www.sunrise-bude.co.uk; 2S/1T/2D/1D or T/1F; ☛; 🐾 £5; WI-FI; £25-37.50pp), and *Tee-Side Guest House* (☎ 01288-352351, 🖳 www.tee-side.co.uk; 4D or T; WI-FI; £30pp, sgl £40), from where, as its name suggests, you can enjoy views overlooking the golf course while eating your breakfast.

Hotels Overlooking the beach from a great vantage point on the edge of Summerleaze Down, *The Beach at Bude* (☎ 01288-389800, 🖳 www.thebeachatbude .co.uk; 2T/13D; ☛; WI-FI; £55-80pp, sgl occ £90-140) is a tremendous place that offers 'luxury B&B'. One of Bude's newer hotels, it has heated floors and a drying room – a delight in bad weather. Even the small rooms are big and the views out to sea and over the beach are fantastic.

On the same road and also boasting drying rooms are *The Edgcumbe* (☎ 01288-353846, 🖳 www.edgcumbe-hotel.co.uk; Mar-Nov; 11D or T; ☛; WI-FI; £38-49pp, sgl occ £53-64) and *Atlantic House Hotel* (☎ 01288-352451, 🖳 atlantichousehotel.com; 11D/4D or T; ☛; WI-FI; £35-48pp, sgl occ £55 but full room rate in peak season). Next door is *The Grosvenor* (☎ 01288-352062, 🖳 www.thegrosvenor-bude.co.uk; 1S/4D/ 2T/2F; ☛; WI-FI in public areas; well-behaved 🐾 £5; £32-40pp, sgl £32-35).

A little more centrally you'll find *The Globe Hotel* (☎ 01288-352085, 🖳 www .theglobehotelbude.com; 1T/3F; ☛; £25-30pp, sgl occ £30-40), and *The Strand Hotel* (☎ 01288-355571, 🖳 www.strand hotelbude.co.uk; 25D or T, 6F; ☛; 🐾; WI-FI on ground floor; 45-47.50pp; sgl occ full room rate).

On the other side of the canal, *Falcon Hotel* (☎ 01288-352005, 🖳 www.falconho tel.com; 4S/7T/18D; ☛; WI-FI; £65-80pp, sgl £65) is an impressive place, whilst, next door, there's *Brendon Arms* (☎ 01288-354542, 🖳 www.brendonarms.co.uk; 1S/ 5D/3T; ☛; WI-FI; £35-40pp).

Where to eat and drink
There are numerous options for food in Bude. Should you arrive in town hungry and in need of lunch or a mid-afternoon snack just a short walk off the path and between the canal and Heritage Centre you will find *The Castle Tearooms* (Thur-Tue 10.30am-5pm, food served 11.30am-3pm) which sells locally made Cornish pasties (£3.20) as well as cream teas and cakes.

The Coffee Shop (☎ 01288-355973; Mar-Nov daily 10am-6.30pm, Dec-Feb 10.30am-5pm), on Lansdown Rd and

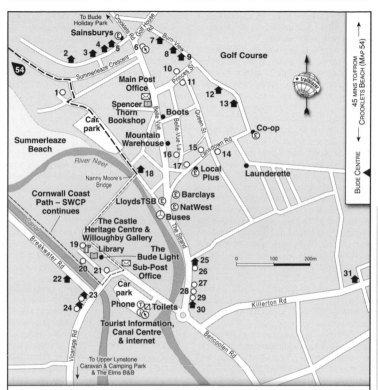

Bude MAP 55

Where to stay
2 The Beach at Bude
3 The Edgcumbe
4 Atlantic House Hotel
5 The Grosvenor Hotel
7 Tee-Side
8 Sunrise
9 Links Side Guest House
12 Sea Jade Guest House
13 Palms Guest House
18 Riverview
22 Breakwater House B&B
23 Falcon Hotel
24 Brendon Arms
25 The Globe
30 The Strand Hotel
31 NorthShore Backpackers

Where to eat and drink
1 Life's a Beach
6 Coffee Pot Café (& internet access)
10 Sizzlers Fish & Chips
11 Urchins
14 Coffee Shop
15 Mirchi
16 KJ's
17 Scrummies
19 The Castle Restaurant
20 Castle Tearooms
21 Olive Tree Coffee House & Bistro
23 Falcon Hotel
24 Brendon Arms
26 Tiandi
27 Silver River Chinese Takeaway
28 Funky Chicken
29 Carriers Inn

nearer the centre of town, sells fresh baked goods (from Landsdown Dairy) which are sure to get you salivating.

Nearer the outskirts of town but accessible from the path before actually entering Bude, *Coffee Pot Café* (Tue-Sun summer 9.30am-5pm, winter 10am-4pm) serves Twinings tea and a typical café menu (a full breakfast costs £5.50); internet access is available.

There are a few particularly good options for pub lunches. Next to the canal, *Brendon Arms* (see Where to stay; food daily noon-2pm & 6-9pm; summer noon-9pm) is a lively and clean no-thrills pub that delivers everything a walker needs including Sunday roasts for £6.95; it also has Sky Sports on the telly. Meanwhile, at the bottom of The Strand, *Carriers Inn* (☎ 01288-352459; food daily noon-3pm & 6-9pm, summer daily noon-9pm; 🐾 allowed in the bar if on a lead), the oldest pub in town, serves real ales and the popular Carriers' beef chilli (£7.25). *Falcon Hotel* (see Where to stay) has a restaurant (daily noon-2pm & 6.30-9pm; booking preferred if wish to eat 6.30-7.30pm) but the menu is fairly standard pub grub.

Offering nourishment throughout the day and with outside tables that overlook the canal, *Olive Tree Coffee House and Bistro* (☎ 01288-359577, 🖳 www.olive treebude.co.uk; summer Tue & Sun 10am-5pm, Wed-Sat 10am-10pm, winter Tue-Sun 10am-4.30pm; WI-FI) serves a good variety of gluten-free and vegetarian dishes – a pasta or risotto dish costing around £5.50 for a small portion or £10 for a large one.

Another café-by-day, bistro-by-night place is the more central *Scrummies* (summer daily 8am-9pm, Sun 9am-9pm; winter days/hours variable) where owner and local fisherman Cliff Bowden catches, prepares and cooks 60-70% of the fish himself and offers a gigantic cod 'n' chips for only £6.95.

A third bistro-cum-coffee house, this time on the corner of Queen St and Princes St, is *Urchins* (☎ 01288-352783, 🖳 www .urchinsbistrobude.co.uk; daily 9am-4pm, Easter-Oct Fri & Sat 5-8.45pm, school

summer holidays daily 5-8.45pm), serving both breakfasts and lunches as well as having a different specials' board each evening – a mussels starter costs £5.95 whilst the larger main is £10.95.

Restaurant-wise there are a few excellent options. *The Castle* (☎ 01288-350543, 🖳 www.thecastlerestaurantbude.co.uk; Mon-Sat morning coffee 10am-noon, noon-2.30pm & 6-9.30pm, Sun 10am-3.30pm; in the winter they may be closed in the evening Mon-Wed) is a lovely restaurant with a terrace (🐾 allowed) that overlooks the back of Summerleaze Beach. In the evening a fillet of salmon costs £17 whilst lunches are also available at very reasonable prices.

Also overlooking the beach but facing south is *Life's a Beach* (☎ 01288-355222, 🖳 www.lifesabeach.info; mid-Feb to Dec café daily 10.30am-3.30pm, evening bistro Mon-Sat 7-9pm, Jan to mid Feb Fri-Sun 11am-3pm) where prosciutto-wrapped halibut costs £18.50.

There are a few ethnic options for those who are literally fed up with fish. Relatively central and both restaurant as well as takeaway are the Indian *Mirchi* (☎ 01288-350300; Sun-Thur noon-1.30pm & daily 5.30-11.30pm) where a lamb chatt kufti masala costs £8.50, and *Tiandi* (☎ 01288-359686, 🖳 www.tiandi.co.uk; Mon-Sat 11.30am-2.30pm & daily 5.30-10.30pm) which advertises Far-Eastern fine dining – a cod Thai-style sweet chilli costs £8.95.

On The Strand there is also *Silver River Chinese Takeaway* (☎ 01288-352028; mid Feb to mid Jan Tue-Sun 5-10.30pm) where a set meal for two costs £19.80.

Other takeaway options include *Funky Chicken* (☎ 01288-353252; Sun-Thur 3-11pm, Fri & Sat 2pm-2am) which sells burgers, pizzas and omelettes as well as fried chicken, and *KJ's* (☎ 01288-355879; daily 4pm-midnight) which is more kebab-orientated. Finally, for the classic British seaside fish 'n' chips you need look no further than *Sizzlers* (daily noon-3pm & 4.30-9pm).

Transport

[See also pp49-51] **Bus**-wise, for destinations north, Jackett's No 219 goes to Hartland where you can connect with Stagecoach's No 319 to Bideford & Barnstaple, where you'll find the nearest **railway station**. Alternatively, First's X9 goes to the main rail hub at Exeter. Jackett's No 76 and Western Greyhound's No 576 head to Plymouth, while Western Greyhound's No 595 service runs to Boscastle.

For a **taxi**, call Bea-line (☎ 07747-196090, 🖳 www.bea-line.co.uk) or Trev's Taxi (☎ 07799-663217).

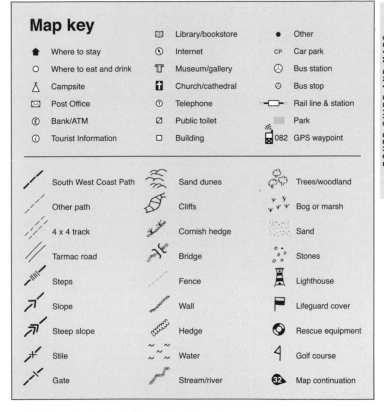

Map key

🛏	Where to stay	📖	Library/bookstore	●	Other
○	Where to eat and drink	ⓢ	Internet	CP	Car park
△	Campsite	🏛	Museum/gallery	⊘	Bus station
⊠	Post Office	✝	Church/cathedral	⊙	Bus stop
ⓔ	Bank/ATM	☏	Telephone		Rail line & station
ⓘ	Tourist Information	☑	Public toilet		Park
		□	Building	📱 082	GPS waypoint

⟋	South West Coast Path		Sand dunes		Trees/woodland
⟋	Other path		Cliffs		Bog or marsh
⟋	4 x 4 track		Cornish hedge		Sand
⟋	Tarmac road		Bridge		Stones
⟋	Steps		Fence	🛆	Lighthouse
↗	Slope		Wall	⚑	Lifeguard cover
⟰	Steep slope		Hedge	◉	Rescue equipment
⟊	Stile		Water	4	Golf course
⟋	Gate		Stream/river	32	Map continuation

ROUTE GUIDE AND MAPS

APPENDIX: GPS WAYPOINTS

MAP	REF	GPS WAYPOINTS	DESCRIPTION
Map 1	01	N51 12.636 W3 28.345	Hands Sculpture – start of SWCP
Map 2	02	N51 13.113 W3 30.671	Start of rugged alternative route
Map 3	03	N51 13.059 W3 31.125	Gate into and out of Holnicote Estate
Map 4	04	N51 13.383 W3 32.352	Metalled road
Map 5	05	N51 13.578 W3 34.057	Reunion of two trails
Map 5	06	N51 13.263 W3 34.928	Turn-off left outside Bossington
Map 6	07	N51 12.967 W3 36.986	Rejoin beach
Map 7	08	N51 13.249 W3 38.086	Arch over path
Map 7	09	N51 13.263 W3 39.490	Culbone Church
Map 8	10	N51 13.325 W3 42.176	Paths to Burford and County Gate
Map 9	11	N51 13.749 W3 42.610	Reunion of two paths
Map 9	12	N51 13.806 W3 43.679	Wild Boar gateposts
Map 10	13	N51 14.096 W3 45.677	Gate into/out of Pudleep Gurt
Map 10	14	N51 14.354 W3 46.949	Turn-off road
Map 11	15	N51 14.304 W3 47.445	Reunion with path from lighthouse
Map 11	16	N51 13.837 W3 49.303	Leave road; zig-zag down to Lynmouth beach
Map 12	17	N51 13.755 W3 51.558	Cattle grid and gate
Map 13	18	N51 13.461 W3 52.865	Start of Woody Bay alternative
Map 13	19	N51 13.398 W3 53.844	White signpost
Map 14	20	N51 13.324 W3 55.618	Heddon's Mouth
Map 14	21	N51 13.138 W3 56.751	Gate with ENP on
Map 15	22	N51 12.857 W3 58.228	Right turning onto good, wide path
Map 15	23	N51 12.538 W3 59.238	Great Hangman National Trust sign
Map 16	24	N51 12.855 W4 00.209	Top of Great Hangman
Map 17	25	N51 12.375 W4 02.185	Combe Martin Beach
Map 17	26	N51 12.723 W4 03.838	Watermouth Valley Camping Park
Map 18	27	N51 12.966 W4 05.208	First view of Ilfracombe and Lundy
Map 19	28	N51 12.548 W4 06.853	Ilfracombe Harbour
Map 20	29	N51 11.829 W4 10.539	Lee Bridge
Map 21	30	N51 11.899 W4 11.993	Bull Point
Map 21	31	N51 11.241 W4 13.738	Morte Point
Map 22	32	N51 10.351 W4 12.448	Tourist information Centre, Woolacombe
Map 23	33	N51 08.543 W4 13.148	Entrance to Putsborough Sands car park
Map 24	34	N51 08.529 W4 15.510	Baggy Point
Map 24	35	N51 07.985 W4 14.163	Croyde Beach
Map 25	36	N51 07.336 W4 14.376	Turn onto road
Map 26	37	N51 07.082 W4 13.086	Turning onto road
Map 26	38	N51 07.013 W4 12.229	Turning off road
Map 27	39	N51 05.622 W4 11.719	Entrance to Braunton Burrows
Map 27	40	N51 04.309 W4 11.496	Turn left onto sand footpath
Map 28	41	N51 06.019 W4 09.788	Velator Bridge
Map 29	42	N51 05.624 W4 07.393	The Braunton Inn
Map 30	43	N51 05.650 W4 06.663	Path goes under bridge
Map 31	44	N51 04.660 W4 03.499	Turn left up steps to access bridge
Map 32	45	N51 04.744 W4 07.168	Fremington Quay Café
Map 33	46	N51 04.237 W4 09.603	Main trail leaves railway tracks here
Map 34	47	N51 04.318 W4 10.113	Start of jetty
Map 34	48	N51 03.384 W4 10.726	Onto road

Bristol Central Library
Tel: 0117 9037200
www.bristol.gov.uk/libraries

Borrowed Items 02/06/2016 10:24
XXXXXX9009

Title	Due Date
0674771	23/06/2016

MAP	REF	GPS WAYPOINTS	DESCRIPTION
Map 34	49	N51 02.987 W4 10.680	Turning off road at Instow
Map 35	50	N51 02.515 W4 11.041	Pass jetty
Map 36	51	N51 00.935 W4 12.002	Bideford Long Bridge
Map 37	52	N51 02.550 W4 11.540	Wooden footbridge
Map 37	53	N51 03.125 W4 11.371	Appledore Quay
Map 37	54	N51 03.203 W4 12.201	Signpost high/low tide route
Map 38	55	N51 03.338 W4 13.543	Information centre at Northam Burrows
Map 39	56	N51 02.451 W4 14.208	Westward Ho! (Bottom of Golf Links Rd)
Map 40	57	N51 01.139 W4 16.446	Green Cliff National Trust sign
Map 41	58	N50 59.605 W4 18.327	Gate at Peppercombe
Map 42	59	N50 59.266 W4 20.635	Buck's Mills
Map 42	60	N50 59.288 W4 21.426	Mary's Rest
Map 43	61	N50 59.171 W4 22.286	Joining Hobby Drive
Map 43	62	N50 59.895 W4 23.980	Gate into Clovelly
Map 44	63	N51 00.213 W4 24.235	The Cabin
Map 44	64	N51 00.621 W4 25.261	Mouthmill
Map 45	65	N51 00.759 W4 26.710	Memorial to Wellington Bomber
Map 45	66	N51 01.153 W4 28.168	Trig Point
Map 46	67	N51 01.235 W4 30.745	Radar station
Map 47	68	N51 00.154 W4 31.648	Blackpool Mill
Map 48	69	N50 59.631 W4 31.968	Hartland Quay
Map 49	70	N50 58.069 W4 31.795	Turn-off to YHA Elmscott
Map 50	71	N50 55.988 W4 32.624	Welcombe Mouth
Map 51	72	N50 54.389 W4 33.720	Hawker's Hut
Map 52	73	N50 53.129 W4 33.531	Right turn by radio station
Map 53	74	N50 51.659 W4 33.224	Wooden footbridge at Sandy Mouth
Map 54	75	N50 50.121 W4 33.129	Lifeguard lookout

INDEX

Page references in bold type refer to maps

TRAILBLAZER TITLE LIST

Adventure Cycle-Touring Handbook
Adventure Motorcycling Handbook
Australia by Rail
Australia's Great Ocean Road
Azerbaijan
Coast to Coast (British Walking Guide)
Cornwall Coast Path (British Walking Guide)
Corsica Trekking – GR20
Cotswold Way (British Walking Guide)
Dolomites Trekking – AV1 & AV2
Dorset & Sth Devon Coast Path (British Walking Gde)
Exmoor & Nth Devon Coast Path (British Walking Gde)
Hadrian's Wall Path (British Walking Guide)
Himalaya by Bike – a route and planning guide
Inca Trail, Cusco & Machu Picchu
Indian Rail Handbook
Japan by Rail
Kilimanjaro – The Trekking Guide (includes Mt Meru)
Mediterranean Handbook
Morocco Overland (4WD/motorcycle/mountainbike)
Moroccan Atlas – The Trekking Guide
Nepal Trekking & The Great Himalaya Trail
New Zealand – The Great Walks
North Downs Way (British Walking Guide)
Norway's Arctic Highway
Offa's Dyke Path (British Walking Guide)
Overlanders' Handbook – worldwide driving guide
Peddars Way & Norfolk Coast Path (British Walking Gde)
Pembrokeshire Coast Path (British Walking Guide)
Pennine Way (British Walking Guide)
The Ridgeway (British Walking Guide)
Siberian BAM Guide – rail, rivers & road
The Silk Roads – a route and planning guide
Sahara Overland – a route and planning guide
Scottish Highlands – The Hillwalking Guide
Sinai – The Trekking Guide
South Downs Way (British Walking Guide)
Tour du Mont Blanc
Trans-Canada Rail Guide
Trans-Siberian Handbook
Trekking in the Annapurna Region
Trekking in the Everest Region
Trekking in Ladakh
Trekking in the Pyrenees
The Walker's Haute Route – Mont Blanc to Matterhorn
West Highland Way (British Walking Guide)

For more information about Trailblazer and our
expanding range of guides, for guidebook updates or
for credit card mail order sales visit our website:

www.trailblazer-guides.com

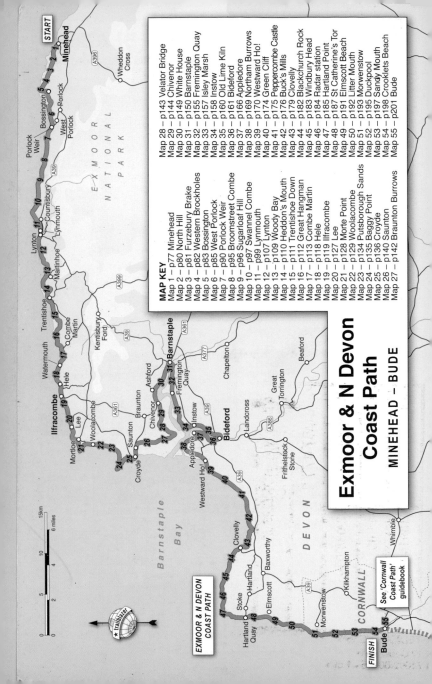

Exmoor & N Devon Coast Path
MINEHEAD – BUDE

START — Minehead

FINISH — Bude

EXMOOR & N DEVON COAST PATH

See 'Cornwall Coast Path' guidebook